AF247458

England, France and Christendom, 1377–99

England, France and Christendom, 1377-99

J. J. N. Palmer

The University of North Carolina Press, Chapel Hill
Routledge & Kegan Paul, London
1972

For my father

Contents

Contents

Tables, Maps and Illustrations

Preface

The title of this book is perhaps slightly misleading. I have not attempted to write a detailed history of Anglo-French relations between 1377 and 1399, still less the history of Christendom in that period. Rather, I have tried to explore some of the fundamental problems posed by this phase of the Hundred Years War: Why did it last for so long, and how was it finally terminated? What were the consequences of the ensuing truce? How did it affect the rest of Europe? Why did it fail to produce a final settlement, and why were its ultimate results so meagre? These and other questions are intimately related to each other, as are the answers I have suggested. Some of these answers are novel, and a few will be regarded as controversial; but they all stand (or fall) together.

In the course of my work I have incurred a number of obligations which I am happy to be able to acknowledge. My debt to other authors is, I trust, apparent in my notes; but I would like to stress my particular indebtedness to the fine works of Perroy, Quicke and Russell. My interest in this period was first aroused by the late K. B. McFarlane, whose friendship I was privileged to enjoy at the outset of my career; and my research into this particular field was initially guided by Professor May McKisack, to whose help and encouragement I owe more than she may be aware. Professor Richard Vaughan first introduced me to the riches of the Burgundian archives and has since frequently placed his time, knowledge and library at my disposal, to the considerable benefit of those parts of this book relating to Flanders. My colleague, Dr J. L. Price, provided me with translations of Flemish documents and then read the whole work in manuscript, as did Dr P. Chaplais. Both have saved me from a number of errors and infelicities; for those which remain I am, of course, alone responsible. Professor G. W. Coopland kindly lent me two otherwise unobtainable works; and Dr D. M. Bueno de Mesquita helped me with a difficult problem in

Italian history. Finally, I would like to thank the staffs of the libraries and archive repositories at which I have worked, and in particular the officials at Lille, who have answered my many queries about documents in the Burgundian archives with great promptness and courtesy.

J. J. N. PALMER

The University,
Hull

Abbreviations

(For the class numbers of manuscripts see bibliography)

ACO	Archives départementales de la Côte-d'Or, Dijon
ADN	Archives départementales du Nord, Lille
AN	Archives nationales, Paris
BARB	*Bulletin de l'Académie royale de Belgique*
BCRH	*Bulletin de la Commission royale d'histoire*
BEC	*Bibliothèque de l'Ecole des Chartes*
BIHR	*Bulletin of the Institute of Historical Research*
BM	British Museum
BN	Bibliothèque nationale, Paris
CCR	*Calendar of Close Rolls*
CChR	*Calendar of Charter Rolls*
CDIHF	Collection de documents inédits sur l'histoire de France
CFR	*Calendar of Fine Rolls*
CPR	*Calendar of Patent Rolls*
CRH	Commission royale d'histoire
DC	*Diplomatic Correspondence of Richard II*
Du Bosc	Du Bosc, *Voyage pour négocier la paix*
EHR	*English Historical Review*
Higden	'Monk of Westminster' in *Polychronicon Ranulphi Higden*, ix
HMSO	Her Majesty's Stationery Office
PPC	*Proceedings and Ordinances of the Privy Council*
RBPH	*Revue belge de philologie et d'histoire*
RC	Record Commission
REH	*Revue des études historiques*
RHD	*Revue d'histoire diplomatique*
RHE	*Revue d'histoire ecclésiastique*
RHS	Royal Historical Society

Abbreviations

RP	*Rotuli parliamentorum*
RQH	*Revue des questions historiques*
RS	Rolls Series
St Denys	*Chronique du religieux de St Denys*
SHF	Société de l'histoire de France
TRHS	*Transactions of the Royal Historical Society*

Chapter One

Introduction

On 18 June 1389 at Leulingham, a hamlet between Calais and Boulogne, a truce was sealed between England and France and their respective allies to last for three years, the longest break in the war since it had begun some twenty years previously, in 1369. Repeatedly renewed, the truce was eventually extended in 1396 to last until 29 September 1426; and although it was to be broken long before that date, it did in fact produce the longest cessation of hostilities during the entire course of the Hundred Years War.

When they put their seals to this truce the rulers of England and France could look back on the longest, hardest, most bitter and wide-ranging war in the history of their two countries. By comparison, the Edwardian phase of the war had been a comparatively mild affair, and England at least was not to be involved in so tough a struggle for another two centuries, if not longer. The Edwardian War was intermittent; the Caroline War (1369–89) unremitting. Some fifteen of the years between 1337 and 1360 were covered by truces, only four of those from 1369 to 1389. Actual hostilities occupied only eight of the twenty-three years of the earlier period but sixteen of the twenty years after 1369. At no time before 1360 did the war continue for more than thirty consecutive months without an equally long intermission; at no time after 1369 did it continue for less than six years without serious interruption.

Not only were the periods of war longer and the intervals of truce shorter but the fighting was more intensive in the second phase of the war. Fourteen major and a handful of minor expeditions were launched against France and her allies after 1369, only nine before 1360. This disparity was further accentuated by the marked increase in naval activity in the later period, particularly after 1377. Campaigns themselves were also generally longer and more arduous. An Edwardian army was normally in the field for three months. The army which besieged Calais was kept together for a year, and the winter expedition of 1359 lasted for over six months; but these were exceptional efforts made with unusually large forces in exceptionally favourable circumstances – after Crécy and Poitiers – which appeared to offer the chance of delivering a knock-out blow. By the later phase of the war the exception had become the norm, practised in normal circumstances. Armies were frequently contracted to serve for a year; and although few completed this term, the average period of service was double what it had been before 1360.

The greater intensity of the war in the 1370s and 1380s was apparent in other directions. Its geographical extent was far greater than it had been before. After Edward III's first mad spending spree, foreign allies had played little part in the struggle; but with the resumption of war under Charles V first Castile, then Portugal and finally Flanders and Guelders joined the fray and so widened the conflict. All the campaigns and battles before 1360 took place on French soil or within a few miles of her borders; but the later wars extended from Portugal to Guelders and from Scotland to Naples. Major English armies fought in Spain, Flanders and Portugal; while French expeditions were sent to Scotland, Flanders, Guelders, Italy and Castile, and on three occasions massive preparations were made to invade England itself. It is symptomatic that the two great battles of the earlier period were fought on French soil, within a few miles of English bases, whereas the comparable battles of the later period were fought at opposite ends of Europe in Flanders and Portugal.

Despite the greater intensity with which the war was waged, a decision seemed more remote than ever. This fundamental fact has been somewhat obscured by the excessive prominence given to the English reverses after 1369. These, it is true, were serious enough. Within the space of just a few years the great principality of Aquitaine, stretching from the Loire to the Pyrenees and from the Bay of Biscay to Auvergne, was reduced to a coastal strip south of the Gironde and a handful of castles on the right bank of the Dordogne. No Crécy or Poitiers shed their lustre on the later period; no captive kings paraded through London, and the Tower was very nearly empty of French aristocrats for the entire twenty years. But the French successes were not un-interrupted, they were not final, and they never looked like being so. By the mid-1370s the position had been more or less stabilized and a long war of attrition, more harmful to France than to her neighbour, had begun.

The reasons both for the French successes and for their limitations are not in themselves obscure. Foremost among them was the calibre of the French leaders, Charles V and his brother Philip the Bold, duke of Burgundy.[1] Charles was a ruler of great political courage, endowed with an iron will and a keen intellect. His greatest weakness was perhaps a certain insensitiveness and inflexibility which led him on occasions to over-reach himself. His mistakes in Brittany and Flanders towards the end of his life, for instance, would have cost him very dearly indeed had he lived long enough to experience their results. Fortunately both for his own reputation and for the integrity of his Crown he died before account had to be rendered. His brother Philip was perhaps an even more gifted ruler; certainly he was a more supple politician. He not only rectified Charles's mistakes in Flanders and Brittany but actually turned the situations there to his own advantage and to that of France. He was the equal of his brother, too, in political courage, and in the first two years of his nephew's reign he guided the monarchy through the gravest crisis it had undergone since the days of Etienne Marcel and the Jacquerie. After his brother's death, Philip's effective control over the French government lasted almost exactly as long as the remainder of the war: he was dismissed by Charles VI on his return from the final campaign of the century. Between them, therefore, he and his elder brother provided the French leadership for the whole of its twenty years, giving France the firm direction she had conspicuously lacked in the earlier phase of the struggle. For the first and only time in the Hundred Years War the French leaders were the equals if not the superiors of their enemies.

It was equally important that they provided themselves with the essential means for waging the war. France was a larger, richer, more populous country than her enemy, but she had hitherto been unable to bring these advantages to bear, very largely because she lacked regular war taxation and an efficient system of public credit. At the beginning of the war, using it as his excuse, Charles V managed to remedy this deficiency. The *aide*, the *taille* and the *gabelle*, first voted by the Estates, were then taken at will for the remainder of the reign. From 1369 the French government derived a steady revenue from both direct and indirect taxation on a national scale, and from that date France actually enjoyed an advantage over her rival in that these taxes, unlike those voted by the English parliament, were completely regular and remained so (with one brief interval) for the remainder of the war. They were not only regular, but enormously lucrative, producing something like ten times the extraordinary revenues of the English government. The financial superiority hitherto enjoyed by England thus passed to France, and this one development does much to explain the new course taken by the war after 1369. With his new resources Charles V was able to maintain a permanent army, some six thousand strong.[2] England could not match this, and as soon as her armies left the field the French forces resumed their seemingly inexorable encroachment against the principality. Within a few years the French were thus able to drive their enemies out of the greater part of Aquitaine without winning a major battle and without establishing any sort of military superiority over the enemy. This was achieved by sheer weight of numbers, made possible by superior financial resources.

On a lower plane of importance France benefited much more than did England from the support of her allies. Throughout the twenty years of the struggle Castile provided regular naval support in Biscay and the Channel. Castilian forces inflicted the only major defeat of the war on the English at La Rochelle, in 1372; and it was Castilian galleys which several times created havoc along the south coast of England, destroying a number of small towns and creating a general feeling of insecurity such as England had not suffered for many decades. The ever-present threat of a major invasion of Aquitaine from Castile added considerably to her value as an ally; for although an invasion materialized on only one occasion (1374), and then with farcical results, the mere threat harassed the English government throughout the period.

No other ally on either side played quite so active or important a role as Castile. Even the Scots were relatively quiescent until the 1380s, though they then made up for lost time. But the inactivity of the remaining countries was mainly to England's disadvantage. Flemish neutrality certainly favoured France rather than England; and when the Flemings did eventually become involved, their participation was very largely detrimental to England. England also lost from the increasing tendency of the Bretons to dissociate themselves from the war. At one period, indeed, the de Montfort party, allies for the better part of forty years, made their peace with France and joined her ranks against an English army. Finally, the king of Navarre, perhaps the most useful of Edward III's allies, took only a minor part in the conflict after 1369.

Thus England was not only without major allies for the greater part of the two decades, but she had to face an enemy already richer, more powerful and more numerous than herself, actively supported by allies of considerable strength in their own right. It became a forlorn theme of English thinking that the country faced the whole world in isolation;

and there was none of the spirit of 'Come the three corners of the world in arms, and we shall shock them'. The first parliament of Richard II's reign complained of the wars of 'France, Spain, Ireland, Aquitaine, Brittany and others', and of the overwhelming number of the king's enemies, who completely encircled the country. Subsequent assemblies echoed the complaint and lengthened the list of enemies. Towards the end of the war, when the increasing strain was having a cumulative effect, this factor dominated all military discussion. Almost every parliament of the 1380s made plaintive reference to the innumerable enemies surrounding the kingdom; all of them rich, powerful and active; all intent on the utter destruction of the country; all inseparably banded together by firm alliances; and all possessing separate and highly dangerous advantages over their isolated and dismayed opponent.[3]

A further advantage commonly credited to France has almost certainly been exaggerated. The quality of leadership on the English side has been consistently denigrated, and much has been made of the internal divisions which allegedly existed during Edward III's dotage and his grandson's minority. Yet it is difficult, if not impossible, to pinpoint any military or political reverse which can be attributed to poor leadership, divided counsel, or sheer incompetence.[4] Division of opinion and argument there certainly was, as was unavoidable in the circumstances; but little if any of this controversy can be shown to have been factious, and once a decision had been taken all parties appear to have given it their support. It was only during the very last years of the war, when Richard II himself began to participate in the government of his kingdom, that really serious divisions appeared, with equally serious consequences. But until that time his uncles provided effective leadership under difficult and trying conditions.

As to leadership in the field, it is arguable that in this period English military superiority reached its peak for the entire Hundred Years War. Despite the far greater resources at his command, Charles V consistently refused to fight English armies, whatever the provocation. They were shadowed and harassed, and when they eventually returned home the French armies resumed their attack on Aquitaine under the capable direction of the duke of Anjou and the constable, du Guesclin. These tactics have been highly praised, with some justice. Consistent pressure from a standing army drove the English from the greater part of Aquitaine, while Charles's refusal to fight pitched battles effectively preserved France from the disasters to which every other of her kings exposed her during the war by offering battle. Yet these tactics had important limitations which have been insufficiently recognized. The English leaders knew that any army they chose to put into the field could march through France with near impunity. This knowledge gave them advantages which they enjoyed at no other period, not even under Edward III at the height of his fortunes. After 1369 quite small English armies of four to six thousand men criss-crossed the heart of France, the duke of Lancaster burning and ravaging Artois, Picardy and Normandy (1369); Robert Knolles leading his men through the Ile de France, round Paris, into Poitou and then back into Brittany (1370); Lancaster marching through the centre of the kingdom from Calais to Bordeaux (1373), a prodigious military achievement which has been unjustly denigrated; his brother, the earl of Cambridge, crossing Brittany from east to west (1375); and finally, the earl of Buckingham, the youngest of Richard II's uncles, burning his way from Calais to Brittany via Paris (1380). By comparison, the much-discussed march of Henry V from Harfleur to Calais was very small beer indeed; and only once before had Edward III flaunted his armies before the French in this way without the aid of a diversionary invasion from another direction.

The amount of damage and destruction wrought by these armies can only be surmised; but the probability is that it was very extensive, and the more effective for being inflicted on the inner provinces of the kingdom. In addition, the blow to French morale and prestige was incalculable, and it must be considered one of Charles V's better claims to fame that he was able to survive it. But it should be emphasized that he did survive rather than triumph. As he lay dying, yet another English army was blazing its way unmolested through the very heart of his kingdom. For something like a fifth of his reign English armies lived on his territories, mocking him and his captains; the peasant who claimed that he dare not get out of bed in the morning for fear of the English was representative of a large percentage of his subjects.[5] His successes were bought at a high price.

While Charles V refused to face the enemy in the field his subjects had to take what was dealt out to them; but his strategy had a more important limitation than this. It avoided the possibility of defeat, but at the cost of the chance of victory. At first this was obscured by the comparative ease with which the English territories were occupied without the need to fight pitched battles. But as soon as the English possessions were reduced to a circle of strongholds around Calais and Bordeaux, the stalemate became apparent. England had the men and the money to defend these limited territories and could only be ejected from them by the thoroughgoing defeat of her armies. Since Charles renounced the attempt to do this, he could not force a final decision. He could only hope to wear his opponent down.

But at this date England showed no desire to withdraw from the struggle. In fact, as soon as the position in Aquitaine had been stabilized she was not slow to produce an answer to Charles V's Fabian strategy. The marked disparity between English and French resources in money and manpower made the reconquest of Aquitaine impracticable, even if it had been desirable: the attempt was not even made. Instead, the government sought to exploit to the limit the invulnerability of its armies while maintaining military pressure on France in the intervals between their *chevauchées*. To do this, it set out to acquire a ring of fortresses around the coast of France. In the mid-1370s England still held Calais, Bordeaux and Bayonne. In 1378 Brest was acquired from the duke of Brittany, and Cherbourg from the king of Navarre; and in the same year the earl of Arundel tried to seize Harfleur, while the duke of Lancaster besieged St Malo for five months.[6] Two years later the earl of Buckingham sat before Nantes for more than two months. In the following year, and again in 1382, attempts were made to subvert the key port of La Rochelle.[7] Bishop Despenser succeeded in taking (though not in holding) most of the Flemish coast between Gravelines and Blankenberghe in 1383, and in 1387 the earl of Arundel came very close to taking Sluys, the greatest port along the entire North Sea coastline. Finally, in the last year of the war the earl of Arundel made a further attempt on La Rochelle.[8] All these efforts were made possible by greatly increased naval activity. No less than eleven major fleets were launched between 1369 and the end of the war.[9]

This new strategy served a variety of purposes. In the first place it greatly strengthened the English defences. French successes, coupled with English isolation, had given a defensive tinge to military thinking at Westminster. The fortresses of Calais, Cherbourg, Brest, Bordeaux and Bayonne were 'barbicans of the realm', and when backed by the increased activity of the navy they guaranteed that the war would be confined to its proper place, on the far side of the Channel. But their purpose was not essentially nor even primarily defensive. They provided not only the security necessary for a successful attacking strategy but also the means to execute it. They were 'fine and noble entries and ports to grieve' the enemy, enabling the government to choose its moment, method and direction of attack with considerable freedom.[10] In the intervals between attacks, the garrisons of Calais, Cherbourg and Brest could maintain military pressure on the enemy, plundering the surrounding countryside and terrorizing the population. In time the cumulative effect of persistent destruction of this kind might produce a political reaction in Paris, and in the meantime French resources were being wasted and large numbers of her troops pinned down. Control of the whole length of the Channel also enabled the English government to keep a stranglehold on French trade with the Low Countries. The extent of the damage inflicted on France by these means cannot be accurately determined, but it was certainly considerable. During the last two years of the war, when Flanders was engaged on the side of France and the entire traffic passing down the Channel came under English attack, her enemies suffered quite staggering maritime losses in a very brief period.[11]

Above all, the new strategy made the best possible use of English resources. Though the 'bastions' were expensive to maintain there were few enough of them to make the burden bearable. They were easy to defend, could be supplied from the sea, and made comparatively light demands on English manpower. In short, they tended to neutralize the advantages enjoyed by the French by virtue of their numerical and financial superiority. The net result was something like a military stalemate.

This stalemate affected the two sides in very different ways. Englishmen were almost exclusively hit financially. The south and east coasts, it is true, suffered from hit-and-run raids from enemy shipping. Several towns on the south coast were burnt – notably in 1377 – and even as far north as Bridlington the priory found it necessary to build an *enceinte* of considerable dimensions to protect itself from surprise attacks from the sea. Though the government allocated substantial resources to new fortifications, particularly at Southampton and Great Yarmouth, there were frequent and vociferous complaints in parliament about the inadequacy of its naval and coastal defences. Nevertheless, the volume of complaint should not be taken as an index to the amount of damage wrought by these raids. It was the novelty rather than the seriousness of the situation which caused so many voices to be pitched so high. It is in the highest degree improbable that all these attacks lumped together did half as much damage as a single English *chevauchée*.

The sufferings of Englishmen were largely confined to their pockets, though here the suffering was real enough. Taxation had never been higher than in the first decade of the reign of Richard II, and throughout the late 1370s and the early 1380s the volume of complaint heard in parliament grew steadily, reaching deafening proportions. Almost every parliament meant a major political crisis for this one reason. In the Gloucester parliament of 1378 the Commons denied that it was their responsibility to finance foreign war, insisting that they could only be taxed for the defence of the realm. Though they were induced to take a more reasonable view by the argument that the English overseas possessions were the bulwarks of English defence, the grant they eventually made produced only £6,000, a derisory sum. The following parliament was a little more co-operative, voting a novel poll tax; but the yield of this tax was only a fraction of what had been anticipated, and in the parliament of January 1380 the chancellor had a sorry tale to unfold. An army of 4,000 men destined for Brittany had had to be reduced to a mere 1,300 effectives, and even this small force had exhausted the grant of the previous assembly. The royal coffers were completely empty; the Crown heavily indebted, and no provision at all had as yet been made for the coming campaigning season. Of the loan of some £14,000 contracted a year previously, not a penny had so far been repaid; the king's jewels were still in pawn; and the garrisons of Calais, Cherbourg and Brest, and the forces in Ireland and Gascony had reveived no wages for longer than the chancellor cared to recall.

On this occasion parliament was moved to make a fairly generous grant; but when its successor met less than a year later, it heard an equally gloomy account from the government. The wages of all English garrisons were now some twenty weeks in arrears; the Crown jewels still in pawn; and the king heavily indebted for loans contracted for the defence of the borders of Scotland, Ireland and Aquitaine. On top of all this, half a year's wages was owed to the army serving in Brittany under the earl of Buckingham, and no provision had as yet been made for the military commitments of the coming year. Impressed by Buckingham's activities in France and Brittany, and no doubt cheered by the very recent death of Charles V, the Commons chose on this occasion to make a very special effort. Although they repudiated any liability for the king's debts, they voted the generous subsidy of £66,000, to be levied as a poll tax.

The fate of that disastrous tax is well enough known. The Peasants' Revolt put an end to the generosity of the Commons and heralded a period of financial stringency without parallel in the previous stages of the war. The first parliament to meet after the Revolt not only produced no grant but made the extraordinary demand that if a peace or truce were negotiated, then the proceeds of the wool subsidy – by this date an indispensable item in the regular revenues of the Crown – should be saved, as a reserve against future emergencies. It was virtually unknown for parliament to refuse to grant a subsidy of some kind; yet not only did the assembly of November 1381 do so, but its refusal was repeated by its successor in May 1382.[12] And even this was not the final extent of the stringency produced by the shock of the Revolt; for although the parliament of October 1382 did vote a modest single subsidy, its immediate successor (February 1383) once again refused a grant, contenting itself with earmarking the proceeds of the subsidy granted in the previous October for a campaign in Flanders in the coming summer.[13]

For three out of four parliaments to refuse a grant of direct taxation was unprecedented, and this defiant opposition to the government was particularly striking in view of the contemporary circumstances. Not only was the government waging a war which entitled it to the financial support of its subjects, but it was doing so under a young king who had just won his spurs and was eager to lead his first army abroad. Though he was barely fifteen, Richard's spirited behaviour during the Revolt had earned him this right, which his council pressed on parliament. In May and in October 1382, and again in February 1383, the council pleaded with the Commons for a sufficiently generous grant to finance an army large enough to be led by the king in person. The plea was supported by the Lords, who in great councils held immediately prior to these parliaments had not only approved the idea of a royal expedition in principle but had promised to serve the king for the period of a year at greatly reduced rates. But neither the pressure exerted by the council, nor the backing of the Lords, nor the example set by their proffered sacrifices were to any avail. The only subsidy granted by the first four parliaments to meet after the Revolt was finally earmarked for a 'crusade' to be led by the bishop of Norwich, on the grounds that this was cheaper than a royal expedition.

The unfortunate results of this economy are all too well known. The crusade was a dismal failure, the bishop experiencing the double degradation of leading the only army of the entire period which the French were prepared to face in the field, an army which then refused the opportunity to fight so eagerly sought by a whole succession of English armies since 1369. The young king's effort to rescue Despenser and attack the French was frustrated, like the previously projected royal expeditions, by lack of money.[14]

Parliament's stubborn and prolonged resistance to taxation marked a turning-point in the war. During the four years after the Peasants' Revolt the only important expedition mounted against France and her continental allies was the Despenser crusade, which was only partially financed by the government and was not strictly comparable to the efforts of previous years. By contrast, three major fleets and three important armies had been launched against the enemy in the four years prior to 1381. And this was by no means the only sign of military retrenchment. Expenditure on Calais, Cherbourg and Brest was drastically reduced. From 7,000 marks a year in 1381, the fee of the captain of Brest had been reduced to a mere 2,000 marks by the end of 1385; and during roughly the same period the fee of the captain of Cherbourg fell from about £10,000 to a paltry £2,000. War subsidies to the duchy of Aquitaine were slashed even more dramatically. After averaging over £20,000 a year between 1373 and 1379, they were cut right back to about £500 per annum from November 1379 and ceased altogether from October 1381.[15]

The result was disastrous, for the decline occurred at the very worst possible moment. The death of Charles V in 1380, the internal convulsions in France during the first two years of the minority of Charles VI, and the potentially highly favourable situation which developed in Flanders during the same period, all combined to present England with the best opportunity she had had since 1369 to make real headway against France. Lack of money alone prevented her from doing so.

If the problems of the English government were almost exclusively financial, those of her opponent were more complex. At first sight, indeed, it might be doubted whether the French had financial problems at all. Except for a short period following the death of Charles V (September 1380 to January 1383), the French Crown enjoyed a regular income from both direct and indirect taxation throughout the war. By English standards the receipts were enormous. It has been calculated[16] that the revenue from the internal sales tax (*aide*) and the tax on salt (*gabelle*) was roughly two million francs, and that the direct tax (*taille*) produced an additional million a year between 1384 and 1388. The receipts would probably not have been much different under Charles V himself. Three million francs (£500,000) was approximately ten times the annual revenue of the English Crown from its extraordinary sources. The discrepancy between the financial resources of the two countries would in fact have been rather greater than these figures suggest, since a variety of local military expenses were paid for by local or regional taxes in France which are unaccounted for in the figures given above.

Yet it would be wrong to conclude that Charles VI and his ministers had no financial problems. The revolts of the years 1380 to 1382 had left their mark. Though taxation was arbitrary thereafter, there were limits beyond which it was not expedient to go, and the pressure of war drove the government dangerously close to those limits. The crushing burden of taxation was the theme not only of chroniclers and moralists but even of government edicts. One writer estimated that no less than fifteen *tailles* were imposed on Normandy during the last five years of the war, and another itemized ten *tailles* levied on a national scale between 1385 and 1388 alone. Clearly this pace could not be kept up. Towns and villages were deserted as their inhabitants fled the tax-collector, and resistance to his demands became commonplace. Yet despite enormous sacrifices imposed on the population, the government lived from hand to mouth, without reserves. Important projects were abandoned for lack of money, and at the end of the war the king's ministers could still claim – with some exaggeration perhaps – that their master had not two francs to his name.[17]

Even in Paris, therefore, financial considerations were a powerful argument in favour of peace. But France had other problems, equally if not more pressing. The war was fought on French soil. The great *chevauchées* of 1369, 1370, 1373, 1375 and 1380 left a trail of devastation and destruction in their wake. On top of this, the Cotentin was plundered and ransomed by the garrison of Cherbourg; Picardy and Artois by that of Calais, and west Brittany by that of Brest. Brittany was intermittently plunged into war throughout the period, and Flanders, soon to come under the rule of a French prince, was ravaged by four years of ruinous civil war and by the passage of several major English and French armies.

To the south the situation was even worse. The whole area between the Charente and the Garonne was in dispute and suffered extremely heavily throughout the war.[18] The plight of the surrounding provinces of Rouergue, Auvergne, Limousin and Quercy was, if anything, more desperate due to the depredations of the mercenaries, or 'the English' as they were familiarly known. Their activities became an increasing problem to the French authorities as the war wore on. By the 1380s they controlled some forty major castles in and around Auvergne, dominating an enormous block of territory from Gascony almost to the Rhône. In the absence of a French army their range of activity was even greater. In 1383, during Charles VI's campaign in Flanders, the garrison of

Carlat raided beyond the Loire, while an Anglo-Gascon force occupied Verteuil and Taillebourg, threatening La Rochelle; and in 1386, when the projected invasion of England drew all the French forces northwards, the 'English' raided to the gates of Toulouse, subjected the whole of Quercy to ransom, and threatened to dominate the Agenais. Other raiders reached Rabastens and Carcassonne.[19]

Finally, in Provence only the armourers thrived.[20] On top of the burden of taxation and the raids of the 'English', the civil wars engendered by the Neapolitan succession and the Schism added to the almost unendurable misery of the population. The *Tuchin* revolt was both an expression of this misery and a consummation of the ruin of the entire region.

With Languedoc and Provence virtually *hors de combat*; Brittany, Normandy, Picardy and Flanders under continual military pressure; the inland provinces periodically devastated; and sea traffic with the Low Countries exposed to staggering losses, it is scarcely surprising that the French government became increasingly anxious for a settlement as the war wore on. This tendency was fostered by the royal uncles of Charles VI, whose particularist interests inclined them in favour of peace. The duke of Berry had nothing to gain from a war which wasted money he would have preferred to lavish on his art treasures. His brother Anjou favoured peace because it would release resources for his conquest of the kingdom of Naples. And the duke of Burgundy favoured peace because of the damage done to his inheritance by the war. As heir to, then ruler of Flanders, Philip had every reason to wish to be on good terms with England. With her monopoly of wool, her powerful mercantile marine, and her geographical position, England could ruin the industrial and commercial prosperity of Flanders if the country was dragged into the war. Moreover, history had shown that the Flemings would sooner revolt against their own ruler than take up arms against England. As a Frenchman and a Clementist, Philip was already unpopular enough in Flanders. He could ill-afford to add to his existing disabilities as its ruler. Yet if he inherited the country while the war was in progress, he could not hope to maintain Flemish neutrality, since this would give a handle to his opponents within France, thus weakening his control (which was never absolute) over the French government. The most satisfactory way out of this impasse was to end the war with England.

Political incentives towards a settlement were reinforced by idealistic considerations, which grew steadily stronger as the war progressed. It was obvious to all concerned that the Anglo-French struggle was the most potent factor favouring the continuance of the Schism, and it was equally obvious that with each passing year an eventual solution to the Schism became more and more problematical and the possibility of a permanent division within the Catholic world more and more likely. At any time such a prospect would have caused serious concern; but in the particular circumstances of the 1380s it held a menace which no statesman in Europe could ignore. For while Christendom was divided within it was under siege from without. After breaking into Europe in mid-century, the Ottoman Turks had expanded at the expense of their Christian neighbours with astonishing rapidity. The battle of Marica (September 1371) established their hegemony in the Balkans, and in the course of the next few years the king of Bulgaria, the princes of Serbia, and even the emperor of Byzantium became tributaries to the sultan. In the 1380s vassaldom began to give way to complete subjection. Serres fell to the Turks in 1383, Sofia about 1385, Nis in 1386, Thessalonika in 1387. In 1388 Bulgaria was once again subjugated and in 1389, at Kossovo, Serbian independence was finally crushed. Thereafter the pace quickened. Independent Bulgaria ceased to exist in 1393, Thessaly was overrun in the same year, and by 1395 the Turks had even established themselves in the Peloponnese. All this was watched with rapidly growing alarm by a divided Europe. It had become imperative for England and France to settle their differences and lead a Christian counter-offensive, for no other country was equipped to do so. From the early 1380s both governments began to show signs of an awareness of this moral obligation and a readiness to act upon it.[21]

All these factors combined to produce a growing desire for peace. Throughout the 1380s the English parliament continued to urge the need for an end to the war. It became an essential ingredient of any argument aimed at persuading them of the superiority of one strategy to another that it would bring the war to 'a good and hasty conclusion' – and since the 'good' was superfluous, the emphasis here was evidently intended to fall on the need for a rapid end to the struggle. When they were asked point-blank to give preference to the continuance of the war or the conclusion of peace in 1384, the Commons plumped decisively for peace, 'the most noble and gracious aid and comfort' that could possibly be devised for them. The same desire is apparent in all the French chronicles of the period, and is also evident in the evolution of the peace talks during the later years of the war.

Until 1374 both sides had shown extreme reluctance to discuss a truce, let alone negotiate peace; but as the pressures of war mounted, this intransigence disappeared. The first major conference was held in 1375, and between that date and the truce of 1389 peace or truce talks were held in every intervening year.

It is unfortunately impossible to determine the exact nature of these discussions, but the broad outlines of their progress can be discerned.[22] Both parties made considerable concessions. England consented to put to one side discussion of her claim to the French throne and was prepared to settle for something less than the restitution of the principality of Aquitaine. The French, too, steadily increased their offers. In 1375 they demanded the total withdrawal of the English from France, but only two years later Charles V was prepared to concede the whole of Aquitaine south of the Dordogne, together with the towns and fortresses of Bourg, Blaye, Libourne, St Emilion and Castillon on the north side of the river. Historians have found these offers surprisingly generous, yet before the end of his reign Charles was prepared to add Cahors and Quercy, Périgord, Saintonge (south of the Charente), Vabres and Rouergue, and even to contemplate the cession of the greater part of Limousin and the whole of Angoumois. A glance at the map will reveal that this offer more than doubled that of 1377; and although it would have left Richard II with substantially less than his grandfather had acquired at Brétigny, it would nevertheless have given him an Aquitaine whose boundaries were far wider than they had been on the eve of the Hundred Years War. Charles V's final offer should dispel any illusions about the degree of French success in the war, which the king himself clearly did not share.

But it was the question of sovereignty rather than the extent of the English possessions which proved the most intractable problem. The king of England demanded complete independence in Aquitaine; the king of France refused to relinquish his sovereignty. This was not an argument over words and formulae, but over the realities of power. Could the king of England legislate for his Gascon subjects? Could he tax them? Settle their disputes without outside interference? Or lead them against his enemies, even against France? Or must he enforce French legislation; seek permission from Paris to levy taxation; allow appeals against his rulings to the *parlement*, and accept that his subjects must serve the French king against their English duke if the interests of the two were to clash? Only force it had seemed could answer these questions. But neither side had in fact been able to achieve the necessary military and political ascendency to enforce its own will. Some *via media* was required before negotiations for peace could even begin in earnest. It is a testimony to the urgency with which peace was sought that no less than three possible solutions were devised.

The most radical of these solutions will be discussed in the next chapter, and the least radical does not require much discussion. It proposed to evade rather than to solve the problem, by the conclusion of a long truce of up to fifty years, during which period the status quo would be maintained and all rights and claims remain in abeyance. Thus for the duration of the truce the king of England would exercise a *de facto* sovereignty in the part of Aquitaine under his control, but would cease to use the title 'king of France'. He would not, however, acquire any right to the sovereignty he used, nor lose his right to the title he ceased to employ. The unsatisfactory nature of this solution is apparent enough, and it is scarcely surprising to find that it was the last resort of both sides.

The third solution – which could be combined with the first – was some sort of agreed limitation on the French king's exercise of his sovereignty. At first the French were very reluctant to agree to this solution. In 1376 Edward III urged his ambassadors to press for 'modifications' (the technical jargon for limitation on sovereignty), which were evidently not much to the taste of the French. In the following year Charles V was still insisting that sovereignty be 'entirely' his. But before 1380 he had backed down and had accepted 'modifications' as the basis for negotiations, even committing himself so far as to persuade the English council to a written agreement on the subject. After his death it was the English who made difficulties, withdrawing their agreement and twice reneging on their commitments under various pretexts, with the French anxiously trying to hold them to their earlier position. Later, 'modifications' became inextricably involved with the first solution; but in the period from about 1377 to 1382 'modifications' provided the main hope for a solution to the problem of sovereignty over Aquitaine, and a formula which at the very least enabled the two sides to discuss peace terms.

With both governments disposed to explore all possible avenues towards peace, and with the pressures upon them to do so steadily mounting, it may appear strange that the war lasted for as long as it did. One of the major reasons for the continuance of the struggle was that it could not be isolated from a number of other conflicts. Succession disputes in Brittany, Flanders, Castile and within the papacy were so closely related to the main conflict that it could not be terminated

1. The Breton succession
= (1) Arthur II (2) =
John III, d. 1341 — Guy de Penthièvre
no issue
JOHN = Joan
d. 1345
Louis de Mâle =
c. bf. Flanders
1346–84
CHARLES DE BLOIS = Joan
d. 1364
d. 1384
JOHN IV (1) = 1361 Mary, d. of
1345–99
Edward III
(2) = 1366 Joan Holand,
d. 1384
(3) = 1386 Joan of Navarre
Margaret = Philip of
Burgundy
Olivier de Clisson
Constable of France
Louis I of = Marie
Anjou
d. 1384
Guy
d. 1385
JOHN = Margaret
Joan
b. 1387
d. 1388
Peter/JOHN V
b. 1389
1399–1442
Joan/Mary
b. 1391
Arthur
b. 1393
House of Anjou
Family of Penthièvre
Dukes of Brittany
Counts of Flanders
(Names printed in capitals are those of Rival Claimants)

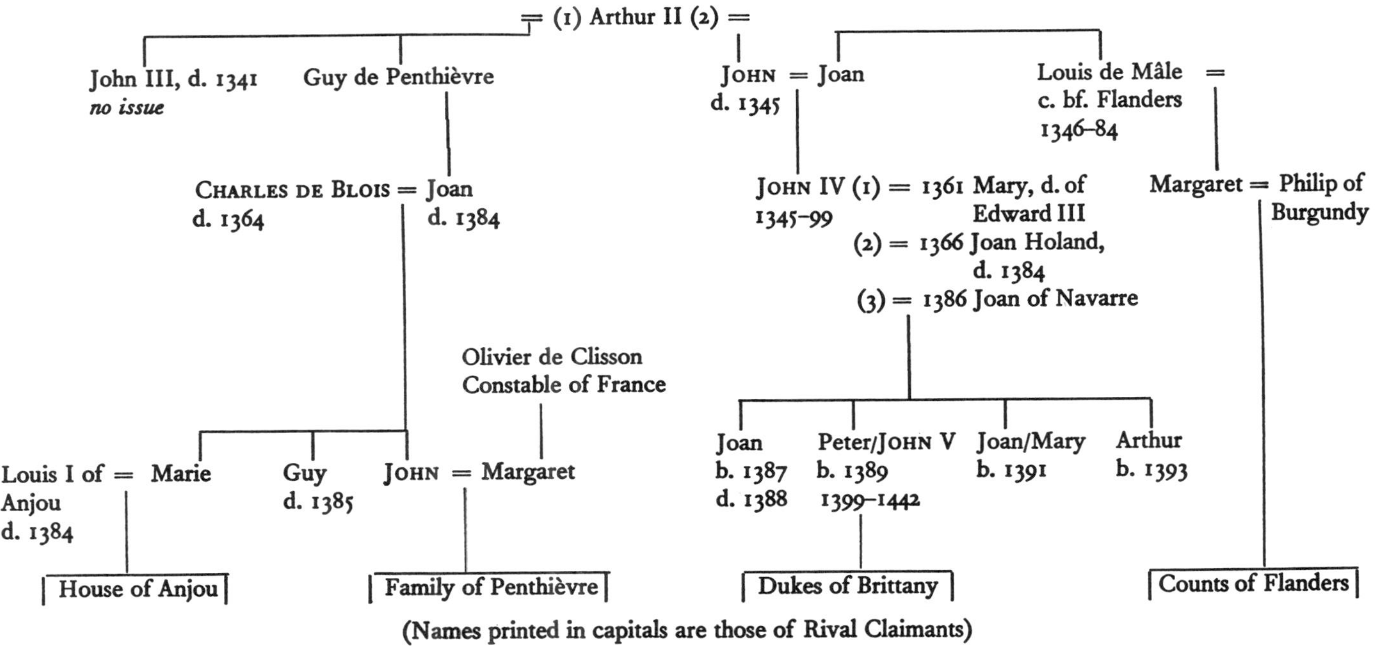

17

without a concurrent solution to some or all of these peripheral disputes. For though they had been provoked or nurtured by the Anglo-French duel, these side-shows had acquired an impetus of their own and could not be terminated by the simple *fiat* of either of the two kings.

The thorniest and most perennial of these issues was the forty-year-old Breton civil war between the houses of Blois and Montfort, which had been given a new lease of life by the renewal of the Anglo-French war in 1369. After lending underhand support to England in the early years of the war, John de Montfort declared openly for Edward III in 1372 and fled to England. The duchy was then occupied by French troops, ostensibly for defensive purposes. But instead of handing it over to de Montfort's rival, Joan of Penthièvre – her son was in an English prison – Charles rather foolishly annexed the duchy to his Crown in 1378. As a result, de Montfort was invited back by the Bretons, whose love of independence was greater than their dislike of his connections. With the backing of an English army, de Montfort was triumphantly reinstated. Had Charles not died at this moment, the consequences of de Montfort's return might well have been extremely serious. But his death liquidated the element of a personal vendetta between the king and the duke, enabling Philip of Burgundy to snatch diplomatic victory from military defeat. By the second treaty of Guérande, concluded on 4 April 1381, John de Montfort was recognized as rightful duke of Brittany in return for his homage, his recognition of French sovereignty, and his promise to aid France against England and Navarre. As security for his good behaviour, he was also obliged to pay a stiff fine which was not, however, immediately exacted. His disappointed rival, John de Blois, was compensated by confirmation of his possession of the counties of Penthièvre and Limoges and of his position as heir apparent to the duchy.[23]

At first it appeared that the treaty would simply produce a change of alliances rather than an end to the war. Angered by de Montfort's duplicity, the English government confiscated his earldom of Richmond and offered to free John de Blois in return for an alliance against France, his homage for Brittany, and his marriage to a daughter of the duke of Lancaster.[24] But John de Blois rejected this offer. To have accepted would have cost him the support of his friends at the French court; and in any case, the treaty of Guérande was not entirely unfavourable to him. It guaranteed both his family possessions and his position as heir apparent to the duchy; and since de Montfort was now over forty and still childless – his second wife being barren after fifteen years of marriage – de Blois's chances of succeeding him peacefully were by no means remote.

De Blois's refusal of the English offer produced a momentary but uneasy calm. England had nothing to gain by attacking Brittany without the support of one of the two rivals, and so for as long as de Montfort refrained from openly and actively assisting France, he was left in peace. Though Richmond was retained in the king's hands, its temporary confiscation was not converted into a permanent forfeiture.

It was obviously in de Montfort's interests to maintain this precarious equilibrium; but the pressure on him to join in the war against England was considerable. He had powerful enemies in France who considered the treaty of Guérande a betrayal and who would not hesitate to exploit any opportunity to embarrass or to unseat the duke. Chief among these was the constable, Olivier de Clisson, head of an anti-Montfortist coalition. De Clisson, himself a Breton, had long been the strong arm of the Blois party. He was closely supported by the Angevins, who were allied by marriage to the house of Blois, and by the Marmosets, a group of influential ministers of the late king. What made this combination particularly dangerous was that it bade fair one day to oust Philip of Burgundy from his control of the French government, and when that day dawned de Montfort could expect no mercy. There was thus a natural community of interests between him and Philip, a bond cemented by family ties and (later) by a certain similarity in their positions as vassals of the French Crown and pawns in the Anglo-French war.[25] Whatever strengthened de Montfort thereby weakened Philip's rival, and any reverse suffered by the duke of Burgundy threatened the security of the duke of Brittany.

In these circumstances it was essential to both that de Montfort act as a 'good Frenchman', yet necessary for him to do so without antagonizing England to the point of provoking serious reprisals. He was quite up to this difficult task and his actions in the mid-1380s were all characterized by ambiguity and ambivalence. He negotiated with England but sought French permission to do so. His subjects served against England but in their private capacities. The duke himself joined the French army in 1383 but claimed that he was assisting his cousin, the count of Flanders, not aiding the French.[26] Finally, de Montfort concluded a private alliance with the dukes of Burgundy and Berry in February 1384. Whether the alliance was directed against de Clisson, against England (the only likely enemies) or against some other party, was not stated, and the omission was evidently intentional.[27] By these means, Brittany was kept 'neutral' and the duchy enjoyed a few years' unaccustomed peace. But it was a precarious peace. It only required the death of de Montfort's wife and a slight shift in English policy at the end of 1384 to upset the fine balance which de Montfort had managed to achieve and so to bring Brittany back into the war.

During the period that Brittany enjoyed her precarious peace Flanders became the focus of Anglo-French rivalries. After 1369 the count, Louis de Mâle, managed to keep Flanders neutral, refusing to be drawn in on either side, whatever the pressures or enticements. The nice balance he achieved was symbolized by the marriage of his daughter and heiress to the duke of Burgundy on the one hand, and a commercial treaty with England and his adhesion to the 'English' pope, Urban VI, on the other. Even the outbreak of civil war with the towns in 1379 failed to upset this balance, and from 1379 until 1382 the struggle between Louis and his subjects remained a domestic concern. But then, quite suddenly, in the spring of 1382, the internal affairs of Flanders were transformed into an international crisis, and England and Ghent lined up against France and Louis. In rapid succession three major armies – one English and two French – invaded the county; and although the tempo slowed down thereafter, Flanders remained the most crucial issue between the two sides for the remainder of the war.

The explosion has been blamed on an economic crisis provoked by Louis de Mâle. According to this view,[28] Louis, unable to reduce Ghent by conventional military means, tried to crush her by placing an embargo on English wool, on which the livelihood of her population depended. The ban was effective beyond all expectation, but with quite unforeseen results. Goaded beyond endurance by blockade, Ghent staked everything on a gambler's chance, offered battle, and unexpectedly and decisively defeated Louis at Beverhoutsveld (3 May 1382). At the same time England, shaken out of her neutrality by the catastrophic decline of her wool exports, rushed to the assistance of Ghent. By July, if not earlier, an alliance was under discussion, and by October the Flemings were ready to receive an English army.[29] In the event the allies were pre-empted by the French, who got their army into the field first, crushing the Flemish militia at Roosebeke on 27 November before England could come to its assistance. But France only intervened to forestall England. The root of the trouble was the English reaction to the threat to her wool trade.

It is difficult to accept this analysis. The English government could not have been unaware that its intervention would provoke French retaliation, with far more serious consequences for its wool trade than a temporary embargo could ever produce. Had her policy been dictated by economic considerations, England would have sat back and prayed that the embargo worked, and worked quickly. Her export figures, which have been cited as evidence that she intervened to protect economic interests, really prove quite the contrary; for though there was a decline during the period of the embargo, the bottom only fell out of the market in the next year, following the irruption of English and French armies into the county.[30] The one other piece of evidence which has been produced to support the economic thesis is even more irrelevant. In the autumn of 1382 the government abandoned the wool staple at Calais and it has been suggested that it did so because the wool shipments through Calais (i.e. to Flanders) had become negligible. The last point cannot be directly verified; but the government gave its reasons for abandoning the staple, and these had nothing to do with a decline in exports to Flanders. The staple restrictions were lifted as a concession to exporters, to induce them to pay the wool subsidy in advance: if they did so, they could ship their wool wherever they chose at reduced rates.[31] This was a fiscal expedient to finance an invasion of Flanders, not an economic repercussion of the civil war there.

There is no good reason to doubt that the English government intervened in Flanders for political reasons. In the spring and autumn of 1382, and again in the summer of 1383 it required the Flemings to recognize Richard II as king of France and sovereign of Flanders – in other words, it required them to help England against France in return for English assistance against Louis de Mâle.[32] Paradoxically enough, the second of these demands was probably the crucial one and provides the key to English intervention. The aid which Ghent would furnish against France was liable to be unimpressive in itself and neutralized by the assistance which Louis gave France, but her support against Louis within Flanders would be invaluable. England had no reason to fight Louis himself, but had every reason to fear and detest his heir, Philip of Burgundy. For over a decade the threat of Philip's succession had been the biggest cloud on the political horizon and any opportunity to disperse it was certain to be seized with alacrity. Flanders was the richest and most densely populated region of western Europe and was bound to England by economic ties of exceptional strength and importance. She possessed the finest harbours between the Mediterranean and the Baltic, a merchant fleet rivalled by England alone, and a strategic situation which was a threat to the security of her island neighbour. In addition, her ruler was poised to secure the succession to Brabant, an inheritance very nearly as rich as Flanders itself. In the hands of a Flemish count these territories represented no real danger, but when they passed to a French prince it appeared that French supremacy would be put beyond question. Any sacrifice which might avert this catastrophe was worth while.

When it decided to intervene in 1382 the English government could not know, of course, that Louis de Mâle was to die less than two years later, when the struggle for Flanders was still undecided. But he was already an old man (fifty-two) by the standards of his day and circumstances were never likely to be better than they were at this time. Nothing would be lost in anticipating his death by a few years for the chance of disturbing the succession. Even while Louis still lived Richard II contemplated using his sovereign power as 'king of France' to depose him and assume the title count of Flanders himself.[33] The struggle for Flanders might very aptly be termed the 'War of the Burgundian Succession'.

Though this explains why England was prepared to intervene, it also makes it difficult to understand why she waited until 1382 to do so. Perhaps the problem has been misleadingly formulated. With so much at stake, England would probably have intervened at any time. But it was not until 1382 that the opportunity arose. Up to this point no one in Flanders had anything to gain by appealing for outside help; but in the winter of 1381–2 Louis's blockade of Ghent and his refusal to accept any settlement short of her unconditional surrender drove the city to desperate measures. Even then, she tried to persuade Charles VI to intervene on her behalf before she took the risk of plunging Flanders into the maelstrom of the Anglo-French war by appealing for English aid. The exact date of this appeal is unknown, but in all probability it was made in the new year. On 24 January 1382 Philip van Artevelde was elected *ruwaert* of Ghent. Until this moment he had played no significant role in the long civil war, and his sudden prominence appears to have been engineered in order to make use of the emotional associations of his name. His father had arranged the Anglo-Flemish alliance at the beginning of the war, and Philip was almost certainly elected to renew that alliance. In all probability therefore he made immediate overtures to England. By the early spring negotiations were already in full swing, for by April Louis de Mâle was sufficiently well aware of what was going on to have posted spies in England to keep himself informed of their progress. The report of these spies[34] is a vital source for the origins of Anglo-French intervention in Flanders. It reveals that England was the first to threaten intervention, and that she did so for political reasons in response to an appeal from van Artevelde. In return for his recognition as king of France and sovereign – and possibly count – of Flanders, Richard offered to lead a major army to the assistance of Ghent that summer. The offer was made in earnest, for his council immediately opened negotiations with the lay lords and the mercantile community to secure the necessary military and financial backing. The lords were enthusiastic and pledged their support on advantageous terms; but the merchants were reluctant, and in the parliament of May 1382 the Commons doomed the entire enterprise by refusing to grant the necessary funds for a royal expedition. Thus France, the last to be involved, was the first to get in her blow, with incalculable consequences for the subsequent course of the war.

The transformation of the Flemish civil war into an international crisis was therefore precipitated by Louis's blockade of Ghent, though

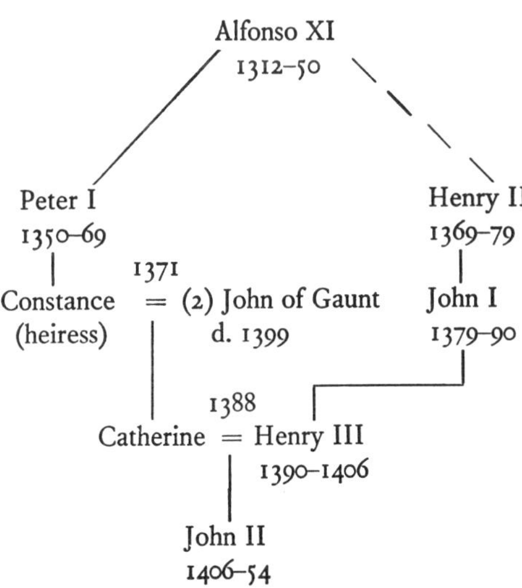

2. *The Castilian succession*

not for the reasons usually given. The blockade drove Ghent into the arms of England, who was only too anxious to receive her. The size of the political stakes involved in Flanders ensured that it would be the most serious obstacle to peace for many years to come. It is much more difficult to explain why England withdrew from Flanders than why she became involved there.

Yet a third obstacle to peace was provided by a third succession dispute, in Castile.[35] By virtue of his marriage to a daughter of Peter I of Castile in 1371, John of Gaunt, duke of Lancaster, had acquired a strong claim to the Castilian throne. Although he made no headway in pursuit of his claims in the decade after his marriage, and although they might not appear formidable after ten years' inactivity and the unopposed accession of the son of the original usurper, they were nevertheless a serious obstacle to peace. One of the reasons for Gaunt's relative inactivity was his preoccupation with the war with France. Once this appeared to be nearing its end, therefore, he was bound to pursue his claim to Castile with more vigour; and since France repeatedly refused to abandon her ally, the Castilian problem seemed doomed to be the last obstacle to peace, and not the least serious for being the last. There was a further, more important reason why it should loom particularly large when peace was in sight. In order to solve the problem posed by conflicting claims to sovereignty over the duchy of Aquitaine, the two sides agreed that the duchy should be settled on John of Gaunt and his heirs, thereby separating it from the English Crown.[36] If Gaunt was to be given Aquitaine, however, both France and Castile were certain to demand that he first renounce his claim to the Castilian throne, since his position in the duchy would otherwise constitute a standing threat to the security of both countries. The Castilian problem was therefore inextricably entangled with the problem of peace with France, and a solution to the one was unthinkable without a prior or concurrent solution to the other.

A fourth succession dispute which would appear to have been highly important but which had in fact little discernible effect on the course of the war can be quickly dismissed. The Schism in the papacy was treated by both sides as a convenience, to be exploited as occasion required. It is true that certain phases of the war were represented as crusades in favour of one or other of the two popes; but it is as certain as these things can ever be that England would have sent an army to Flanders in 1383 and to Castile in 1386 had the Schism never occurred. The Schism did make it easier to finance these armies; but such slight encouragement as this gave to the continuance of the war was more than counter-balanced after 1383 by the effect of the religious split in Flanders, where a Clementist prince (Philip of Burgundy) ruled Urbanist subjects, making him more than ever anxious to see an end to the war.

The Schism had even less effect upon the course of the peace negotiations than it did on the continuance of the war. Prior to 1378 papal mediators were responsible for every meeting between the two sides, but their absence made no discernible difference after that date. Between 1378 and 1389 peace or truce talks were held in every single year, usually through the mediation of neighbouring lay princes. At one time or another the king of Armenia, the duke of Brittany, the count of Flanders, the ruler of Holland and the emperor himself were invited or offered to mediate. After 1389 talks continued as frequently as before, though the two sides dispensed with mediators altogether. It is difficult to believe that a united papacy would have achieved more notable results.

One final problem was certainly more serious than this and may well have been the most important single reason for the dogged continuance of the war in the years 1377–83. During that period one or other of the Crowns was worn by a minor. It was remarked by one observer of a projected treaty in 1384 that 'there was a law in latin which forbade the sale of the property of infants',[37] a remark intended to imply that the agreement was invalid because of the minority of Charles VI. In fact Charles was technically of age in 1384, even though only fifteen years old. But before 1383 the objection would have been a formidable one. No minority government would have been anxious to court the political dangers of a sell-out, and in any case no formal agreement would have been worth the parchment it was written on. In these circumstances the apparent lack of progress towards a settlement in the years following the death of Edward III is not perhaps as surprising as it would at first appear. After 1383 more determined efforts were possible and they were duly made.

NOTES

1 For Charles V see the magnificent work of Delachenal, *Histoire de Charles V*; and for Philip, the perceptive study by Cartellieri, *Philipp der Kühne.*

2 Delachenal, *Charles V*, iv, 226–33; Contamine, 'Batailles, Bannières,

Compagnies', *Cahiers vernonnais*, iv, 29–30. The army was in fact larger, since this figure does not include the contribution of Languedoc.

3 *RP*, iii, 6–7, 73, 134, 150, 184.

4 Bailey, 'The Campaign of 1375 and the Good Parliament', *EHR*, lv, 370–83, points to one possible instance.

5 Deschamps, *Oeuvres*, iii, 63.

6 *Chronique des quatre premiers Valois*, 272–5; Delachenal, *Charles V*, v, 231.

7 *Foedera*, vii, 332; C 61/96, m. 13; *Lettres des rois*, ii, 229–30.

8 *Higden*, ix, 188.

9 Sherborne, 'The Battle of la Rochelle and the War at Sea, 1372–5', *BIHR*, xlii, 17–29; and 'The English Navy: Shipping and Manpower, 1369–1389', *Past and Present*, xxxvii, 163–75, two valuable studies.

10 *RP*, iii, 34, 36.

11 Below, chapters 4–5. Some idea of the damage done by the Calais garrison can be gleaned from the laconic remarks of the Westminster chronicler (*Higden*, ix, 12, 67–8, 71, 90, 93, 188–9). For the French forces tied up in defence see Rey, *Finances royales*, 372–85.

12 The customs grant of 1378 was renewed and earmarked for coastal defence.

13 *RP*, iii, 34–6, 72–3, 88, 111, 114 for last three paragraphs.

14 *RP*, iii, 122–3, 140, 144–8; *Higden*, ix, 23, for last two paragraphs. For a different view of the Despenser episode see Aston, 'The Impeachment of Bishop Despenser', *BIHR*, xxxviii, 132, 138–41, 144–7.

15 Jones, 'Brest sous les Anglais', *Cahiers de l'Iroise*, xvi, 9–10 (for Brest and Cherbourg); Fowler, 'Les finances et la discipline dans les armées anglaises en France au XIVe siècle', *Cahiers vernonnais*, iv, 60–1 (for Aquitaine).

16 Rey, *Domaine du Roi*, 164–76, 324–40, 390–404 – an indispensable work.

17 For complaints see Le Fèvre, *Journal*, i, 330–7; Cochon, *Chronique normande*, 182; *Chronographia regum francorum*, iii, 74–91; *St Denys*, i, 350–3; de Mézières, *Songe*, i, 328–30, 583–5; ii, 362–7, 392–3; *Ordonnances des rois de France*, vii, 186–9; for desertion and tax evasion see Froissart, *Chroniques*, xiii, 134–5; Lehoux, *Jean de Berri*, ii, 173–4; and for the Crown's financial difficulties, le Fèvre, *Journal*, i, 332–3; Froissart, *Oeuvres*, xiii, 352–4.

18 Boutruche, *Crise d'une société*, 209–18.

19 Durrieu, *Gascons en Italie*, 17–21; ACO B 1461, fos 138, 147; *Recueil des documents concernant le Poitou*, v, 278, 290; *Histoire de Languedoc*, x, 1711–16.

20 *Annales avignonnaises de 1382 à 1410*, xii, 56. For what follows see *ibid. passim*; *Histoire civile . . . de Nismes*, iii, 59–77; Lehoux, *Jean de Berri*, ii, 89–101, 130–7, 170, 176–8, 190–3. For the affairs of Languedoc and Provence, this last book is essential reading.

21 Below, chapter 11 *passim*. For what follows see *RP*, iii, 73, 89, 93, 133, 137, 170.

22 *Anglo-French Negotiations at Bruges; Du Bosc*, 307–60.

23 *Mémoires . . . Bretagne*, ii, 298–301.

24 *CFR, 1377–83*, 274–5; *Registrum Honoris de Richmond,* 199–203; Jeulin, 'Un grand "honneur" anglais', *Annales de Bretagne*, xlii, 294–5, for the confiscation; and Froissart, *Oeuvres*, ix, 462–3; Pitti, *Cronica,* 57; *Anglo-Norman Letters*, no. 265, for the negotiations with John de Blois.

25 Some of the effects can be seen in Philip's correspondence with his wife while in Brittany in 1394 (ADN, B 1276/12981; B 18822/23294; and *Documents pour servir à l'histoire de la maison de Bourgogne,* 89, 96.

26 *Mémoires . . . Bretagne*, ii, 453–4.

27 Text in Froissart, *Oeuvres,* xviii, 564–6, and *Choix de pièces inédites*, i, 51.

28 First argued by Coulborn, 'Economic and Political Preliminaries of the Crusade of 1383', 83–92, 278–81; and adopted by Perroy, *L'Angleterre et le grand Schisme*, 171–5; and Quicke, *Les Pays-Bas*, 330–2, and others.

29 Quicke, *Les Pays-Bas*, 332–5. This book is essential for events in the Low Countries up to 1384.

30 Wool exports to the nearest hundred sacks for 1380–1, 1381–2, and 1382–3 (September to September) were: 18,400, 18,000 and 14,000 (*England's Export Trade,* 51).

31 *RP*, iii, 123–4.

32 Appendix 2; Froissart, *Oeuvres,* x, 464–6; *Foedera*, vii, 396–7.

33 Appendix 2.

34 Appendix 2; and cf. below, p. 45.

35 Russell, *English Intervention in Spain and Portugal,* is indispensable on this subject.

36 See chapter 2 below.

37 Deschamps, *Oeuvres,* iii, 62; for the date see appendix 1 (b).

Chapter Two

A New Policy
1375–95

Throughout the Hundred Years War negotiations for a final settlement were repeatedly frustrated by the seeming impossibility of devising a satisfactory solution to the problem of conflicting claims to sovereignty over the English territories in France,[1] a problem which was never more acute than during the second phase of the war. Since only the most thoroughgoing defeat could induce either king to contemplate relinquishing his claims to sovereignty over the duchy of Aquitaine and other English possessions, the military stalemate which developed in the 1370s appeared to preclude the possibility of a negotiated settlement. The protracted negotiations of the period between 1375 and 1395 have consequently been considered little more than a farce, or at best a rather forlorn attempt to solve a problem which in existing circumstances was inherently insoluble. Despite the manifest goodwill on both sides during their final stages, the ultimate failure of the negotiations has therefore occasioned no surprise, nor indeed any feeling that this failure requires anything particular in the way of explanation.

The assumption that the negotiations were doomed to the failure which eventually overtook them was not, however, shared by contemporaries. On a number of occasions well-placed observers were convinced that a final peace was not only possible but even imminent. Twice, at least, a draft treaty was agreed upon; and the historian Froissart had reason to believe that the last of the series of summit conferences held in the early 1390s resulted in the conclusion of a secret treaty. We have no means of verifying his belief, but the events of that period certainly support the view that the two sides came very close to reaching a final agreement. Their friendliness, their co-operation, and their mutual plans to end the Schism and prepare a joint crusade against the Turks all point to this conclusion, as does the opposition which fears of a final settlement provoked in certain quarters. News of impending peace precipitated a serious rebellion in the north of England in the spring of 1393, and at roughly the same time the count of Armagnac and a number of the provinces of southern France came dangerously close to rebelling against the French Crown for similar reasons. The Gascon revolt of 1394 also appears to have been provoked by the imminence of a settlement which was thought to endanger the independence of the duchy; and indeed the entire sequence of events in Gascony between 1390 and 1395 can only be understood by reference to the peace negotiations and to the fears aroused in Aquitaine by the prospect of their success.[2]

It is difficult to believe that these protests were all without foundation, or that contemporaries were so obtuse as to believe in the possibility of a final settlement where none existed. But if we accept their evaluation, then it becomes necessary to question the validity of the accepted version of the nature, course and outcome of the peace negotiations. In particular, it becomes necessary to find an alternative explanation of the fundamental basis of those negotiations; for if the two sides came anywhere near to reaching a final agreement, they must have found a possible solution to the problems created by the continued existence of a king of England who was also duke of Aquitaine and a peer of France.

The first clue as to the possible nature of this solution was provided by the monk of Westminster's account of the results of the summit conferences of 1392 and 1393, an account which had rather astonishingly been overlooked. The first of these two conferences took place at Amiens in March and April 1392, and in May the duke of Lancaster – the head of the English delegation at Amiens – reported to a specially convoked 'quasi parliament' at Stamford that the French had demanded that the king renounce his claims to the kingdom of France and to the old Angevin empire and allow the duke of Berry to retain those parts of Aquitaine in their hands during his lifetime. In return they offered that

> after the death of the duke of Berry Aquitaine and Gascony, together with all their appurtenants, *should revert to the duke of Lancaster and his heirs forever, provided that the duke and his heirs performed the customary homage to the king of France.* But these proposals did not please the Commons, who said that it would be foolish and excessively injurious to the king and his Crown to alienate forever such fine lordships, which had been ruled by hereditary right by the kings of England for so long, for the

benefit of a single person. After these dissensions, however, the
lord king – on the advice of the duke of Lancaster – was prepared
to agree to some of the demands of the French in order to secure
a good peace, despite the opposition of the Commons.

The negotiations were accordingly resumed, and the results of the next
summit conference – held in the spring of 1393 – were laid before a
parliament held at Westminster in January 1394, where they provoked
considerable displeasure,

> first because it was absurd that the king of England should render
> homage and fealty to the king of France for Aquitaine and his
> other continental possessions and become his liege man; for in
> this way all Englishmen whatever of the king's allegiance would
> be subjected to the king of France and held in bondage forever
> after. Secondly, despite this the dukes of Berry and Burgundy
> were to hold freely for their lives certain of the most desirable
> provinces of Aquitaine *which, after their deaths, were to revert to the
> duke of Lancaster and his heirs, to the great prejudice of the Crown of
> England and the perpetual and damaging disinheritance of the king of
> England.* Having carefully considered this and other factors,
> neither the Lords nor the Commons would assent to such an
> agreement. For truly, if lesser men than the duke of Lancaster had
> done this, then they would immediately have incurred the taint of
> treason, not unreasonably. But the duke of Lancaster did as he
> pleased, ignoring this opposition . . .

Unfortunately, the chronicle terminates abruptly a few lines further on,
and the author's views on the third and final summit conference of this
period will probably never be known.[3]

What remains, however, is sufficient to cast very grave doubts on
the conventional view of these negotiations. For if we accept this
account, then the fundamental premise of the conferences of 1392 and
1393 was that England and Aquitaine should be forever separated,
thereby eliminating the basic source of the perpetual conflicts between
England and France. And there is no good reason to reject it. It could
scarcely have been invented, and in any case the Westminster chronicler
was not given to flights of fancy. As a source of accurate and often con-
fidential information his chronicle has no rival.

In the light of his version of these conferences a number of other
episodes assume a quite new significance. Perhaps the most interesting

and important of these is Froissart's account of the causes of the Gascon revolt of 1394. Froissart had the good fortune to visit England early in 1395, when Gascon affairs still preoccupied the king and his council to the exclusion of most other business. In his customary manner he set about collecting information for his history and was lucky enough on this occasion to find two unimpeachable informants in Sir Richard Stury, a member of the royal council, and Sir John Grailly, one of the envoys sent to present the Gascon case to the king and his counsellors. According to these two men – whose accounts Froissart purports to record verbatim[4] – the revolt had been provoked by the grant of Aquitaine to John of Gaunt in the previous year. By this grant the king, with the assent of his council, had provided that

> *the duke of Lancaster and his heirs should be forever lord and inheritor of the whole country of Aquitaine* . . . And then the letters of donation were drawn up, engrossed, examined and passed with great deliberation in council, in the presence of the king of England, his uncles the dukes of York and Gloucester, the counts of Salisbury, Arundel, Derby (son of the duke of Lancaster), Marshal, Northumberland and Huntingdon . . . and of all the lords and prelates of England who ought to have been present.

Now if Froissart's information was accurate – and his sources would seem to guarantee that it was – Aquitaine was alienated to Gaunt and his heirs at about the time of the final summit conference of this period, which met in the spring of 1394. The two events were evidently related, although Froissart himself did not realize that his story had any connection whatever with the progress of the peace negotiations. Like the conferences of 1392 and 1393, that of 1394 proposed to base a final settlement on the separation of England and Aquitaine. There is also evidence – which will be discussed more fully below – that this proposal was made as early as 1390, at the very outset of the peace negotiations of the post-war period; and so it would seem reasonable to conclude that it provided the fundamental basis for negotiation throughout all the conferences of the early 1390s.

But what of the war-time negotiations? At an earlier stage in this inquiry I was forced to conclude that they had been based on quite different and more conventional premises.[5] There were two reasons for this, both negative but none the less convincing for that. In the first place, the journal of the French ambassador, du Bosc, for the conferences of 1379–85 contained no reference at all to the proposal to grant Aquitaine to the duke of Lancaster. In itself this was not necessarily conclusive since the journal is a rather threadbare compilation, more concerned with points of detail and of procedure than with matters of substance. Moreover, the comparable official documents relating to the conferences of the 1390s were equally – and in their case misleadingly – taciturn about this crucial point. But in the former case there appeared to be no means of controlling the official record, which had perforce to be accepted. Secondly, and more convincingly, the secret journal of the papal mediators at the Bruges conferences of 1375–7 was almost equally silent. It did, it is true, record that at the outset of the first conference the mediators proposed that Aquitaine be settled on the duke of Lancaster; but, as the editor of the journal remarked, the proposal appeared to be merely 'a tentative suggestion', made only to be 'dropped without further discussion'.[6] This seemed conclusive; for of all the official documents relating to the peace negotiations of this phase of the war, this journal is by far the most revealing. Where most of the other materials do little more than note procedural points and the formal territorial offers made by the two sides, the journal records – if only briefly – the principal topics of discussion and the main proposals made to solve the crucial central issue of the negotiations, the conflicting claims to sovereignty over the English territories in France. This being the case, its apparent failure to make more than passing reference to the proposal to alienate Aquitaine to the duke of Lancaster was negative evidence of a very persuasive kind.

Some time after reaching these conclusions, however, the discovery of two slight but suggestive pieces of evidence prompted me to reconsider them. I had for some time been searching for clues as to the nature of the two summit conferences of 1383 and 1384. Attention was concentrated on these two conferences for a variety of reasons. They were the only top-level meetings between 1377 and 1392; they were the only set of negotiations to produce a break in the war between 1377 and 1389; and they came very close to reaching a final settlement. Unfortunately, they are also the worst documented of all the conferences of the period. The draft peace which was agreed upon at the first meeting has not survived, and no hint of its terms can be found in any other sources. Even the journal of the French ambassador, du Bosc, is more than usually unhelpful, since the conduct of the negotiations was very largely taken out of his hands by the royal uncles. There are no other sources to fill these gaps. Our ignorance of these crucial meetings is therefore almost complete; we do not even possess a single one of the formal territorial offers made by either side at either of the main meetings.

In these circumstances any new evidence, however slight, was likely to upset our views as to the nature of these conferences. The first piece to do so was supplied by the poet and diplomat, Eustace Deschamps, in a poem which is well-enough known but whose significance had been missed because – among other reasons – it had been generally taken to refer to the peace negotiations of 1394. However, it undoubtedly describes the conference of 1384, at which Deschamps himself was present and at which, he says, the English delegation demanded that the homage due to the French Crown for Aquitaine be henceforth performed by its duke, and not by the king of England.[7] The duke and king were evidently to be two different people, and the duke of Lancaster was presumably to be the duke. This inference was rendered unnecessary, however, by the appearance of a second source in a rather unexpected place, in the materials collected for the history of the southern provinces of France. In an undated letter which can confidently be assigned to the year 1384, the Lord Albret informed his 'nephew', the count of Armagnac, that the probable outcome of the peace conference which was about to open at Boulogne was that 'you and I and all our country in those parts [Aquitaine] will be given to the duke of Lancaster, who is to be our duke.'[8] Given the intense personal interest which both Armagnac and Albret would have in such an arrangement – both would become vassals of the new duke of Aquitaine – this was not the sort of matter on which the writer was likely to have been mistaken. Like the conferences of the 1390s, therefore, those of 1383 and 1384 posited as their fundamental premise the separation of England and Aquitaine; and since these last two conferences were the only summit meetings between 1377 and 1392, it is quite probable that this premise held good for the less important conferences held after 1384.

It also appeared probable that this might be true too of those held prior to 1384, and this prompted a more careful analysis of the journal of the mediators at Bruges, in the course of which it became apparent that the proposal to alienate Aquitaine to the duke of Lancaster played a larger role in the proceedings than appeared at first sight. After some preliminary skirmishing, the mediators opened the really serious business of the conference on 31 March 1375, when they proposed that:

(1) Either the duke of Lancaster be created duke of Aquitaine, relinquishing his English lands to his father, Edward III, and giving

homage for Aquitaine to the king of France, who would retain certain parts of the duchy for himself;

(2) Or, that the greater part of Aquitaine be retained by the king of France, the area south of the Garonne remaining to Edward III in full sovereignty.

The whole of the following week was then devoted to the consideration of these proposals. Eventually, the French rejected the second one out of hand but accepted the first, while the English rejected the first but grudgingly accepted the second as a possible point of departure. But the mediators did not let matters rest there. They immediately returned to the attack, asking John of Gaunt himself to reconsider the reply given by his delegation. His reply was illuminating. While ostensibly supporting the stand taken by his co-ambassadors, he qualified it by saying that the rejected proposal was unacceptable 'especially because of the homage to be done to the king of France, which did not please him'. In other words, he did not object to becoming duke of Aquitaine, nor did he dismiss the possibility of an Anglo-French settlement on this basis, provided he were free of tenurial obligations to Charles V and his successors.

There was room for negotiation on this point. Having recorded Lancaster's reply, the mediators noted in their journal that they then 'opened a certain way' to the two embassies. From the context it would appear that this 'way' was designed to meet John of Gaunt's objections to giving homage, and it is therefore particularly unfortunate that no further information is given on this point. However, given the circumstances it may be surmised with reasonable probability that the 'way' they suggested was a compromise whereby the French would retain their sovereignty over the duchy but accept certain 'modifications' or restrictions on its use. The concept of 'modifications' was first introduced into the negotiations during the course of Gaunt's first embassy at Bruges, and its introduction at this point would have gone halfway to meet the objections he had raised to the mediators' first proposal.[9]

In any case, when the talks were resumed in May the basis of negotiation remained the projected separation of England and Aquitaine, though in a modified form which combined elements of the two proposals made at the outset of the negotiations. Now, a two- or threefold division of the duchy was envisaged, one part being allocated to the king of England, a second to one of his sons or nephews, and the third to the king of France. For present purposes the third share can be ignored. The concept of a 'share' for the king of France was a legal fiction designed to allow the ambassadors to pretend that they were negotiating on the basis of the last peace between the two countries, the treaty of Brétigny. The twofold division of those parts of the duchy allocated to England, however, demands careful consideration, for at first sight it represents a retreat from the proposal to separate the duchy from the English Crown. But this appearance is very largely illusory, for the two shares were to be different in character and unequal in size. By far the larger of the two was still earmarked for the duke of Lancaster,[10] who was to hold it from the French Crown in a modified form of sovereignty. Edward III's share was to be smaller but held in full sovereignty. The English embassy agreed to this as soon as the talks resumed in May, and as late as August 1376 Edward was still prepared to negotiate on this basis. On this last occasion he indicated the territories he intended to keep for himself: Bordeaux, Bayonne and Dax. In other words, his share of the duchy was to be a group of strong-points accessible from the sea – 'bastions' like Calais, Cherbourg and Brest. This choice was clearly dictated by strategic rather than feudal or dynastic considerations and must be viewed in the light of English military activity in the years following the failure of the Bruges negotiations, when a determined effort was made to add to the number of English bastions around the French coast.

Apart from one period when the conference confined itself to the discussion of a long truce, the proposal to confer most of the duchy on the duke of Lancaster appears to have remained the basis for negotiations until the summer of 1376, when the larger share of the duchy was earmarked for the heir to the throne. Since Edward III was now in his dotage and his heir was a mere boy, a settlement along these lines would have produced only a brief and nominal separation of Crown and duchy. Despite its apparent resemblance to the original proposal, therefore, this amounted to a rejection of the basic principle on which the negotiations of the previous year or so had been founded. The reason for the English volte-face must be a matter of surmise; but it may be remarked that it occurred immediately after the death of the Black Prince and at a moment when John of Gaunt himself was popularly believed to be intriguing with the French king to disinherit his nephew, the future Richard II. In these circumstances it would have been political suicide for Gaunt to have negotiated a settlement which entailed his own acquisition of Aquitaine at the expense of his nephew's inheritance.

The domestic situation in England may therefore have been ulti-mately responsible for the failure of the Bruges conferences. It was at this juncture following the death of the Black Prince and the English volte-face that the royal dukes withdrew from the conference, herald-ing its final failure. But it is also possible to isolate another reason for this failure. Time and again the papal mediators emphasized the diffi-culties of reaching any sort of compromise on the issue of sovereignty. This may appear surprising, since it was not French sovereignty over the whole duchy which was at stake. Edward III expressed himself ready to accept a modified form of French sovereignty over the greater part of the duchy, that part to be given to the duke of Lancaster. But he insisted that Calais and its march, and Bordeaux, Bayonne and Dax be granted to him absolutely, and on this point Charles V was adamant: he would not relinquish the essential attributes of his Crown over any corner of his kingdom. Every ingenuity was exercised to circumvent this impasse, to no avail. Precisely the same obstacle was to confront the two sides in the 1390s, when the problem of French sovereignty over Calais and La Rochelle was reserved for the special attention of the two kings themselves while the details of the modified sovereignty which the French were to exercise over Aquitaine were left to under-lings to work out. In each case the reason was the same. Both Edward III and Richard II were determined to obtain absolute possession of the 'bastions' they intended to keep in their own hands; the remaining English territories – the greater part of Aquitaine – did not so much concern them, and they were quite prepared to concede the French a modified sovereignty there. The difficulties created by conflicting claims to sovereignty over Calais and one or two other towns serves to high-light the importance of the projected separation of England and Aqui-taine and of the degree to which it had approximated the positions of the two sides.

It can now be seen that at every one of the summit conferences between 1375 and 1394 it was proposed to base a final settlement upon the separation of England and Aquitaine. But this separation could take different forms, each of them different in their implications. All involved the donation of Aquitaine to John of Gaunt, but they were distin-guished by the precise nature of the terms on which he was to hold the duchy. In the first place, he could hold it merely for the term of his life. During that period he would act as an independent ruler, responsible for the services due to the French Crown; but after his death the duchy would return to the English Crown, encumbered with French sovereignty and all that that entailed. At best, therefore, this could provide only a temporary solution to the problem of Aquitaine, and one which consequently found little favour with either side.

The remaining alternatives were far more radical. In both cases the duchy could be settled on John of Gaunt *and his heirs*, thereby establishing a new ducal dynasty in Aquitaine. This dynasty could then be made subject to either the French, or to both the French and English Crowns. In practice the difference between these possibilities was not likely to be as important as it might at first appear. If the duchy were made directly dependent upon the French Crown, then its separation from England would be complete, legally as well as practically. If on the other hand it was held from the king of England, who himself held it from the king of France, then legally speaking England would remain tied to both Aquitaine and to France. But the tie was likely to be a fragile one. Once actual possession and the power to rule had been alienated to a separate dynasty English interest in Aquitaine would inevitably diminish, and with it the constant friction with France.

Because of the brevity and ambiguity of the evidence, it is not always possible to distinguish which of these three methods was under consideration at any given moment. On the whole, however, the evidence suggests that the most radical of the three alternatives was the one consistently preferred. Both the Westminster chronicler and Froissart state quite categorically that it was proposed to alienate Aquitaine to Gaunt *and his heirs* in 1392, 1393, and 1394; and although the papal journal for the Bruges conference does not record in so many words that Gaunt was to start a new dynasty in Aquitaine, it implies as much by its statement that he was to renounce all his English lands to Edward III and pay homage to Charles V alone. As for the conferences of 1383 and 1384, the testimony of Deschamps and Albret is too vague on this point to warrant any conclusions at all; but it may be remarked that at the first of these meetings Gaunt was accompanied by his son and heir – then a mere youth – whose presence may conceivably indicate that the permanent alienation of Aquitaine was under consideration on that occasion too.

Though the precise nature of the proposals made in 1383 and 1384 must remain open to some doubt, the remaining summit meetings concurred in proposing the final separation of England and Aquitaine and it is therefore tempting to conclude that this was the basis of the negotiations throughout the entire period. However, there is evidence that on at least one occasion a temporary separation of Crown and duchy was also contemplated. On 2 March 1390 John of Gaunt was created duke of Aquitaine *for life only*, and a month later the English ambassadors to the first of the post-war peace conferences were issued with instructions which clearly envisaged a final settlement based upon Gaunt's life tenure of the duchy.[11] But although this would seem conclusive – for this occasion at least – there is reason to believe that it may be misleading. When the Gascons were informed of Gaunt's appointment they expressed their gratification yet objected to the precise terms of the grant which, they insisted, threatened to entail their final separation from the English Crown. Their reason for fearing this is to be found in the curious formula employed to express the tenurial link between John of Gaunt and Richard II. The grant stipulated that Gaunt was to hold the duchy from the king and his heirs 'as kings of France' and to pay homage to them in the same capacity. *This was a title which Richard was proposing to relinquish.* When he did so, his uncle would be left holding Aquitaine from Charles VI. The king of England's promise that the grant was for life only would then be an irrelevance.

This was almost certainly why the formula was employed. It had been carefully considered,[12] and its implications would have been apparent to those versed in the legal subtleties of Anglo-French relations. The king of England never made grants in Aquitaine by authority of his title to the French throne. He might exercise sovereignty in the duchy by virtue of that title, since he had no legitimate claim to its exercise as king of England. But the lordship of Aquitaine belonged to him as king of England, and in all matters affecting his lordship he acted as king of England and duke of Aquitaine. These distinctions were recognized in theory – they were clearly stated by Richard's own ambassadors at about this date[13] – and always acted upon in practice. When Richard granted the duchy to his uncle as 'king of France' he was suppressing his right to it as king of England. His only possible motive for doing so was to prepare the ground for the final alienation of the duchy; and this being the case, his promise that the grant was for life only cannot be believed.

The Gascons therefore had very good reason to suspect the king's ultimate intentions. It looks as if the short-term separation of England and Aquitaine was designed simply to deceive them: to lull them into accepting Gaunt as their duke – thereby making subsequent opposition more difficult – until the actual conclusion of peace with France allowed his metamorphosis into a French peer *in perpetuum*. One wonders whether this were not its only purpose, and whether the temporary alienation of Aquitaine were ever seriously considered as a viable basis for peace.

Before any attempt can be made to answer this question it is necessary to examine the only other certain reference to the short-term proposal, which is contained in the draft treaty concluded in June 1393.[14] Here it is stated that the French ambassadors requested that if Richard II made his uncle duke of Aquitaine for life, then Gaunt should do homage for the usufruct of the duchy and the king himself for his proprietary right. As it stands this clause makes no sense, for the duke of Lancaster was already duke of Aquitaine for life. The word 'only' must be implied: if the king granted the duchy to his uncle for life *only*, then a double homage was required. In other words, although the treaty was based upon the assumption that Aquitaine would be finally alienated to Gaunt – as the monk of Westminster had stated – it also made provision for a temporary alienation of the duchy.

These two alternative solutions are therefore found side by side both in 1390 and 1393. What is the explanation of this? It is surely improbable that the two kings were simply unable to choose between the two. Other possible explanations also seem rather far-fetched when the two episodes are taken together. It is quite possible, for instance, that the English government expressed a preference for the temporary solution in order to push up the price of the permanent one, which would certainly be preferred by the French. This might easily explain the instructions given to the English ambassadors in 1390. But it is scarcely likely that such tactical weapons were still being wielded more than three years later when a final treaty was in sight. Again, while it is very likely that the grant of 1390 was intended to deceive the Gascons, it is scarcely conceivable that the provisional treaty of 1393 was drafted with this purpose in mind. Nevertheless, the Gascons almost certainly provide the key to this problem. The possibility of their opposition to the final separation of England and Aquitaine was one which confronted the English government throughout the 1390s.[15] Prudence would have dictated that contingency plans be made; and since the Gascons repeatedly protested their readiness to accept John of Gaunt as their duke for his lifetime, this provided an obvious basis for such plans. But it was clearly a second-best solution, and the lack of enthusiasm it aroused is evident from subsequent events. When the more radical proposal was defeated by the Gascons the entire scheme was abandoned.

It remains to consider how Gaunt and his heirs were to hold their duchy. On the whole the evidence suggests that England was to renounce all interest in Aquitaine, leaving the duke directly dependent on the French Crown, *sans moyen*. This was clearly the implication of the grant of 1390. By reserving homage to himself as 'king of France', Richard denied that it was due to him as king of England. The same conclusion can be drawn from the Bruges journal, which states that Gaunt was to pay homage to Charles V but is silent about any tenurial link between England and Aquitaine. Against this can be set the statements of the Westminster chronicler and Froissart. According to the former, it was stipulated in 1393 that Richard perform homage for his uncle's duchy; while according to Froissart, the grant of Aquitaine to Gaunt and his heirs in 1394 provided that they were to do homage to Richard and his successors for the duchy. We have already seen that both writers command respect and it may seem perverse to doubt their assurances on this point. Yet there is reason to do so. The provisional treaty of 1393 did not stipulate that the king do homage for the duchy except in the event of his grant to his uncle being only for the term of his life; but the provision was a complex one and it is easy to see how confusion could arise. Whether this is what happened, or whether the chronicler was better informed than can now be established, must remain open to some doubt.

In Froissart's case there is perhaps less doubt. Though his sources of information were excellent, the circumstances in which he acquired his information precluded accuracy on this particular point. He learnt about the alienation of the duchy only in the context of the opposition it provoked from the Gascons and never realized that it was in any way connected with the peace negotiations with France. His informants had evidently been reticent about this particular aspect of the question and it could therefore never have occurred to the chronicler that homage for the duchy could be given to anyone other than the king of England. Even if he were not told in so many words that the duchy was to be dependent upon the English Crown, Froissart would have assumed as much. In these circumstances his evidence on this point is worthless. Since a question mark also hangs over the statement of the Westminster chronicler, it must be considered doubtful whether it was ever proposed to combine the perpetual alienation of the duchy with the maintenance of its tenurial links with England.

Whatever the truth of this matter, it is apparent that the proposal to separate England and Aquitaine in some form or other provided the basis of the peace negotiations for the entire twenty years or so of their duration. And though it is not always possible to distinguish with complete certainty between the different versions of this proposal, it is at least clear that on the majority of occasions – and possibly even on all of them – the total alienation of Aquitaine, and the creation of a new ducal dynasty subject to the French Crown was preferred to the other alternatives.

The importance of this proposal scarcely requires comment. Though England and Aquitaine had been separated before, their separation had always been temporary and had always been intended to be so. In most cases, moreover, it had been made for reasons which had nothing whatever to do with diminishing friction between England and France. Henry III's grant to his son, the lord Edward, preceded the treaty of Paris and the re-establishment of the feudal bond between the two countries; and Edward III's donation to the Black Prince was subsequent to the treaty of Brétigny, which had apparently destroyed that bond. Whatever the reasons which prompted Edward I to give the duchy to his son in 1306, he did so only when he had one foot in the grave. Only the grant to the future Edward III in 1325 was obviously intended to reduce friction between England and France, but that experiment had a short life and was not repeated. Far from wishing to separate the duchy from their Crown, in fact, successive kings were at pains to stress its dependence. From the reign of Henry III it was held that Aquitaine was annexed to the Crown, from which it could only be detached as a temporary apanage for the heir to the throne. This constitutional rule was observed by every king until the late fourteenth century. The proposal to confer Aquitaine on John of Gaunt in any form was therefore in defiance of all previous precedent; and the proposal that the duchy be granted to him *and his heirs* reflected a radical change of attitude towards the problem of feudal relations with France. Quite clearly, the two sides were acutely conscious of the fact that they had outlived their feudal past. The very persistence of the plan to separate Crown and duchy – through some twenty years and the reigns of four kings – shows that they were convinced that they could never enjoy a tolerable relationship until 'France should belong to the French and England to the English'.[16]

Had this proposal been implemented, England and France would have become separate kingdoms for the first time since 1066, thereby eliminating the root cause of their persistent hostility. But this was not the only virtue of the proposal. Not only did it offer hopes of a stable peace, it also promised to make the task of negotiating it rather easier. France could afford to be more generous if her provinces were to be given to the duke of Lancaster rather than to the king of England, and England could more easily accept a settlement which involved the transfer of extensive territories to one of her royal family (even if technically speaking he thereby became a French prince). The critical problem of sovereignty over Aquitaine would also become less intractable once it ceased to be an issue between the two kings themselves. In short, the proposed separation of England and Aquitaine provided the basis of a settlement which was acceptable – even attractive – to both sides, and one which promised to facilitate the conclusion of a treaty which there was every reason to hope would prove more durable than any of its predecessors.

The proposal also throws a very revealing light on certain aspects of the political history of the period. Since it can no longer be accepted that the peace negotiations were inherently doomed to fail, it becomes necessary to find a more positive explanation of their ultimate lack of success. Seen from this angle, the virtually unknown Gascon revolt of 1394 becomes one of the most important events in the late fourteenth century.[17] Secondly, the proposal throws a startling new light on the position of John of Gaunt, around whom everything revolved. The domestic implications of his role in Anglo-French affairs do not concern us here, but the proposal to alienate Aquitaine to him and his heirs clarifies a number of obscure features of the foreign politics of the period, the most important of which is the place occupied by the Castilian problem. Gaunt's claim to the Castilian throne was clearly a far more serious obstacle to peace between England and France than has yet been realized. For if he was to be established in Aquitaine – astride communications between France and Castile, having a common frontier with the latter, and in close proximity to potential allies in Navarre, Aragon and Portugal – then it was imperative from a French and Castilian viewpoint to secure his prior renunciation of the Castilian throne. While it is not impossible that the French might have sacrificed their ally in order to make a separate peace with England in other circumstances, they would certainly not do so in these. The problems of an Anglo-French and an Anglo-Castilian peace were therefore inextricably entwined. It is no coincidence that the war with France ended a few months after John of Gaunt renounced his claim to the throne of Castile.

NOTES

1 Palmer, 'The Peace Negotiations, 1337–1453', *The Hundred Years' War*, 51–74.
2 Below, chapters 8–11.
3 *Higden*, ix, 266–7, 281–2.
4 *Oeuvres*, xv, 135–6, 147–67; cf. chapter 9.
5 The argument to this point was first presented in my essay 'Anglo-French Peace Negotiations, 1390–1396', *TRHS*, 5th series xvi, 81–94, where a more elaborate discussion of some of the points will be found. Cf. Vale, *English Gascony, 1399–1453*, 28ff., who rejects this thesis on what seem to me to be completely inadequate grounds.
6 *Anglo-French Negotiations at Bruges*, xvi, xvii.
7 *Oeuvres*, iii, 63 (for date, see appendix 1(b)):

> En Guyenne sont ii$^\mathrm{m}$ et cinq cens
> Villes, chasteauls qu'Engles veulent qu'on doingne,
> Et grant tas d'or, *et que le roy esloingne*
> *De roy en duc l'ommaige qui est fais.*

8 *Histoire de Languedoc*, x, 1691–2; for date see appendix 1(c).
9 *Anglo-French Negotiations at Bruges*, 11, 78; and *passim* for what follows.
10 He was not named again by name after the initial proposal.
11 *Foedera*, vii, 659–60; *PPC*, i, 19–23; below, chapter 9, for what follows.
12 There are two enrolled versions of the grant (C 61/101, mm. 7–6), the first of which – cancelled – does not contain this formula.
13 E. 30/1629, m. 1; BN, MS. Fr. 2699, fos 105v–6.
14 Palmer, 'Articles for a Final Peace between England and France, 16 June 1393', *BIHR*, xxxix, 182–5.
15 Below, chapter 9.
16 BM, Royal MS. 20 B VI, fo. 15v. (the *Epistre* of Philip de Mézières, 1395).
17 See chapter 9.

Chapter Three

The Years of Appeasement
1383–6

With the appointment of Michael de la Pole as chancellor of England on 13 March 1383 the determined pursuit of peace may be said to have become the cardinal feature of English foreign policy. A leaning towards peace had been apparent in previous years; but it had been a hesitant and wavering tendency, inhibited by the conditions of the minority, unsupported by any definite group or party, and too weak to resist the tempting prospects opened out by internal upheavals in Brittany, Portugal and Flanders. Unlike his predecessors, de la Pole was prepared to resist such temptations and to pursue his main objective wholeheartedly. His single-mindedness introduced a new element into domestic politics. As his policy became clear and its disastrous results all too evident, it served to polarize opinion and divide the ruling class into two parties, one supporting the government, the other favouring the continuation and more vigorous prosecution of the war. For the next five years this was to be the most crucial issue between the government and the aristocratic opposition. Ultimately it was to produce a situation in which the country was simultaneously pursuing two diametrically opposed foreign policies; and in the meantime it did more to determine the nature and alignments of the constitutional crises of 1386–8 than any other factor.*

Though peace talks had continued without serious interruption since 1375, their prospects had been poor during the minority of Richard II. As he grew to manhood, however, hopes of peace grew with him. For the first time in the reign parliament referred to the possibility of a peace or truce in February 1382, and a month later a

---

* The thesis outlined in this paragraph and elaborated in the next five chapters is fundamentally new and I have therefore not thought it necessary to note where my views on particular points diverge from those of other writers.

summit conference was arranged for 1 June, the two sides agreeing to put no major armies into the field in the interval. Though it stopped short of even a brief general truce, this agreement was the most hopeful sign since the failure of the Bruges conference in 1377. Well-informed observers anticipated the conclusion of an eight- to twelve-year truce.[1]

These hopes were short-lived. Events in Flanders wrecked the conference before it had a chance to meet. At almost exactly the moment that it was arranged, Ghent appealed to England for aid against its count, offering in return an alliance against France. The government found the offer more attractive than the prospect of peace, and accepted eagerly. Although the French tried to avert the crisis by inviting Louis de Mâle to attend the conference, and presumably to submit his quarrel with Ghent to its arbitration, their move was unsuccessful.[2] Throughout April and May the English government pursued its efforts to raise the funds necessary to finance a large expeditionary force to Flanders, and in so doing destroyed all hope of an immediate settlement with France.[3] The conference fixed for 1 June never met, and its failure to do so was followed by the longest break in the negotiations throughout the war, as both sides devoted all their energies to the struggle to control Flanders.

After the cancellation of the June summit conference the alignment of England and Ghent against the count of Flanders and France was never in any real doubt. Throughout the summer of 1382 Philip van Artevelde pursued his negotiations for an alliance with England, openly recognizing Richard II as rightful king of France and overlord of Flanders. Louis de Mâle had no choice but to enlist the support of Charles VI. The ensuing race to put armies into the field was won by France, due to the refusal of the English parliament to grant sufficient funds for a major campaign. The results of its cheese-paring were little short of disastrous. The French cavalry annihilated the Flemish militia at Roosebeke on 27 November 1382, destroying the unity of the Flemings and killing their leader, van Artevelde.[4]

Despite the magnitude of the Flemish defeat, Roosebeke did not end the war. Though most of Flanders submitted to Charles VI, Ghent remained unsubdued. The terms imposed on Bruges in November, and offered to Ghent herself in December, ensured that she would not submit and that England would continue to support her. For the two towns were required to recognize Clement VII as the true pope; to obey Charles VI as rightful king of France; to renounce their alliance with

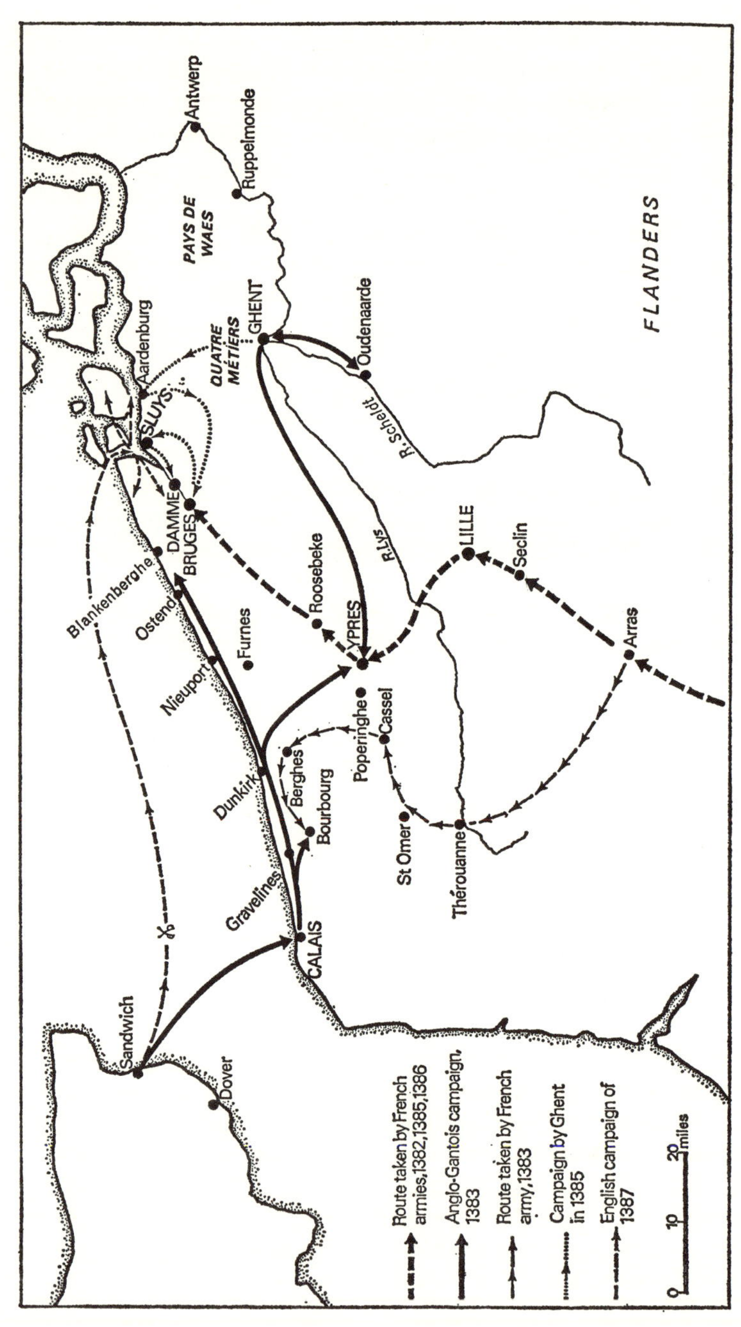

1. Flanders, 1382–7

England; to join in the war against their late ally; and, finally, to cease all trade with her.[5] These last two demands impelled Ghent to reject the terms. At a pinch she might abandon her cherished neutrality to enter the war on the English side; but her hatred for France, and fear for her wool supplies, made it inconceivable that she would do so to aid France while she had any alternative. Since an alliance with England was available, Ghent refused to submit to France.

Negotiations between England and Ghent continued throughout the winter of 1382–3. A small Flemish fleet which had escaped the clutches of the French after Roosebeke came over to England and was enrolled in the service of the Crown. Its admiral, Francis Ackermann of Ghent was to become the key figure in Anglo-Flemish relations in the next few years. He had been the leading spirit in the revolt against Louis de Mâle from the very beginning, long before Philip van Artevelde came to the fore. According to one redaction of the Flemish chronicles, he and his friend and ally Peter van Bos were responsible for the outbreak of the revolt in 1379, and had since laboured to keep it going. Another tradition held that van Artevelde himself was only a front for these two men, put up in the moment of Ghent's greatest danger in the winter of 1381–2 to make use of the emotional associations of his name. Whatever the truth of these accounts,[6] it is certain that the death of Philip van Artevelde at Roosebeke made no difference to the alignment of Ghent with England, except possibly to make it more definite.

England remained as determined to continue the struggle as Ghent and even acute financial difficulties were not allowed to get in the way. Though the two parliaments of October 1382 and May 1383 could be induced to vote only a single subsidy, an army was raised by entrusting the campaign to the Bishop of Norwich, who was able to supplement the inadequate parliamentary grant with the proceeds of the sale of indulgences, granted by Urban VI for a crusade against the Clementist heretics of France and Flanders. By the spring of 1383 Bishop Despenser was ready to dispute possession of Flanders with Charles VI.

This was the situation inherited by de la Pole. Negotiations with France had been suspended for almost a year, neither side showing any inclination to renew them; and both countries were preparing for a major conflict in Flanders. The prospects of peace had never seemed worse. Yet within six months the chancellor had called a halt to the war; three months later he had concluded the first general truce since the beginning of the reign; and within a year of taking office he had negotiated a provisional peace.

None of this was accidental. On his appointment de la Pole had taken careful stock of the situation and decided that he had no viable alternative to a settlement with France. Over the previous few years the Commons had displayed a steady determination to reduce taxation or to refuse it altogether. Already encumbered by years of accumulated war debts, the government was unable to wage war with any prospect of real success, and its failures abroad combined with its acute financial distress to undermine its stability at home. It did not require prophetic powers to see that if this situation were allowed to continue, the independence of the Crown would be seriously endangered. From the chancellor's point of view there were two possible solutions to this dilemma. Either he had to persuade the Commons to be vastly more generous, or he had to end the war.

The first possibility was perhaps never a very real one, though de la Pole did make an attempt to realize it. He was careful however to put his case in such a way that if the Commons rejected his plea for a great deal more money, they were thereby morally committed to support his bid for peace. In his first address to parliament, and on subsequent occasions, he argued[7] that the nation was confronted by two possible courses of action: it could either attack the enemy with all the force at its command, or it could conclude peace. There could be no half-measures and there were no alternatives. England was the claimant and the aggressor in the war and could not honourably pursue a defensive strategy. In any case, such a strategy was liable to prove as dangerous as it was dishonourable since it would invite the enemy to transfer the war to English soil. The deceptively attractive policy of relying on a subsidized merchant fleet to keep the enemy at bay – the policy preferred by the Commons – must therefore be discarded in favour of a more energetic, if more expensive approach. France and her allies must be hammered by armies led by the king in person, even though this would necessarily involve considerable financial sacrifices.

De la Pole realized, however, that it was unlikely that parliament would vote funds on a scale sufficient to tip the balance in favour of England, and until there was evidence to the contrary he proceeded on the assumption that he must try to end the war before the situation deteriorated even further. His first move was to explore the possibilities of a solution to the Castilian problem. On 1 April 1383, eighteen days after taking office, he appointed ambassadors to negotiate with King John of Castile. This was the first time that an English government had formally admitted that John of Gaunt's claims to the Castilian throne were negotiable. Though the English ambassadors were also commissioned to negotiate offensive alliances with the kings of Navarre and Aragon, it appears that these negotiations were designed to put diplomatic pressure on Castile to accept a settlement rather than as serious preparations for war, since the king of Aragon was told that no military intervention in Spain was contemplated for at least two years. Two years was of course a euphemism for 'within the foreseeable future'.[8]

But the real obstacle to peace lay in Flanders rather than Spain, and here de la Pole's freedom of action was severely circumscribed. Preparations for the crusade of the bishop of Norwich were already well-advanced when he took office and he appeared to have no choice but to await its outcome. Even so, there are signs that he attempted to cancel the expedition, despite the obvious political dangers involved. According to Thomas Walsingham, a last-minute effort was made to halt the crusade, and it was frustrated only by the zeal of the bishop, who deliberately ignored his recall and placed himself and his army out of reach of the government with the utmost celerity. Unlikely as it sounds, the story may well contain a grain of truth. Not very long afterwards a visiting ambassador expressed his belief that the crusade had been launched against the king's wishes; and although he had his own reasons for wishing to believe this version of events, he would scarcely have dreamed up so improbable a story without some basis in fact or rumour.[9]

Whether or not de la Pole attempted to cancel the expedition, its successful beginnings deprived him of all freedom of action. After landing at Calais in the middle of May, Despenser, guided by Francis Ackermann, took most of Flanders without encountering effective opposition. Early in June he settled down to besiege Ypres assisted by the militia of Ghent and some smaller towns. The outcome did not appear to be in doubt, and the surrender of Ypres would have brought the whole of Flanders under the control of England and Ghent. The bishop's astonishing success to this point produced a change in the government's attitude. On 1 June he was granted extensive diplomatic powers to treat with the count and towns of Flanders for the first time, and on the following 20 June these already wide powers were significantly enlarged.[10] But by this date the tide had begun to turn. Ypres put up an unexpectedly stubborn resistance, depriving Despenser of the support of a united Flanders, weakening his army, and enabling Charles VI to raise one of his own. On 2 August the French king left Paris to take up the *oriflamme* at St Denys; by 31 August he was at the Flemish border.[11]

At this point de la Pole intervened, the speed of his intervention emphasizing his desire to do so. On 8 September 1383, before he was even aware that the French were in Flanders, he commissioned the duke of Lancaster to treat for peace. The commission was couched in the most extravagant language, denouncing war and its attendant evils in forceful and vigorous terms. The sentiments were not unusual but their mode of expression certainly was, and bore witness to the urgency of the chancellor's desire for peace. So too did the contents of the commission. If he could not obtain peace by conventional diplomatic means, the duke was empowered to terminate the war immediately by a duel, to be fought out either between the two kings themselves, or the kings and their uncles, or between equally matched forces chosen from amongst their subjects. Four days later, on 12 September, these powers were supplemented (or possibly replaced) by a more conventional commission which authorized the duke to conclude a general settlement with both France and her allies on all outstanding issues between the two sides.[12]

At first it appeared that this would be achieved. A summit conference was arranged for the end of the year and actually met in December. By the new year, it had agreed on the articles of a provisional peace, subject to the approval of the two kings. To allow time for their examination, a general truce was concluded on 26 January 1384 to last until 1 October, and the conference was adjourned until 1 June.[13] The truce was the first break in the war since Richard II ascended the throne, and the provisional treaty was the nearest the two countries had so far come to an agreement since the war began.

The provisional treaty was laid before a parliament which met at Salisbury at the end of April, and the proceedings[14] reveal with great clarity the government's anxiety to secure its approval. The chancellor approached the two houses separately, hoping no doubt that a favourable reply from one would strengthen him in his dealings with the other. The Lords were tackled first. They declared a preference for peace rather than war but would neither approve nor reject the particular proposals laid before them. The chancellor then turned to the Commons, who returned a similarly evasive reply. Though they declared peace to be 'the most noble and gracious aid and comfort that could possibly be devised for them', they refused to give it their express consent. In desperation, de la Pole appealed to them to put themselves in the king's shoes. A choice must be made; there could be no middle course between war and peace. In making the choice, the chancellor urged the Commons to bear in mind the king's innumerable enemies, their power, wealth and solidarity, and the poverty, weakness and isolation of England herself. But the Commons resisted both his appeal and his scarcely veiled advocacy of the peace proposals. They stolidly repeated their previous reply, reminding the chancellor that the Lords had committed themselves no further. The government would have to make its own decision and accept full responsibility for it.

When the summit conference reconvened in the summer of 1384 its sole accomplishment was a brief extension of the existing truce until 1 May 1385. Since the extension covered only the winter months when campaigning was unlikely, it was of very limited value. No provision was made to continue the negotiations, and both sides set about preparing for war long before the truce had expired.[15]

This dismal failure was not due to the refusal of the English parliament to endorse the provisional peace terms, for all the sources agree that the French were responsible for the breakdown. According to de la Pole himself, the French ambassadors had tried to wreck the conference from its very inception, first by threatening to withdraw altogether, then by their constant procrastination, and finally by refusing to negotiate on the basis of the articles to which they had assented in January. On top of all this, they had refused to consider any other 'rational and honest way to peace', despite the readiness of the English delegation to make concessions on points of substance. His account, echoed by the Westminster chronicler, is substantiated by the journal of the French ambassadors, which records little other than the wrecking tactics they employed throughout the brief life of the conference.[16]

The reason for the French attitude is not at first apparent. Between the first and second meetings of the royal uncles serious hostilities had broken out between England and Scotland, following the end of the 'great truce' in February; and a number of raids from both sides of the border had culminated in a two-week invasion of Scotland by the duke of Lancaster in April. But it is improbable that these events were a cause, let alone the sole cause of the failure of the second summit conference. France had agreed to the truce of January knowing full well that it could leave Scotland at the mercy of her neighbour. Scotland could have been included in the truce had she so wished, but the French made no effort to inform her of this until the damage had been done. Due to long disuse, the 'old alliance' was not functioning too smoothly at this date, and the meetings between the allies in August, during the second summit conference, were devoted rather to mutual recrimination than to plotting against England. The French attitude during these meetings reveals that they had no intention of waging war on behalf of Scotland; and since the English government had been anxiously seeking to extend the truce with her northern neighbour for some time prior to 1384, it does not seem that Scotland was any very serious obstacle to peace.[17]

Much the same can be said of Castile. It is easy to see how the Castilian problem could prevent a peace settlement, but not why it should make the French eager to resume the war, as they were clearly intent on doing in the late summer and autumn of 1384. If Castile had been the cause of the breakdown of the summit conference, then the onus would have lain on England and should have been apparent in her conduct of the next stages of the war. Yet all the sources agree that France was responsible for the breakdown of the peace talks; and the resumption of war was to show that England had no real appetite for the struggle. Like Scotland, Castile served only to exacerbate an impossible situation.

The basic cause of the breakdown was undoubtedly the situation in Flanders. Louis de Mâle had died in the middle of the first peace conference and had been succeeded by Philip of Burgundy. Thereafter there was no possibility of peace with France without a concurrent settlement of the entire Flemish problem, both in its internal and its external aspects. This put both sides in an almost impossible position. Philip could not accept any settlement which left him with less than absolute freedom in Flanders; and although de la Pole was already committed to a withdrawal from the county, he could not simply abandon his ally Ghent to the mercies of her new French ruler. This dilemma very nearly wrecked the first peace conference, when a breakdown was only averted by a compromise, made very largely at the expense of Ghent and England. Flanders was included in the truce of 26 January, the position of Ghent being independently guaranteed by a separate agreement.[18] In effect this meant that Philip was recognized as count of Flanders, that England was excluded from the county, and that Ghent was isolated. In the interval between the two peace conferences Philip was thus able to assure his hold on the remainder of Flanders and so prepare for the submission of Ghent, without opposition. On 10 May, in return for a pardon for their recent rebellion, Bruges and Ypres, together with fifteen other towns and the feudal nobility of the *Franc* of Bruges, agreed to pay Philip sums ranging from ten francs to twelve thousand francs a month until Ghent and her allies had been reduced to

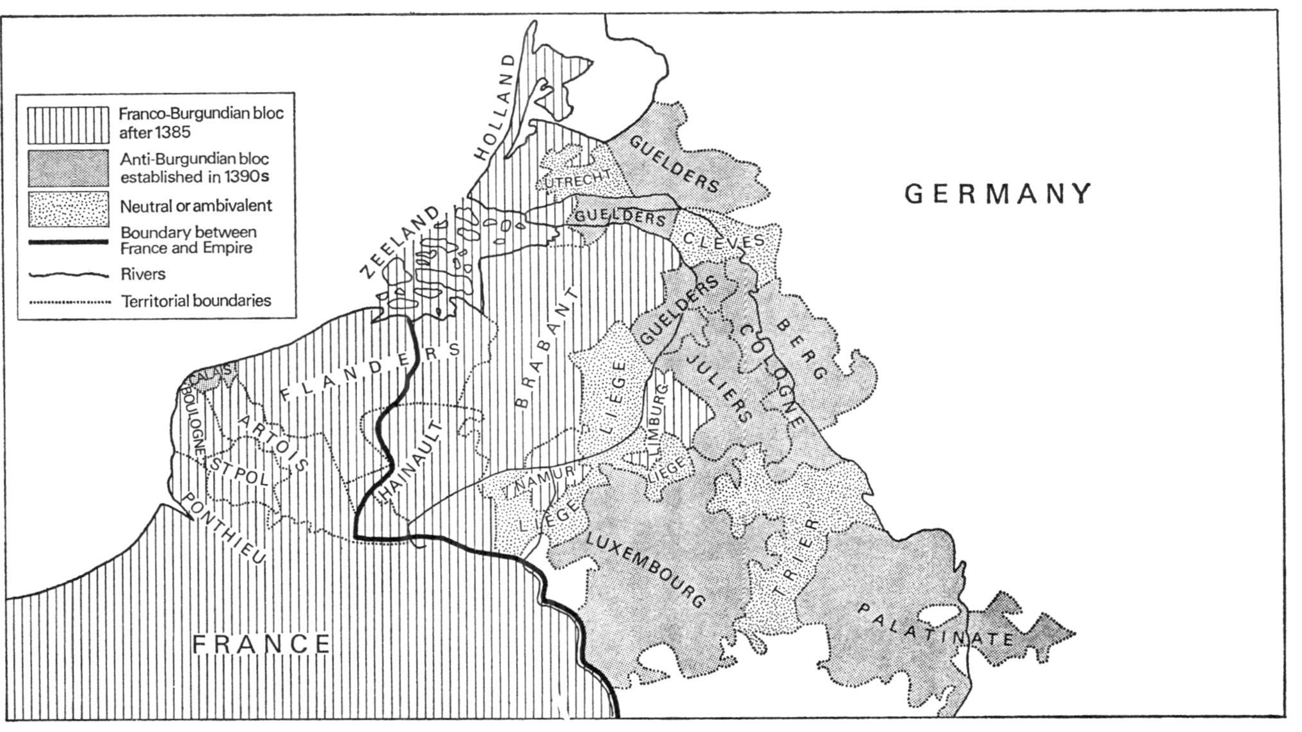

2 The Low Countries after 1384

obedience. At the end of the same month one of Philip's supporters seized Oudenaarde, Ghent's only major ally, in a manifest breach of the truce for which no reparation was made. Finally, during the same period Philip began a major programme of repair and reconstruction, and put in hand the building of Sluys castle, 'among the most elaborate and expensive of all his architectural and military enterprises'. These measures effectively isolated Ghent, and each of them was a separate humiliation to the English government.[19]

From this point onwards it was against Philip's best interests to extend the truce or to continue the peace negotiations unless Ghent were excluded from their scope. This was the one concession the English government could not make. Short of actually abandoning its ally to the mercies of the duke of Burgundy, it made every other possible concession. No issue was made of Philip's activity in Flanders; and if the government protested about the breach of the truce, it did nothing further. Philip was recognized as count of Flanders, and the king of England withdrew his claim to the homage of the county. This was of course a fundamental concession not only to Philip but to Charles VI, and it was only revoked when the negotiations had patently broken down.[20] But it did not go far enough to satisfy the duke of Burgundy, and his insistence on a free hand to deal with Ghent doomed the negotiations to the failure which quickly overtook them. When the truce of January 1384 was extended in September, Ghent was once again excluded and made the subject of a separate agreement; she was the only party accorded this special treatment.[21] But the problem could not be indefinitely postponed in this manner. But for the approach of winter, the truce would probably not have been extended at all; for by the autumn of 1384 it had become clear that war could not be avoided in the following year, and that the struggle would centre on Flanders.

The size of the stakes involved had meanwhile been substantially increased by the death of Duke Wenzel of Brabant on 8 December 1383. Wenzel left no issue, and although he was duke of Brabant only *iure uxoris*, his death raised the problem of succession to the duchy[22] since his wife Jeanne was old (sixty-one) and ailing and had in fact long been expected to predecease him. The right to the succession was by no means clear, but of the possible candidates Philip of Burgundy was undoubtedly the best-placed. If Brabant and Flanders were united, they would dominate the Low Countries with ease; and united under a French prince, they would have England at their mercy. After two centuries of continued effort, the French monarchy was poised to absorb

the greater part of the Low Countries and so to achieve an overwhelming economic, political and strategic superiority over its enemy.

From an English point of view this awful prospect was accompanied
by certain immediate advantages. For years England had had to wage
her war single-handed; but in threatening to dominate the Low
Countries, France acquired a number of enemies who could be enlisted
on the English side. Foremost among these were the emperor, Wenzel
of Bohemia, and William, duke of Guelders, both of whom had a direct
interest in the succession of Brabant. Wenzel had a double claim to the
duchy, by treaty and by devolution. By an act dated 20 February 1357,
Duchess Jeanne de Brabant had agreed that the duchy should return
to the house of Luxembourg in default of heirs to herself or her husband.
Even if this act were regarded as invalidated by subsequent events,
Wenzel could, and did, claim that as an imperial fief Brabant could not
descend to a female and must therefore return to the Empire on the
death of the duchess.

In opposing Philip's claims, Wenzel was vigorously supported by
William of Guelders. As ruler of Guelders, Duke William was naturally inclined towards enmity with any ruler of Brabant, and as heir to
the duchy of Juliers this tendency was exacerbated; for both territories
had a long history of bad relations with Brabant. In addition, the duke
hoped to make use of the claims of the Duchess Jeanne's youngest
sister Marie, the widow of his predecessor, to secure a share in Brabant
on Jeanne's death. The height of his ambition seems to have been to
persuade the emperor to transfer to him his own rights in Brabant. This
was by no means an unlikely eventuality. Occupied at the other end of
the Empire, Wenzel could only intermittently attend to the affairs of the
Low Countries and would find it difficult to compete with Philip of
Burgundy. Any alternative was preferable to a French succession, and
William of Guelders was an aggressive and vigorous ruler who could be
counted on to make the most of any imperial powers conferred on him.
For all these reasons, Duke William rather than the emperor was to
become the 'bastion of the Germanic Low Countries against Franco-
Burgundian influences and infiltration'[23] in the years following the
deaths of Louis de Mâle and Wenzel of Brabant, and as such he was the
key figure in any system of alliances which England might try to raise
against Philip and Charles VI.

No other power had so direct an interest in the succession to Brabant;
but two others were affected by the possibility of a union of the duchy
with Flanders.The towns of Brabant were alarmed at the prospect,

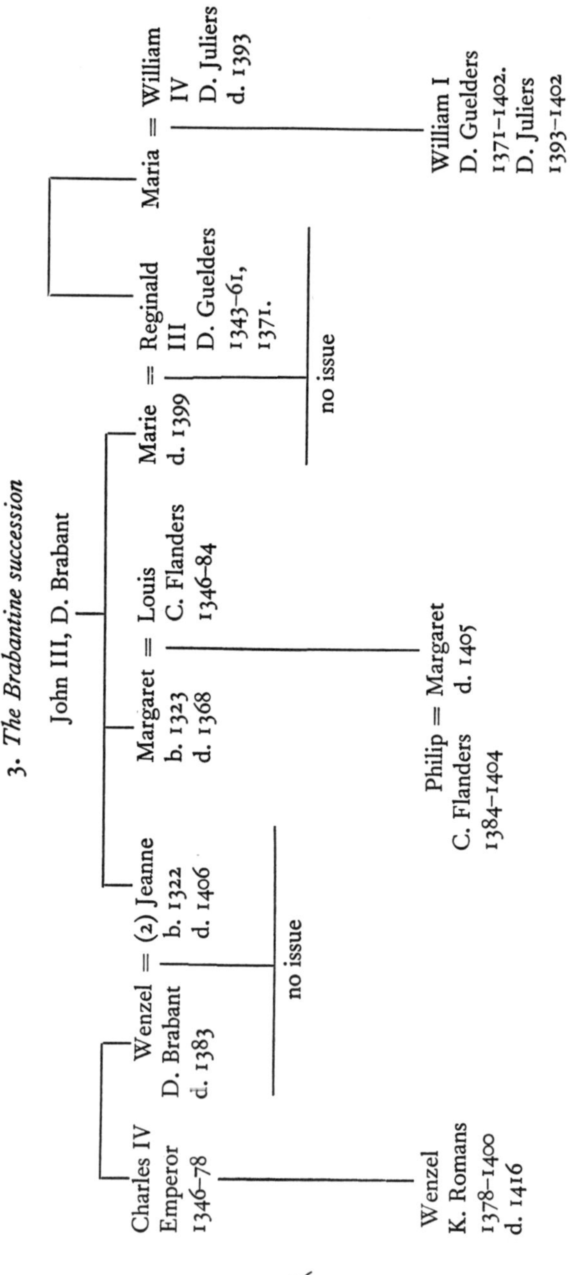

3. The Brabantine succession

John III, D. Brabant

Charles IV
Emperor
1346–78

Wenzel = (2) Jeanne
D. Brabant   b. 1322
d. 1383   d. 1406

no issue

Margaret = Louis
b. 1323   C. Flanders
d. 1368   1346–84

Marie = Reginald
d. 1399   III
          D. Guelders
          1343–61,
          1371.

no issue

Maria = William
        IV
        D. Juliers
        d. 1393

Wenzel
K. Romans
1378–1400
d. 1416

Philip = Margaret
C. Flanders   d. 1405
1384–1404

William I
D. Guelders
1371–1402.
D. Juliers
1393–1402

which threatened the subjection of their economic interests to those of Flanders. This made them potential allies, whose co-operation might easily be further encouraged by judicious manipulation of the wool staple, a time-honoured device for enlisting the support of the powerful industrial communities of the Low Countries. The same weapon might also have been employed against the ruler of Holland, Zeeland and Hainault, who had his own reasons for finding the sudden expansion of Burgundy distasteful. Not only did it threaten to diminish his own stature, but the union of Flanders and Brabant would leave him at the mercy of their ruler, whose territories would separate the various units of his own inheritance from each other.

Thus when it became apparent that the negotiations with France were going to be fruitless, the English government could turn with some confidence towards its potential allies in the Low Countries. But instead of doing so, it followed a policy of deliberate disengagement. The consequence was the rapid consolidation of Burgundian power. It was a high price to pay for the end of the war, but the only one which might end it quickly. It is a measure of de la Pole's determination to secure peace that he was prepared to pay this price.

The most conspicuous example of his inactivity is to be found in his relations with the Empire. Richard II's marriage with Wenzel's sister had produced the closest contacts with the Empire since the early years of the Hundred Years War.[24] They had not immediately resulted in an alliance directed against France; but once Wenzel's dynastic interests were threatened by French expansion, such an alliance appeared inevitable, particularly as Wenzel himself displayed a quite unwonted energy in pursuit of his rights. At the end of 1383 he concluded an alliance with the dukes of Guelders, Juliers and Berg against anyone who might harm his interests in the Low Countries; and in the autumn of 1384 he followed this up with an extended visit to the Low Countries in an attempt to secure his succession to Luxembourg and Brabant.[25] The moment appeared propitious for the alliance which de la Pole's predecessors had so eagerly sought. Yet no attempt was made to secure it. There is no sign that Wenzel was approached during his residence in the Low Countries, and in the ensuing months he was almost equally ignored. In the entire period between the death of Wenzel of Brabant and de la Pole's loss of office, only one English embassy – and that an unimposing one – was sent to the emperor.[26]

A little more attention was paid to the duke of Guelders. Towards the end of December 1384 one Peter Wenk was sent to the duke on the king's secret business, and in the following February Hugh Fastolf and George Felbrigg were dispatched on a similar mission.[27] As late as May, there is evidence of diplomatic contacts with Nimwegen.[28] But nothing came of these missions, and negotiations then hung fire for almost a year and a half. It is not known why; but in view of the speed with which an alliance was concluded as soon as de la Pole was removed from office, it is highly probable that his own lack of interest was the only obstacle to an agreement.

Negotiations with Duke Albert of Holland, Zeeland and Hainault and with the towns of Brabant were pursued with even less energy and were if anything less successful. Since the autumn of 1383 the duke of Lancaster had been trying to arrange a marriage between his daughter Philippa and Albert's heir, William of Ostrevant;[29] but the negotiations did not even get as far as the conclusion of a contract, and in the summer of 1384 they were superseded by negotiations between Albert and Philip of Burgundy, conducted through the mediation of Jeanne de Brabant. By January 1385 they had agreed on a double marriage between Philip's heir, John de Nevers, and Margaret of Bavaria; and Albert's heir, William of Ostrevant, and Margaret of Burgundy. This grave political defeat prompted the English government to make one last effort to save the situation, and in February 1385 Fastolf and Felbrigg were instructed to visit Albert on their way to Guelders and to try to dissuade him from the Burgundian alliance. But it was a forlorn effort. The ambassadors were received ungraciously and left empty-handed.[30] On 12 April, the day after they returned to London, the double Burgundian-Wittlesbach marriage was celebrated at Cambrai before Charles VI himself, Duke Albert, Philip, and Jeanne de Brabant. The marriage contract of John de Nevers and Margaret of Bavaria settled the succession to Brabant on John and his heirs, thereby proclaiming the solidarity of all parties on the most important outstanding political issue in the Low Countries and aligning them behind Philip and France. Never before had the rulers of Holland, Zeeland, Hainault, Brabant and Flanders identified themselves so completely with either England or France. Coming on top of the Burgundian succession to Flanders, the Cambrai weddings constituted the most serious political and diplomatic defeat suffered by England since the war began, and perhaps the most radical alteration in the balance of power in Europe since the beginning of the century. To a very large extent the English government had invited its defeat by its refusal to lend whole-hearted support to its friends and allies in the Low Countries.

The policy which dictated this neglect of the princes of the Low Countries and of Germany also ensured that Ghent would be given every incentive to make her peace with her ruler. Though she was not actually abandoned to his mercies, she was given no real assistance in the months which followed the failure of the peace conference. Despite a constant stream of envoys between Ghent and Westminster[31] no treaty resulted, and later events were to show that no common military policy was agreed upon. In view of Ghent's subsequent conduct, it is difficult to believe that she was in any way responsible for this lack of co-ordination and co-operation. Throughout her association with de la Pole she made the running and he was the laggard.

A typical example of their relationship is provided by their different attitudes towards the question of the appointment of a *ruwaert*, or governor, of Ghent. Abandoning her normal attitude of jealous independence, the town made the unprecedented request that the English government should fill the post, asking for the nomination of a prince of the Blood, evidently hoping in this way to secure a closer alliance. The request was not refused; but instead of a prince of the Blood, Ghent had to be content with Lord Bourchier (November 1384). Bourchier was a worthy enough peer, with forty years service and some nine major campaigns to his credit. But he had never before held an independent command and was never to do so again. He was not a prominent figure at court; he was scarcely ever employed on important royal business, and he is not known to have wielded any political influence at all. In short, his talents were largely, if not exclusively military, and even these were not of the highest order. His presence in Ghent constituted no real commitment by the English government.[32]

Negotiations with France in the spring of 1385 reveal a similar lack of enthusiasm for Ghent and her cause. The truce was due to expire on 1 May, and as this date approached efforts were made to avert a renewal of the war. Once again the principal obstacle was Ghent. Her situation made the discussion of any sort of peace out of the question and even an extension of the truce difficult to obtain. The French would agree neither to a general suspension of hostilities nor to a local truce for Picardy and Flanders unless Ghent were excluded from their scope. In the end the English ambassadors were unable to satisfy this demand and the negotiations promptly broke down. But not before they had made every effort to accommodate Philip of Burgundy. At one point they proposed a truce covering Picardy and Flanders but not Ghent, and at another expressed their willingness to seek the agreement of their ally to a local truce which excluded her. But with her armies poised to invade England and Scotland, France held out for the complete isolation of Ghent and the negotiations broke down, having achieved nothing more substantial than a local truce for Picardy and the Flemish coast until 15 July.[33]

Before that date the war had been renewed, and the course it took once again emphasized the government's wish to dissociate itself from its Flemish ally. Towards the end of May, the French sent a small army of 1,600 men to Scotland while concentrating a far larger force at Sluys, preparatory to an invasion of southern England.[34] The obvious *riposte* was to call out the northern earls in force against the Scots and to send the bulk of the English troops to co-operate with Ghent in an attack on the French army in Flanders. What in fact happened was that a tiny contingent of 400 men was sent to aid Ghent in July,[35] while in the same month the king himself set out for Scotland at the head of an army almost twelve thousand strong[36] – easily the largest army sent against the Scots in the Middle Ages and possibly the largest English army of the entire war.

The disproportion between these two efforts was accentuated by the invaluable contribution made by Ghent to the joint war-effort.[37] As soon as the truce expired, the Flemish militia under Francis Ackermann attempted to seize first Aardenburg, then Bruges, then Sluys and finally – and successfully – Damme. All four strongholds controlled key points between Ghent and the Zwin, and thus between Ghent and England. Their capture would have made possible closer military co-operation between the allies, and by that token would have endangered the position of the French army at Sluys. In fact, the immediate consequence of the capture of Damme on 16 July was the cancellation of the projected invasion of England in favour of an attack on Damme.

A secondary effect should have been to attract substantial English reinforcements for Damme, and at first it seemed that they might be forthcoming. The king was already on his way to Scotland, but a council left to manage affairs in London made a desperate effort to raise men, money and materials. Artillery and provisions were rushed to the coast; loans were hastily contracted; and although he was approaching his seventies, Robert Knolles, the most famous of Edward III's captains, was brought out of retirement to lead a relief force.[38] But it does not appear that this force ever reached its destination,[39] and the French were able to proceed with the subjection of Flanders without outside interference. A Flemish attempt to subvert Sluys in the name of the

English King and to destroy the French fleet at anchor in the Zwin was ruthlessly suppressed; Damme was retaken; and the *Quatre-Métiers,* the area on which Ghent relied for supplies, was systematically ravaged.

But Ghent herself remained unsubdued; and although her position was not a happy one, she had several times recovered from equally desperate situations in the previous six years. Yet she now chose to make her peace with France and Philip, on highly unfavourable terms. Her reason for doing so is not in much doubt. Without English support, Ghent could not for long resist both her own ruler and her French overlord, and the events of the past year had made it clear beyond all doubt that England would not supply assistance on anything like an adequate scale. This left Ghent with no alternative but to seek an agreement while she still had some power to bargain. Unfavourable though they were, the terms of the treaty of Tournai (18 December 1385) did at least allow her to retain her religious allegiance and her municipal independence and saved her from the ravages of a French army.[40] Given her isolation, this was about all she could have expected to salvage.

The submission of Ghent and the consolidation of Burgundian power in the Low Countries had thus been brought about by English policy towards France. It may be added that no attempt was made to disrupt the treaty of Tournai during what remained of de la Pole's period of office. Within a few weeks of the treaty, in fact, peace negotiations with France had been resumed, and one of their first fruits was a truce covering Picardy and Flanders until 1 May 1386.[41] The main beneficiary of this truce was the duke of Burgundy, who was able to consolidate his recent diplomatic victory at Tournai. De la Pole's other activities at this time were equally conciliatory. Lord Bourchier was recalled from Ghent; English reinforcements for the city were switched to the Scottish frontier;[42] and so far as is known, no attempt was made to secure anti-Burgundian alliances with Guelders, Juliers, the Empire or with dissident elements within Flanders itself. One of the few remaining links with the Low Countries was severed in the summer of 1386 when William de Coudenberghe – the Urbanist bishop of Tournai who had negotiated the Anglo-Flemish alliance after Roosebeke – was bought out of the pension granted him on that occasion.[43]

The immediate results of this policy were uniformly unfavourable. Once the whole of Flanders had been brought under Burgundian control, it still remained to be decided whether the county would resume its previous neutrality in the Anglo-French war or whether it would throw its weight into the struggle against England. The previous history of

Flanders made it improbable that she would follow the latter course, yet this is precisely what happened. During the negotiations which resulted in the treaty of Tournai, Ghent pressed for a declaration of Flemish neutrality and insisted that no obstacles be placed in the way of trade.[44] But on both these points she had to give way. The treaty of Tournai did indeed specify that commerce be free, but it did so in such general terms that Philip was not precluded from imposing a ban on the merchants of any particular nation. Ghent fought hard to secure a more precise formula which would prevent Philip interfering with trade with England; but to no effect. As for the declaration of neutrality, not even a hint of this found its way into the treaty. Philip subsequently used the freedom of action this gave him to draw Flanders into the war on the French side. No previous count had managed to dictate to his subjects in this way on matters vital to their economic well-being; and the fact that Philip was able to do so was largely, if not entirely due to the policy of the English government, which had denied Ghent the support which would have enabled her to take a firm stand on this vital point.

His dealings with the Low Countries provide the acid test of de la Pole's foreign policy, as this was easily the most important area of conflict during his tenure of office. But his determination to appease France and to disengage England from the Continent is equally apparent in other areas. His treatment of the duke of Brittany provides a case in point.

To begin with, the chancellor did nothing to disturb the peaceful if precarious state of equilibrium established by the second treaty of Guérande (April 1381). Brittany's internal peace and her effective neutrality in the Anglo-French war both favoured his policy towards France, and his dealings with de Montfort were consequently marked by a positive cordiality, despite a number of very real causes for bad feeling. There were no reprisals for de Montfort's part in opposing the Despenser crusade, and he was even accepted as a mediator at the peace conference which followed. When his ambassadors appeared at the Salisbury parliament in May 1384 seeking the restoration of Richmond and Brest and the free exercise of the right to sell licences to shipping sailing around Brittany, they were given a friendly welcome. The third request was conceded and they were told to renew the others at the peace conference due to open a month later.[45] This was a fairly broad hint that if the conference was as successful as it was expected to be, then Richmond and Brest would be returned.

But when the peace talks failed the English attitude changed, suddenly and drastically. In the autumn of 1384, Joan of Penthièvre died, leaving her son John de Blois the leader of the Penthièvre party. Within three months de la Pole was negotiating his release; and although the identity of the other principal in these negotiations is concealed, all the circumstances point to it being de Montfort's inveterate enemy Olivier de Clisson, the French constable. In this same month (January 1385) John de Blois appointed de Clisson his lieutenant in Brittany. De Montfort retaliated by refusing to accept homage for the Penthièvre lands by deputy and seized them himself. The efforts of de Clisson and Marie of Anjou, the sister of John de Blois, to secure the intervention of the French royal council were blocked by the duke of Burgundy.[46]

The renewal of the Blois–de Montfort struggle was provoked and exacerbated by de la Pole's readiness to release John de Blois, which threatened de Montfort's security. It was an unfriendly act and it was intended to be so since it was accompanied by the total confiscation of the earldom of Richmond. Richmond had been in the king's hands since 1381, but only as a temporary measure; and as recently as May 1384 the duke had been led to believe that its return was imminent. But in November he was declared to have forfeited it completely and it was promptly assigned to the queen.[47]

Superficially this sudden change of policy was motivated by simple fiscal considerations and made possible by an opportune death. There was no question of releasing de Blois in return for an alliance against de Montfort or Charles VI; his ransom was to have been a simple cash transaction. The government was desperately hard up and hoped to obtain something like £45,000 for de Blois, as much as parliament had voted in direct taxation in the three years following the Peasants' Revolt. The death of de Montfort's wife and Richard II's half-sister, Joan Holand, in November 1384 had broken the last remaining bond which might have inhibited the king from taking his profit at the duke's expense, and the confiscation of Richmond and the ransom negotiations followed hard on its heels.

Yet this cannot be the whole explanation. The very fact that de la Pole could give precedence to fiscal considerations points to a major change in English policy towards Brittany. For the first time in almost half a century England was prepared to cut her ties with the duchy and renounce any influence in its internal affairs. The profits of this renunciation were to be devoted to the reconquest of Ireland by the king's favourite, Robert de Vere, who was created marquis of Dublin for this purpose in November 1385, and granted the proceeds of de Blois's ransom to finance an expedition to Ireland.[48] England was symbolically turning her back on France, and the symbolism was surely too perfect to be accidental. It portrays de la Pole's policy to perfection.

In Brittany, as in the Low Countries, appeasement produced highly unfavourable results. Once it was clear that de la Pole was serious in his intention of releasing John de Blois, de Montfort was forced to rely more heavily than ever on Philip of Burgundy for his security, and modified his policy accordingly. Though he appealed to the English parliament to forbid the ransom of his rival, and renewed contacts with the king of Navarre, whose daughter he married in September 1386, he could scarcely have anticipated the success of his appeal to England, or have expected much in the way of assistance from Navarre. He therefore aligned himself more closely with France. Important Breton contingents joined the great invasion force of 1386 and in the same year the duke himself undertook the siege of Brest. For something like a year – a crucial year – Brittany was thrown into the scales against England, with results which were very nearly disastrous. They were the inescapable consequences of the chancellor's foreign policy.

Throughout the years 1383 to 1386 de la Pole's efforts to create the conditions for an Anglo-French *détente* had led to one reverse after another, each further weakening the English position abroad and his own position at home. Their combined effect was to invite the French to transfer the war to English soil, and to raise the domestic opposition to the government to a point where something had to give. In 1386 these two currents met and mingled. The result was the gravest constitutional crisis of the century and the most serious invasion threat of the Middle Ages.

NOTES

1 *RP*, iii, 114; *Foedera*, vii, 347–8; Le Fèvre, *Journal*, i, 26; Russell, *English Intervention in Spain and Portugal*, 329–30.
2 ADN, B 277/14452–4; see appendix 1(d) for date.
3 *RP*, iii, 122–4; appendix 2.
4 Perroy, *L'Angleterre et le grand Schisme*, 166–81; Quicke, *Les Pays-Bas*, 332–5; Vaughan, *Philip the Bold*, 24–8; Lehoux, *Jean de Berri*, ii, 68–73.
5 *Chronique rimée des troubles de Flandres*, 106–9; Froissart, *Oeuvres*, x, 484–6, 494–6.
6 *Istore et croniques de Flandres*, ii, 223, 247; Froissart, *Oeuvres*, ix, 372–8.
7 *RP*, iii, 149–50, 203, 215.

8 *Foedera*, vii, 386–90; *DC*, no. 40n.

9 Walsingham, *Historia Anglicana*, ii, 88; *Mémoires . . . Bretagne*, ii, 454.

10 *Foedera*, vii, 395–7.

11 For this campaign see Perroy, 196–7; Quicke, 341–55; Vaughan, 29–30; Lehoux, ii, 81–3.

12 *Foedera*, vii, 407–8, 410.

13 *Du Bosc*, 328–30; *Foedera*, vii, 418–21.

14 *RP*, iii, 170.

15 *Foedera*, vii, 438–45; Froissart, *Oeuvres*, x, 306.

16 *RP*, iii, 184; *Foedera*, vii, 444–5; *Higden*, ix, 44, 49–50; *Du Bosc*, 331–40.

17 *Higden*, ix, 44, 49–50; *Du Bosc*, 331–40; Campbell, 'England, Scotland and the Hundred Years' War', *Europe in the Late Middle Ages*, 206–9.

18 *Istore et croniques de Flandres*, ii, 331, 336, 367–9; Froissart, *Oeuvres*, x, 276–7; *Croniques de Tournai*, 263.

19 *Ordonnances de Philippe le Hardi*, i, no. 27; Vaughan, *Philip the Bold*, 31–5, quote from *ibid.* 33.

20 *Foedera*, vii, 428–9 (cf 413), 448–9.

21 *Ibid.* 442; *Du Bosc*, 342; C 47/28/6/23.

22 On this Quicke, *Les Pays-Bas*, and Laurent and Quicke, *Origines de l'état bourguignon*, are indispensable. See also Stengers, 'Philippe le Hardi et les Etats de Brabant', *Hommage au Professeur Bonenfant*.

23 Vaughan, *Philip the Bold*, 97.

24 Perroy, *L'Angleterre et le grand Schisme*, 129–65.

25 Laurent and Quicke, 98–117.

26 Bernard van Zetles, a German squire, left London on 20 December 1384 and returned on the following 2 May (E 364/18, m. 7).

27 E 403/505, m. 16; E 101/319/18, 19 (cf. n. 30).

28 E 403/505, mm. 8, 10, mention gifts to the duke's envoys, one of them in England on behalf of the bishop of Liège, another natural enemy of Brabant.

29 Toth-Ubbens, 'Een dubbel vorstenhuwelijk in het jaar 1385', *Bijdragen voor de Geschiedenis der Nederlanden*, xix, 101–6. For what follows see also Laurent and Quicke, 118–30.

30 Froissart, *Oeuvres*, x, 306–16. The English ambassadors, who left London on 11 February and returned on 13 April, were sent 'versus Duces Aubret et Gelre ac alios diversos milites et probos homines diversarum villarum' (E 101/319/18, 19; cf. E 403/505, m. 24).

31 E 403/499, mm. 13, 14, 17, 19, 20; E 403/502, mm. 17, 16; E 403/505, mm. 12, 13, 16; E 403/508, mm. 17, 18–20, 22, 24; E 403/510, mm. 2–4, 6.

32 Froissart, *Oeuvres*, x, 303; *Foedera*, vii, 448–9.

33 Du Bosc, 343–9; *Foedera*, vii, 466–8, 470.

34 Terrier de Loray, *Jean de Vienne*, 179–205; Mirot, 'Une tentative d'invasion en Angleterre', *REH*, viii, 262–3.

35 Not in the previous November as generally stated (E 101/40/11; E 403/508, mm. 18–19; E 403/510, m. 7).

36 Lewis, 'The Last Summons of the English Feudal Levy', *EHR*, lxxiii, 1–26.

37 Froissart, *Oeuvres*, x, 339–42, 353–64; *Croniques de Tournai*, 271–81; *Istore et croniques de Flandres*, ii, 350–2; Brandon, *Chronique*, 5–14; *St Denys*, i, 370–85; *Higden*, ix, 63, 75; Walsingham, *Historia Anglicana*, ii, 127, 133–5 for next two paragraphs.

38 E 403/508, mm. 22, 24; E 403/510, m. 6; E 403/512, m. 9; *Calendar of Letter-Books, H*, 269.

39 There are no surviving accounts in E 101 or E 364 and no record of prests issued to Knolles and his captains.

40 Froissart, *Oeuvres*, xxi, 555–6; *Istore et croniques de Flandres*, ii, 367–83; *St Denys*, i, 404. Cartellieri (*Philipp der Kühne*, 120–3) lists the surviving documents.

41 *Foedera*, vii, 499–500.

42 Lewis, 'Article VII of the Impeachment of Michael de la Pole', *EHR*, xlii, 402–7.

43 E 403/512, m. 17; Perroy, 'Un evêque urbaniste protégé de l'Angleterre, Guillaume de Coudenberghe', *RHE*, xxvii, 103–9.

44 The essential documents are published in Froissart, *Oeuvres*, x, 569–78, xxi, 555–8; *Rekeningen der stad Gent*, 505.

45 *Mémoires . . . Bretagne*, ii, 450–6.

46 C 76/69, m. 12; *Mémoires . . . Bretagne*, ii, 482–3; Le Fèvre, *Journal*, i, 56, 68, 74, 75, 89, 92, 93.

47 *RP*, iii, 279.

48 Palmer, 'The Parliament of 1385 and the Constitutional Crisis of 1386', *Speculum*, xlvi, 477–90 for this and previous paragraph.

Chapter Four

The Great Invasion Scare
1386

During the three years which followed de la Pole's appointment as chancellor, England suffered one reverse after another on the Continent. Flanders was lost, the Low Countries subjected to French influence, and Brittany alienated; the French made serious inroads into the duchy of Aquitaine; and at home the country was exposed to a series of invasion scares which humiliated the nation even if they did little material damage. Initially, these reverses were accepted as the necessary price of peace, only a small aristocratic opposition insisting on a more vigorous prosecution of the war whatever the cost. But as the war dragged on and the level of taxation remained as high as ever, the Commons were gradually driven into an unholy alliance with the opposition Lords, despite the irreconcilable nature of their respective objectives. By 1386 their alliance had been forged and it had become apparent that the chancellor could not maintain either his own position or his policies for very much longer. That autumn the impending crisis was precipitated by the threat of a major French invasion. But it was very nearly averted. Throughout the year de la Pole made desperate efforts to snatch a last-minute peace with France from the apparent ruins of his policies, and almost succeeded. Had he done so he would have pre-empted the domestic opposition by driving a wedge between the Commons and the war party. But his failure sealed his own fate and that of his foreign policy. When parliament met in October the chancellor was swept from office, a baronial council headed by the king's uncle seized power, and a revolution in English foreign policy ensued.

At the beginning of the year, however, the prospects seemed better than this. The settlement of the Flemish question at the end of 1385 had not only removed the main obstacle to peace but had made the French as eager as de la Pole for a settlement. His hold on Flanders secure, Philip of Burgundy could only lose from a continuation of the war, which would put an intolerable strain on the loyalty of his new Flemish subjects. Flanders had already suffered immensely more from internal strife and the passage of English and French armies than any other part of France; and since the county would be an obvious target for English attacks in the event of a full-scale renewal of hostilities, this was something Philip was now anxious to avoid. As virtual ruler of France his interests tended in the same direction. France had gained as much as she could expect to win, and the burden of taxation was beginning to evoke complaints reminiscent of the early 1380s, with all the dangers this implied. Peace could consolidate the French successes and Philip's own hold on the government.

For the first time since the Flemish crisis arose, therefore, both governments were inclined to favour a settlement. Immediately after the conclusion of the treaty of Tournai serious negotiations were resumed at a high level through the mediation of King Leo of Armenia, who moved between Westminster and Paris acting as a personal intermediary between the two kings. The result of his *démarche* was an agreement for a personal interview between Charles VI and Richard II in March 1386. The end of the war appeared to be just around the corner, for a meeting between the two kings would never have been arranged unless its success were virtually guaranteed in advance. In March, Charles VI and Philip of Burgundy duly made their way towards Boulogne to await Richard's arrival at Calais.[1]

But Richard did not cross the Channel. With success in his grasp, de la Pole appeared to change his course. During preliminary meetings held at Leulingham at the end of February and in the early part of March, he insisted on a free hand for the duke of Lancaster in Castile, which the French refused to concede. Though he promised to delay John of Gaunt's preparations until Easter, in the hope that his claims might be settled privately by that date, this was not enough to save the conference. Charles VI and his uncle returned to Paris, and the negotiations hung fire.[2]

Superficially, this volte-face is easy enough to explain. In the two years before de la Pole took office an invasion of Castile had been a serious alternative to intervention in Flanders, and it was natural enough that John of Gaunt's ambitions should come to the fore again once England had disentangled herself from the Low Countries. Moreover, just as this disengagement was nearing completion in the latter half of 1385, news arrived of the unexpected Portuguese victory over the Castilians at Aljubarrota on 14 August. The combination was irresistible and plans for an invasion of Castile were at once put in hand.

This is a tempting explanation; but in view of de la Pole's policy over the previous three years, a highly dubious one. It seems more probable that the Castilian venture was forced upon him by the war party. Pressure to do something had been growing for some time,[3] and Aljubarrota both increased the pressure and provided an obvious outlet. Forced into action of some kind, the chancellor had good reason to prefer an invasion of Castile to any other course. Since it could be represented as a private venture, it might not entail a full-scale resumption of hostilities with France. Moreover, the Castilian dispute had to be resolved in some way or other, for it was an essential pre-condition for peace with France. Finally, there is some reason to believe that Gaunt pledged himself to secure a rapid settlement in Castile if he were given the chance.

Gaunt's motives in invading Castile have never been very closely examined. It has been assumed rather than proven that his objective was the Castilian throne, but there are a number of reasons for believing that his expectations were much more limited than this. In the first place, the meagre results of his father's life-long struggle for the French Crown can scarcely have made him too sanguine as to his own chances of wresting Castile from his rival, however good his claim and whatever the military victories he might win. He was granted only limited resources for a limited period by his government, and even these were only extended on a credit basis. In these circumstances he can scarcely have hoped – let alone have expected – to conquer Castile. Moreover, his entire approach to the enterprise implies more modest aims. Both before and after the invasion, and for almost the whole of 1386, he was negotiating with King John of Castile. At different points in the year hopes of an agreement were high enough to allow for an extension of Anglo-French peace talks, then to attract the mediation of the king of Aragon, then to induce the Scots to agree to a general peace conference, and finally to persuade Charles VI to authorize the conclusion of a three-way treaty between himself, Gaunt and the Castilian king. All of this suggests that these negotiations were taken very seriously; and if this were the case, then Gaunt's real concern was to sell his dynastic claims as dearly as he was able. His army increased his bargaining power. It was not for social reasons that he took his two daughters to Spain: they were essential to the 'Lancastrian settlement', a settlement which was clearly foreseen before they left Plymouth.

In taking his daughters with him, John of Gaunt may simply have been providing for all possible contingencies; but his diplomatic and military preparations also suggest that his ultimate object was to sell his claim and his daughter to his rival at as high a price as he could command. The most conspicuous feature of these preparations was his decision to 'go it alone'. Despite the overwhelming military and political advantages it offered, he carefully refrained from concluding an alliance with Portugal. Though he was represented at the negotiations which produced the Anglo-Portuguese treaty of Windsor in May 1386, he made no agreements with King John of Portugal in his capacity as 'king of Castile and Leon', even though King John himself sought an alliance.[4] He made no attempt to invade Castile in co-operation with the Portuguese king, and he conducted the initial stages of his campaign entirely with his own resources. These sacrifices were borne in the hope of a compromise with Castile, which would have been jeopardized by collusion with Portugal because of the intense bad-feeling between these two kingdoms. Only when his negotiations with John of Castile were finally broken off did John of Gaunt approach Portugal, and the rapidity with which a military and political alliance and a marriage contract were then concluded serves to emphasize his previous restraint. Talks with Castile petered out in October; discussions with Portugal began at the end of the same month and were consummated by Gaunt's ratification of the treaty of Ponte do Mouro on 11 November less than a fortnight later.

If this interpretation of Gaunt's aims is correct, then his invasion of Castile was not intended to herald an escalation in the English war effort. Rather than a reversal of policy towards France, it represented a temporary change of tactics governed largely by domestic politics. Other considerations suggest a similar conclusion. While Gaunt pursued his preparations his government did all it could to avoid provoking France, and at times even seemed to dissociate itself from his enterprise. It was also studiously inactive on every other front. No effort was made to attack France herself, to renew alliances with her enemies, to stir up disaffection in the Low Countries or to woo the duke of Brittany back into the English camp. The only other important military activity of the government was the preparation of an Irish expedition, to which the king devoted far more attention than he gave to the Castilian enterprise. While ostentatiously ignoring his uncle's departure from Plymouth, Richard personally supervised the Irish expeditionary force from his headquarters at Bristol. His activity typified the attitude of his government.[5]

The story of the peace negotiations in the first six months of the year tells a similar tale. Discussions in February and March were conducted by the chancellor in person, a certain sign of his concern.[6] Though the Castilian problem prevented any progress, he was loath to break off the talks, and provision was made for a further meeting at the end of June if there were any chance of Gaunt's claims being settled peacefully before then. In the event, this meeting did not materialize; but at precisely the moment it should have done so a different conference produced an agreement which throws a very revealing light on English policy. One of the principal clauses of a one-year truce with Scotland concluded on 27 June provided that the two sides should reconvene on 14 March 1387 'for to trete for a pees perpetuel, or a lang trewe' between England, Scotland and France.[7] It appears from this that in nine months at the outside, the chancellor expected a solution in Castile. He apparently saw no further obstacle to peace.

When this truce was sealed, John of Gaunt was on the point of departure. Diplomatic and military preparations had been pursued steadily since the beginning of the year, the former culminating in an alliance between England and Portugal on 17 May (treaty of Windsor), and the latter in the concentration of the Lancastrian army at Plymouth a little over a month later. On 9 July, Lancaster's army, perhaps some five thousand strong, sailed from Plymouth Sound for north Spain. It was to remain in being for about a year, during which time its activities – and its inactivity – were to determine to a considerable extent the changing course of Anglo-French relations.

Its first effect was to provoke an invasion of England, the French *riposte* to the assault on their ally. An invasion was no new project. On several previous occasions the French had tried to carry the war to their enemy, without however ever getting very far with their preparations. Their most formidable effort before 1386 had in fact been in the previous year, when the 'first army of England' invaded the country from the north in collaboration with the Scots. This was scheduled as a diversionary attack; for the 'second army of England', by far the larger of the two, was to have fallen on the south of England from Flanders. The whole enterprise was in a sense the first fruit of the acquisition of Flanders, which had placed greatly increased naval resources and a first-class port at the disposal of France. The Zwin estuary before Sluys could shelter a fleet of any size, and from Sluys itself the whole of the southern and eastern coasts of England were exposed to attack, making it possible to disguise its direction and so disperse the enemy defences. But France had not been able to profit from these advantages in 1385 because of the insecurity of her hold on Flanders. By capturing Damme, Ghent had disrupted the whole enterprise. By the time Damme had been retaken the northern prong of the invasion was badly blunted, the season was late, and supplies were low. The invasion of southern England had consequently to be cancelled.

In 1386 the prospects for the 'third army of England' seemed far brighter. With the submission of Ghent in the previous December, Flanders was fully under French control and could contribute to the success rather than the subversion of the invading forces. Another ex-ally of England, the duke of Brittany, also threw his weight into the scales against her. Angered by the negotiations for the release of his rival, de Montfort openly supported France for the first time. He contributed a substantial body of 500 men to the main invasion force, and in June he himself undertook the siege of Brest, employing – so Knighton assures us – 1,000 labourers guarded by 10,000 troops to construct a fort to blockade the town. Although the siege was temporarily raised by John of Gaunt on his way to Castile, de Montfort soon returned to the attack, diverting a considerable fraction of England's meagre resources to the defence of Brest.[8]

Thus for the first and last time in the Hundred Years War, the two great fiefs of Flanders and Brittany supported their French overlord; and while France appeared to be stronger than ever, England seemed almost defenceless. John of Gaunt's campaign had stripped the country of most of its seasoned troops and many of its experienced commanders. It had also practically exhausted the limited financial resources of the government; and after the outcry against excessive taxation in the autumn parliament of 1386, the chancellor dared not summon another assembly for some time to come.[9] Finally, the appeasement he had practised over the past three years left de la Pole without friends or allies abroad at this critical juncture.

Heartened by these circumstances, the French threw themselves into their preparations with enormous enthusiasm. Before the end of February the English government had taken its first precautionary measures against the expected invasion. On 26 February the two admirals contracted to guard the seas until the end of the summer, initially with a small force of ten ships and 500 men, and then through-out July, August and September – when the major threat was antici-pated – with 62 ships, 1,000 men-at-arms and 1,500 archers.[10] Before the end of March the Burgundian Estates had granted the duke a subsidy for the 'passage of England', and in April the French council imposed a new and stiff war aid 'for the passage of the sea' throughout the entire kingdom.[11] By this date the English government was looking to its defences in real earnest. Throughout April, May and the early part of June commissioners were directed to array troops in the southern and eastern counties to defend the country against the imminent invasion of 'French, Flemings and Bretons'. Special arrangements were made for the defence of such key ports as Southampton and Great Yarmouth, and considerable reinforcements were thrown into Calais 'in the hope', as a chancery clerk wryly observed, that the French would attack the town.

But just when the French build-up was becoming dangerous it came to a sudden halt. In the latter half of May, throughout June and for most of July virtually nothing was done, and after the beginning of June English defensive preparations also ceased. The reason for this stand-still was almost certainly the serious illness of Philip of Burgundy. Towards the middle of May he was stricken down by a high fever which recurred in successive bouts, each one leaving him weaker than the last. It was touch-and-go whether he would survive. Meanwhile every effort was made to keep his condition secret, and it was in fact success-fully concealed until it had ceased to matter. At the beginning of July the English government received a report of his death; but by this date he was well on his way to recovery and the government could have derived no profit from its belated information.[12]

Nevertheless, Philip's illness had an important, perhaps decisive effect on the fate of the French undertaking. The time factor was to prove crucial, and the loss of several weeks in the middle of the summer ensured that the French concentration would not be completed before late autumn, when the weather could no longer be relied upon. Even in the short run the repercussions were singularly unfortunate. When he was stricken down, Philip was on his way to Avignon, presumably to concert plans with Clement VII and John of Castile to resist the Lan-castrian invasion of Castile.[13] After his recovery it was too late to fulfil this mission and King John was left to fend for himself. Even more serious, however, was the loss of Scottish support. Up to this point the Scots had refused to come to terms with England, despite the hammer-ing they had received from the English counter-attack in 1385; but when the 'third army of England' failed to concentrate at the begin-ning of the campaigning season, they were not prepared to risk a repeti-tion of that experience. On 27 June they concluded a one-year truce with the English government, which was thus able to concentrate its defences in the south, thereby lessening the chances of a successful French landing.[14]

Despite these setbacks the French were not deterred. By July Philip was back in Paris, and towards the end of that month the French resumed their preparations. On 23 July the admiral, John de Vienne, was ordered to assemble the nucleus of the invasion fleet from the Norman, Flemish and Picard ports, and this appointment was followed by a steady stream of orders and instructions which was not to dry up until the great armada had finally assembled at Sluys. By the beginning of October its concentration was virtually complete.[15]

The invasion force of 1386 represented the most deadly threat to England throughout the entire Middle Ages. It was led by the French king in person, accompanied by his uncles and the cream of the French nobility. Their avowed aim was to deal a knock-out blow, to end the war in a single campaign by forcing the English government to capitulate on their terms. To achieve this they had assembled the most powerful striking force of the entire war. Their fleet was acclaimed as the finest and the largest ever seen in Europe by all the English and French chroniclers, by Froissart (an expert judge), by the marquis of Saluzzo, and by the Italian diplomat Buonaccorso Pitti. Only the Bible and Homer, it was claimed, furnished comparable examples, and there was even some disagreement about this. Though one writer compared it to the fleet which destroyed Troy, another declared it had no peer since the Creation. According to Froissart all the ports between the Baltic and the Pillars of Hercules were scoured for shipping, and no one estimated the result at less than a thousand vessels. The army was on a similar scale. All the provinces were put under contribution and troops came from as far afield as Savoy, Germany and the Low Countries. Arms sales boomed as far south as Avignon, and in Aquitaine French officials were seriously concerned for the safety of Languedoc following the mass exodus of men-at-arms towards Sluys.[16] Sluys itself was far too small to accommodate the entire army, which spread out as far afield as Bruges. Its precise size cannot be calculated; but contemporaries agreed that it was quite exceptional and there is no good reason to doubt that it was the largest army raised by either side during the Hundred Years War. Though the figure of 100,000 favoured by some chroniclers is incredible, it is probably not so much of an exaggeration as it first appears. The unusually precise estimate of 28,500 given by the Tournai chronicler, who appears to have had access to official information, may not be very wide of the mark; and since it expressly excludes certain minor categories of troops, the total fighting force was probably somewhere around 30,000 men.[17] It is very doubtful whether the army which John of Gaunt took to Spain was even a fifth of this size.

The task of landing this huge force in England was no easy one. Without a foothold on English soil and with the enemy waiting to meet them, there was a serious danger that the French troops would be pushed back into the sea before they had landed in sufficient numbers to establish a safe bridgehead. The difficulty was met with great ingenuity. A prefabricated wooden castle, some seven leagues in circumference, was constructed to cover the the disembarkation and to protect the army during its first days on enemy soil. It could be erected in a matter of hours – a crucial consideration – and so would enable the army to withstand any attempt to push it back into the sea and dispense it from the need to capture a major port as a preliminary to disembarkation. It was not given the chance to do so however, for its master architect and part of the structure were captured on their way to Sluys.[18]

The English used the prefabricated sections which fell into their hands to supplement the existing fortifications at Dover, one of the many measures taken at this time to strengthen the coastal defences. Within weeks of the renewal of the French build-up, orders began to stream out of Westminster. All the major towns and fortresses from Southampton to Newcastle were surveyed and put into a state of defence, particular attention being paid to the area around Orwell in East Anglia. A major fleet was concentrated on the mouth of the Thames, and from about mid-August to early December commissions of array were issued for almost every English county. At the height of the invasion scare the troops were actually called out and they then numbered about 11,000. Although this was only a third of the French force, it was a very considerable army by English standards, among the largest half-dozen raised during the entire war.[19]

According to Froissart, the English council had drawn up contingency plans to oppose the French landing. Units of the English forces were to be concentrated at likely spots on the coast, with instructions to retire before the enemy, burning and destroying as they went. When the French army had been lured inland to a depth of three or four days march, a determined effort would then be made to destroy their fleet; and if this were successful, the army could be attacked and destroyed piecemeal. His account is very largely substantiated by what is known of the disposition of the English forces. The fleet sheltered well up the Thames, keeping out of reach of the French and making no serious attempt to disturb their preparations. Sections of the English army were dispersed around the coast as predicted by the chronicler, and a large strategic reserve was concentrated in the vicinity of London, about three or four days' march from any point on the south or east coasts.[20] The local units would presumably retire towards this central army once landings were made.

The plan was probably the best that could be devised in the circumstances, but it is scarcely surprising that it was unpopular. The English were not accustomed to stand on the defensive, and their sense of security had not been seriously disturbed for a very long time. Under the threat of the sort of treatment they had been handing out to the French for the past half-century, they showed up very badly. Local authorities ignored orders to pay their contingents, with predictable results. The troops were such a menace to life and property that they were forbidden to approach within fifty miles of the capital, and many units were disbanded and sent home as soon as they arrived. The northern and midland contingents in particular distinguished themselves by the scale of their depredations, leaving a trail of destruction in their wake across the midland counties on their return home. All this served to intensify the general feeling of nervousness and insecurity, particularly in the south and south-east where the brunt of the invasion was expected. Despite the protection of the fleet, Londoners tore down the suburbs of the city to strengthen its defences; and according to Froissart the entire population of the southern counties indulged in a frenetic spending spree during the summer months in a despairing effort to enjoy their worldly goods before they were stripped of them by the French. In a sense, the constitutional crisis which erupted when parliament met in October was the final manifestation of the panic induced by the threat from across the Channel.[21]

Despite John of Gaunt's presence in Castile and the build-up of the French armada at Sluys, negotiations between England and France were never completely broken off, and in the late autumn they were resumed at a formal diplomatic level. One reason for this was undoubtedly the improved prospects of a settlement in Castile. Hope of a diplomatic solution to Gaunt's claims had not been extinguished when he set sail from Plymouth in July. In fact at almost precisely this moment the King of Aragon offered to mediate between the duke of Lancaster and King of Castile and between Charles VI and Richard II. His ambassadors were instructed to follow John of Gaunt if he had already left England when they arrived.[22] Whether or not they did so is unknown; but in any case direct negotiations between Gaunt and King John were initiated shortly after the Lancastrian conquest of Galicia and lasted for most of September and October. Their prospects appeared so good that on 11 September Charles VI dispatched an embassy to Castile with instructions not only to ensure the continuance of the Franco-Castilian alliance but also to conclude 'all manner of confederations and alliances' with the duke of Lancaster in conjunction with the King of Castile.[23] Between this date and the arrival of news of the failure of the negotiations in the latter half of November, a peaceful solution to the Castilian problem was always on the cards. It was this which permitted the French to reopen negotiations.

But if the situation in Castile allowed them to negotiate, it was their position at Sluys which forced them to do so. Within a few weeks of agreeing to the negotiations Charles VI cancelled his invasion plans, and there is no good reason to doubt that it was the prospect of having to do so which prompted him to agree to negotiate in the first place.

The reason for this anticlimax to what had undoubtedly been the most serious threat to England during the entire course of the Middle Ages has been the subject of considerable discussion. There are two schools of thought. One, following Froissart, believes that the invasion was cancelled because of the opposition of the duke of Berry; the other, based on most of the remaining literary sources, puts the blame on bad weather and contrary winds.[24] The weight of testimony is clearly with the latter, but against this must be set the fact that Froissart was present at Sluys and gives the most circumstantial account of what happened there. Though a majority of historians have been inclined to doubt his statements, they have consequently found it impossible to reject them outright, and the discussion has remained inconclusive.

Froissart's account really falls into two parts. On the one hand he states that the duke of Berry arrived at Sluys so late as to jeopardize the entire expedition, and on the other that the duke then persuaded the French council that the whole venture was far too dangerous to be pursued. The first of these statements can be disproved. Two Flemish chroniclers relate that Berry was with the king before he entered the Low Countries and was then sent back to Paris to act as god-father to Charles's first son, born at Bois-de-Vincennes on 25 September. This last statement is independently warranted by a southern source, making it necessary to reject Froissart's story. How he came to make such a mistake when he was actually at Sluys at the time is something of a mystery.[25] It is worth remarking, however, that in making the mistake Froissart drew attention to one of the more important factors in the final fiasco, the late date of the French mobilization. Philip de Mézières thought that this alone was sufficient to account for the failure of the whole enterprise.[26] He may well have been right. But the delay in mobilizing the French forces was due to the illness of the duke of Burgundy, not to the alleged dilatory behaviour of his elder brother Berry.

On the face of it the second part of Froissart's story is even less plausible than the first. Nothing in Berry's career supports the belief that he was capable of persuading the nobility of France to a course of action so at variance with all its chivalrous instincts. It is more than probable however that he would have acted as spokesman for a peace party, had one existed; and if it is assumed that in blaming Berry for the cancellation of the expedition Froissart was dramatizing a split in the French council, then his account makes sense and falls into line with other sources. The Tournai chronicler shows that the council developed grave doubts as to the viability of the whole enterprise; Deschamps gives a vivid picture of the objections it aroused, and as far away as Avignon it was reported some time before the invasion was finally called off 'that there is great debate as to whether the king will invade or not'.[27]

There were very good reasons why the French council should have developed last-minute doubts about their plans. The ease with which John of Gaunt had established himself in Galicia had weakened the French position in the south, and the defection of the Scots had even more seriously affected the military situation in the north. The situation nearer home had also deteriorated since the beginning of mobilization. In September war broke out between the duke of Guelders and the duchess of Brabant, and although there is no evidence of collusion between the duke and the English government, it is scarcely surprising that it was suspected at the time, and the suspicion caused what was otherwise merely a trivial annoyance to assume the proportions of a dangerous threat.[28] Most alarming of all, however, was the degeneration of the position in Flanders itself. For the fourth year out of five the county was experiencing the presence of a French army, and memories of 1382, 1383 and 1385 did nothing to make the French more welcome. The possibility of an explosion increased with every week they spent on Flemish soil and became particularly acute towards the end of October and early in November, when large numbers of unpaid troops resorted to pillage to maintain themselves. All the chroniclers agree on the widespread nature of the damage, one asserting that an enemy army could have done no more. The discontent was sufficiently intense and sufficiently widespread to be politically dangerous. At one point the citizens of Bruges – traditionally on the side of the law, order and authority – tried to close their gates in the face of the duke of Berry, and then assaulted him with such violence that he was subsequently confined to bed for three weeks (which may have contributed to the rumour that he was late in arriving at Sluys). For most of the period of the French concentration the citizens of Bruges stood to their arms – and not to assist the invasion. Less surprisingly, Ghent defeated by force an attempt to introduce French troops into the city prior to a visit by Charles VI. Nowhere in Flanders were French troops safe from the hostility of the local population. Murder – and reprisals – were commonplace.[29] While the French army was encamped around Sluys a major rising was of course unlikely; but once it put to sea the consequences were unpredictable. The mere absence of the army might result in rebellion, and certainly any check the French forces received would encourage the Flemings to give vent to their discontent. And once the armada had put to sea any disturbance in Flanders might well prove fatal since it would cut lines of supply and communication and divide the loyalties of the fleet, the greater part of which was composed of Flemish ships or Flemish sailors.

If there were excellent reasons for staying at home, there were increasingly great obstacles to any other cause of action. The most obvious of these was the weather. The majority of the chroniclers blamed the cancellation of the expedition on bad weather and contrary winds. This was also the *official* explanation of the French council,[30] which is no doubt why it was so widely circulated and universally accepted. But like most official explanations this one was meant to conceal as much as it revealed. This is evident from the circumstances in which the final decision was taken. A very detailed account of these circumstances, which has every appearance of being based on official information and the report of a well-placed eye-witness, has been preserved by the Tournai chronicler and is substantially corroborated by the Florentine diplomat, Buonaccorso Pitti, who was at Sluys and in attendance on the king at the time. According to these sources, the royal council failed to come to any decision of its own after prolonged discussion and sought the advice of the ships' masters. After a four-day debate, the masters advised against the expedition in the following terms:

> Most feared and powerful lords: in truth, the sea is foul, and the
> nights are too long, too dark, too cold, too wet and too windy.
> We are short of victuals, and we must have a full moon and a
> favourable wind. Moreover, the English terrain and all the
> harbours of England are dangerous. Too many of our ships are old,
> and too many are small and may be swamped by the large ships.
> The sea is at its worst between 29 September and 25 November.

Their advice was taken and the expedition cancelled.

It is clear from all this that the weather was being cast as the villain of the piece, and equally clear that the casting was designed to obscure other factors. The weather was bad of course; but had it been manifestly impossible the council would not have required the advice of the ships' masters and they would not have taken four days to reach a decision. Moreover, as the masters themselves admitted, the weather was liable to improve at the end of November. But it was not given the chance to do so. A mere fortnight beforehand the expedition was cancelled.

The reason for this seemingly precipitate action was almost certainly the grave financial situation. The huge armada required colossal sums to keep it in being, and the delay caused by the weather and other factors imposed an enormous strain on French resources. The *monthly* cost of the army and navy must have exceeded the overall cost of the duke of Lancaster's expedition by a considerable margin, and would have come very close to the annual revenue of the English government. According to Froissart the expedition cost three million francs, or £500,000 sterling, a staggering but not incredible figure.[31]

By the later stages of mobilization financial stringency was having serious repercussions. The report of the ships' masters refers to shortage of food and supplies, and pillaging by French troops shows that this scarcity was not confined to the navy. The widespread looting universally attributed to these troops was not due to lack of discipline but rather to a lack of pay. According to Froissart the wages of the army were up to six weeks in arrears towards the end, and if this figure is anywhere near the truth, then the government was indeed in dire financial straits. The Tournai chronicler thought that shortage of money was the fundamental cause of the final fiasco, and reported that royal credit sank so low that only a few loyal souls would lend, and even they were loath to extend their credit beyond the end of the week.[32] Without wages, the troops had begun to disperse of their own accord before November; by the middle of the month it had proved impossible to hold the remainder together any longer and so the expedition was cancelled, despite the imminence of better conditions.

Diplomatic, military, financial and natural factors all combined to cast grave doubts on the wisdom of the whole enterprise and so to pre-dispose the French to listen to the English overtures for peace. The balance may well have been tipped by a domestic crisis in England.

Ever since de la Pole committed his government to a policy of *rapprochement* with France there had been signs of unrest and opposition among the nobility led by the dukes of Lancaster and Gloucester and the earl of Arundel.[33] It may be no more than coincidence that the first public quarrels between the king and his uncles date from the early months of de la Pole's chancellorship, but it is morally certain that the earl of Arundel's attack on the government in the parliament of April 1384 was inspired by intense dislike of its foreign policy. The earl claimed that the country was going downhill as a result of governmental mismanagement; and although he did not specify the nature of the decline, his interest in military affairs and foreign policy make it very probable that his wrath had been roused by the withdrawal from Flanders and the provisional peace with France laid before this parliament.

Even more revealing was a quarrel which divided the council in the following spring, when military strategy for the coming summer was under discussion. The 'court party' favoured an invasion of Scotland; the king's uncles advocated a royal expedition to the continent. Behind this division of opinion about military strategy lay a more fundamental divergence over political objectives. The opposition implicitly rejected the chancellor's policy of appeasing France and demanded that he dispute her possession of Flanders, while he was determined to divert attention from Flanders by an invasion of Scotland. The debate degenerated into a verbal brawl, the court party declaring that a continental expedition would add nothing to the king's *gloire* – a very singular opinion – and the opposition threatening to withdraw its support for the government unless the king crossed the Channel. Tempers reached such a pitch that the council dispersed without coming to a decision. Its dissolution was followed by an attempt on the life of the duke of Lancaster.

In the end this particular quarrel was patched up and the chancellor had his way. But it is scarcely surprising that he felt obliged to make some concession to the war party in the following year by sanctioning the Castilian expedition. In a sense, however, this only made matters worse. John of Gaunt had always acted as a restraining influence on his brother and Arundel and in his absence they abandoned even the pretence of tolerating the government's policies. Throughout the summer of 1386 Gloucester made no attempt to hide his opposition but rather gloried in it. When parliament met in a critical atmosphere in the autumn he did not hesitate to exploit the situation, and one of his first acts was to lecture the king on the military glories of his ancestors and rebuke him for the humiliating failures in his own reign.[34]

By themselves Gloucester and Arundel and their aristocratic supporters would probably have been unable to shake the government, but the failure of its peace plans drove the Commons into an unholy alliance with them. The continuation of the war meant continuing demands for taxation, which military reverses made more unpalatable than ever. But it was the cost rather than the course of the war which drove the Commons into opposition, as their subsequent dealings with Gloucester himself were to make very plain; and as the cost of the war mounted, so too did their opposition.

To begin with relations between the chancellor and the Commons were eased by the rapid conclusion of a truce in January 1384, and by the promise of a peace which would entail a permanent reduction in taxation. But when the peace failed to materialize, and the truce was allowed to expire in May 1385, a confrontation became only a matter of time. Despite eighteen months without war, the government was still financially embarrassed. To finance the brief Scottish campaign of 1385 de la Pole tried to resurrect the scutage – a tax which had not been levied for half a century – and may also have attempted to secure gratuitous feudal service from the magnates. His government also defaulted in its debts on a large scale at this time, and by the autumn it appears to have been in the red to the tune of some £120,000, considerably more than its annual income.[35] Neither the military expenses of the year nor the king's reckless generosity adequately account for this situation, which is most plausibly explained by the backlog of debt inherited from previous administrations. But the Commons ignored this and fastened on to the young king's extravagance as the sole explanation of all their financial sufferings. In the parliament of October 1385 they forced him to concede a number of important reforms which strengthened their own hold over taxation and restricted his independence. The scutage was cancelled and the wool subsidy withheld for six weeks, thus emphasizing parliamentary control. The king was then compelled to promise to reduce the cost of administrative departments and of the military establishment and to make no further grants on the revenues for a year, a measure reminiscent of the days of the Ordainers. In return for all this he was granted a subsidy on minutely specified conditions.

These humiliating concessions averted a major constitutional crisis; but since none of them went anywhere near the root of the trouble, a further confrontation was inevitable unless the war could be brought to an end. The chancellor avoided calling parliament until the very last possible moment, in the hope of obtaining peace first, but in so doing he only built up trouble for the future. Almost without resources, he had to resort to constitutionally dubious measures to pay for a defence force. The counties were ordered to foot the bill for half the 11,000 men, and forced loans were imposed on the towns to pay the other half.[36] Even so de la Pole was unable to pay his way, and was obliged to summon parliament for 1 October. When it met, he asked for a quadruple subsidy to be paid in a single year, the most onerous direct tax ever proposed. His request precipitated the long-impending crisis.[37]

The long parliamentary session which followed was dominated by the financial grievances of the Commons, which were exploited by Gloucester and his adherents for their own ends. The aim of the Commons was to resuscitate the reforms of the previous year, which had been largely neglected by the government, and to punish those who had consigned them to oblivion. The second of these aims was achieved by the removal and impeachment of de la Pole, who was charged with failing to implement the reforms of 1385, with misusing parliamentary taxation, and with peculation. His punishment was tailored to fit his alleged crimes, and he was condemned to pay a substantial fine and to forfeit his ill-gotten gains. To ensure the implementation of the reforms he had neglected, the Commons then secured the appointment for one year of a 'great and continual council', headed by the duke of Gloucester, to investigate the income and expenditure of the Crown and to institute reforms on the basis of its findings. Gloucester subsequently abused these powers by seizing control of the government in order to intensify the war against France, an objective which could not possibly be reconciled with the purpose for which they had been granted. From the very beginning the alliance between the duke and the Commons was unnatural, and doomed to a short life. But for the moment this was obscured by their common antagonism to a government which was both unsuccessful and expensive. The council seemed to offer the hope of curing one or the other (if not both) of these failings, and with its appointment on 19 November the crisis was past. A little over a week later parliament dissolved.

The crisis had developed *pari passu* with the French concentration at Sluys. Parliament opened on 1 October just as Charles VI arrived at the Flemish border, and dissolved only a few days after he left Sluys to return to Paris, on 16 November. Throughout this period events at Sluys and Westminster interacted upon each other. The mere existence of the camp at Sluys was of course an essential ingredient in the English parliamentary crisis, and the French decision to reopen negotiations and to abandon their invasion plans was undoubtedly influenced by the struggle between Richard II and his parliament. Seen from Sluys this struggle appeared as a fight between a war party and a peace party, and it was apparent that the balance was weighted heavily in favour of the former by the threat of invasion. Yet the last thing the French desired was an English administration determined to widen and intensify the war, and the prospect lent yet another argument to those who, like the duke of Berry, had grave doubts as to the wisdom of the whole enter-prise.

It can be seen that the factors which prompted Charles VI to give serious consideration to the English peace offers, then to cancel the invasion, were highly complex and cannot be reduced to a simple choice between bad weather and the unpatriotic behaviour of the duke of Berry. In the final analysis the combined effect of the weather and the financial situation proved decisive; but the combination was only made possible by the delay in mobilization caused by the illness of Philip of Burgundy. Long before the cancellation, moreover, the French had become divided over the wisdom of their plans and consequently vacillating in executing them. Military reverses in Spain, the desertion of the Scots, the threat from Guelders and the danger of internal up-heaval in Flanders all made the invasion appear an increasingly hazardous enterprise, while the threat of a more aggressive government in England and the possibility of a settlement in Castile enhanced the attractions of peace. It is against this background that the negotiations must be seen.

They were apparently initiated by the King of Armenia from Paris early in September, immediately after the possibility of peace in Castile became known. The nature of Leo's proposals is unknown, but they were evidently well received at Westminster; for on receipt of Richard's reply on 4 October, the Armenian king left Paris for Bruges to lay it before the French council. There followed a number of exchanges via the captain of Calais which were so promising that it was rumoured that Richard II had crossed the Channel to pursue the negotiations in person. Finally at the beginning of November Charles VI authorized King Leo to commit his government to a formal resumption of peace talks. On 2 November Leo informed the English king of this, and asked for a safe-conduct to come to England to pursue his mediation.[38]

At this point the two governments were apparently back where they had started at the beginning of the year, both without further military ambitions and both disposed to peace. But the appearance was misleading. France had indeed come full circle in its policies but England had executed a sharp about-turn. In September the king had welcomed Leo's approach, but by October he had lost control of his government. When the letter of 2 November arrived, Gloucester and the council were in command and dictated the reply.[39] The request for a safe-conduct was refused and the negotiations broken off. They were not to be renewed during Gloucester's tenure of power.

The French army was demobilized on 16 November. As it made its way south from Sluys Gloucester's reply would have been received, and at about the same time news arrived from Spain of the failure of the negotiations between King John and John of Gaunt, and of Gaunt's alliance with Portugal for a joint invasion of Castile in the following spring. It was clear that the war with England would now continue into 1387 and the French reacted accordingly. At Amiens, in the very last days of November, the council reassembled to consider the changed situation and there decided to make yet another attempt to invade England in the following year.[40]

NOTES

1 *St Denys*, i, 418–28; *Higden*, ix, 76–9; Froissart, *Chroniques,* xiii, 86–92 (under wrong year); *Foedera,* vii, 480–1; 491–4; *Séjours de Charles VI*, 431 (cf. Petit, *Ducs de Bourgogne,* i, 459).

2 *Du Bosc,* 349–60; *Foedera,* vii, 496–7.

3 Below, 81–2.

4 *Foedera,* vii, 518. For the remainder of this paragraph see Russell, *English Intervention in Spain and Portugal*, 435–42. It may also be noted that the treaty of Windsor, despite its subsequent fame, is remarkable chiefly for its vagueness.

5 *Foedera,* vii, 506; *CPR, 1385–9*, 157, 163; E 403/512, mm. 6, 8, 9, 10, 13.

6 *Du Bosc*, 349–60; *Foedera*, vii, 496–7. Only once before had the chancellor left England unaccompanied by the king.

7 *Foedera*, vii, 526–7. For the next paragraph see Russell, chapter 17.

8 BM, Additional Charter 3350; Knighton, *Chronicon*, ii, 208–10; Froissart, *Chroniques*, xii, 181–3, 364; *St Denys*, i, 432–7.

9 Perroy, *L'Angleterre et le grand Schisme*, 236–7; Russell, 412–13; and below, 82–3.

10 BM, Harley Charter 49 D 3 (original indenture).

11 Appendix 3 (Burgundy); Terrier de Loray, *Jean de Vienne,* appendix 119 (general *aide*). For remainder of paragraph see *Foedera*, vii, 507; *CPR, 1385–9*, 175–7, 181; C 76/70, mm. 22, 18, 10, 8, 4; E 403/512, m. 1. Mirot, 'Une tentative d'invasion en Angleterre', *REH*, lxxxi. 249–87, 417–66, documents the French preparations in some detail.

12 Le Fèvre, *Journal*, i, 275–7; ADN B 1279/23563 (letter describing Philip's illness, dated by reference to Le Fèvre); E 403/512, m. 13.

13 Le Fèvre, *Journal*, i, 257.

14 *Foedera*, vii, 526–7.

15 Lehoux, *Jean de Berri*, ii, 181ff, and Mirot (see n. 11) give further detail. For beginning of next paragraph see appendix 3.

16 *Annales avignonnaises*, xii, 92; *Histoire de Languedoc*, x, 1711, 1715.

17 *Croniques de Tournai*, 286 for this and next paragraph.

18 Mirot, *REH*, lxxxi, 285–7.

19 *CPR, 1385–9*, 214–17, 242, 258–60, 263; *CCR, 1385–9*, 169, 174–5, 186–7, 190–1, 193–4, 253–4, 264–7; E 403/515 *passim*.

20 Froissart, *Oeuvres*, xi, 372–4; E 101/40/21; E 403/515 *passim*.

21 *CCR, 1385–9*, 187, 193–4; E 403/515 *passim*; Knighton, *Chronicon*, ii, 212–13; Walsingham, *Historia Anglicana*, ii, 145–6; Froissart, *Oeuvres*, xi, 368–9.

22 Perroy, *L'Angleterre et le grand Schisme*, appendix 9 (Aragonese instructions); and Russell, 435–8, for what follows.

23 Daumet, *Etude sur l'alliance de la France et de la Castile*, appendix 34 (French instructions).

24 Froissart, *Chroniques*, xiii, 75–101; *St Denys*, i, 458; Pitti, *Cronica*, 71; Walsingham, *Historia Anglicana*, ii, 151; Knighton, *Chronicon*, ii, 213; *Memorieboek der stad Ghent*, i, 119.

25 *Croniques de Tournai*, 282; Brandon, *Chronique*, 14; *Petit Thalamus*, 410.

26 *Songe du vieil pèlerin*, ii, 437.

27 *Croniques de Tournai*, 289ff.; Deschamps, *Oeuvres*, v, 350–2; *Annales avignonnaises*, xii, 94.

28 *Croniques de Tournai*, 282; *Istore et croniques de Flandres*, ii, 388; Vaughan, *Philip the Bold*, 97.

29 *Croniques de Tournai*, 284–7; Froissart, *Chroniques*, xiii, 94–9; *Inventaire . . . Bruges*, iii, 102–3; Knighton, *Chronicon*, ii, 214; *Memorieboek der stad Ghent*, i, 119.

30 Appendix 3; *Croniques de Tournai*, 289–91 (translation slightly abbreviated)
 Pitti, *Cronica*, 72.
31 Rey, *Finances royales*, 406 provides a basis for calculations; see also Perroy,
 L'Angleterre et le grand Schisme, 235–7; Froissart, *Chroniques*, xiii, 101.
32 *Ibid.*, xiii, 84–5; *Croniques de Tournai*, 292.
33 *Higden*, ix, 26, 32–3, 55–6 for the incidents which follow.
34 Froissart, *Chroniques*, xiii, 87–8; Knighton, *Chronicon*, ii, 218–19.
35 Palmer, 'The Last Summons of the Feudal Army in England', *EHR*,
 lxxxiii, 771–5; and Palmer, 'The Parliament of 1385 and the Constitutional
 Crisis of 1386', *Speculum*, xlvi (1971), 477–90 for next three paragraphs.
36 *CCR, 1385–9*, 187, 193–4; *Foedera*, vii, 543–5.
37 Knighton, *Chronicon*, ii, 215.
38 *DC*, no. 66; *Croniques de Tournai*, 285–6, 296. Froissart (*Chroniques*, xiii,
 85–92) has confused these negotiations with those of the previous winter.
39 *DC*, no. 66; Walsingham, *Historia Anglicana*, ii, 151.
40 *Croniques de Tournai*, 295–6; Le Fèvre, *Journal*, i, 326; Cochon, *Chronique
 normande*, 181; Froissart, *Chroniques*, xiii, 100–1; *Hansisches Urkundenbuch*,
 iv, 370–1.

Chapter Five

The Council's War
1387

Led by the duke of Gloucester and the earl of Arundel, the great council appointed on 19 November arrogated to itself for a year – the term of its commission – the government of the country and used its position to infuse new vigour into the war with France. This revolution in foreign policy entailed several serious consequences. In the first place it widened the existing gulf between the king and his council to a point where it became unbridgeable. The king, by now taking an active part in government, had made de la Pole's policies his own, and would neither acquiesce in their rejection nor in the loss of his own power. Secondly, the council's aggressive foreign policy clashed violently with its domestic commitments, with unfortunate results both at home and abroad. The council owed its very existence to the Commons, which had secured its appointment in order to reform the royal finances and to reduce taxation. These conditions were not only written into the commission which gave the council its authority but were also implicit in the grants made by the parliament of 1386.[1] Apart from the customary renewal of the wool subsidy and the small import-export tax earmarked for naval defence, the Commons voted only a half-subsidy – a mere eighth of what de la Pole had requested at the beginning of the session. A second half-subsidy was, it is true, made available; but only on condition that the council should dispense with it if its financial reforms enabled it to do so, a condition which exerted a moral pressure the council could not lightly ignore given the circumstances of its appointment. Though its period of power was not remarkable for financial reforms, let alone for financial retrenchment, it chose to do without this part of the subsidy.

It was evident – or at least it should have been evident – that this obligation to economize could not be reconciled with the pursuit of a more aggressive foreign policy. Even if the council had ignored the manifest wishes of the Commons and taken the whole subsidy, it would still have been unable to finance a single major campaign without plunging the government even further into debt. As for the half-subsidy, this could easily be swallowed up by some quite minor military project like the relief of Brest; and if the truth were known, it was probably not even sufficient to pay the interest on existing royal debts.

Yet the council either failed to appreciate this simple fact – which is hard to believe – or simply closed its eyes to it. This self-delusion was evident from the very beginning. On the eve of his seizure of power the duke of Gloucester had an interview with his nephew during which the king threatened to call in the French to suppress his rebellious subjects. This unguarded remark prompted Gloucester to review the recent history of relations with France.[2] Intended to discredit royal policy, his speech does more to discredit its author if read critically. With propagandist zest he recalled the triumphs of Edward III's middle years, emphasizing the vast amount of blood and money which that king had expended on his effort to conquer France. Turning to Richard's own reign, he recounted in some detail the prodigious demands which the king – or more accurately, his council – had made on his subjects, reducing them (he said) to 'unbelievable poverty, so that they could neither pay their rents for their properties, nor aid the king, nor minister to the necessities of their own lives'. Thus far, allowing for a pardonable element of exaggeration, it would be difficult to argue with this analysis of the effects of the French war. But from this point Gloucester abandoned reason in favour of rhetoric; and after a circumlocution on the evils of poverty, he triumphantly concluded his peroration with the claim that the straits to which the nation had been reduced were entirely due to the machinations of 'evil counsellors'. He was evidently unable – or more probably unwilling – to recognize that the central portion of his speech had provided a more accurate diagnosis of the situation.

The consequence of this failure to look facts in the face was that both the foreign and domestic policies of the council were foredoomed to failure. All attempts at financial reform went by the board, and during the council's term of office the financial difficulties of the government were seriously aggravated by the use of a series of short-sighted expedients designed to finance the war effort. By these expedients the council was in time to forfeit the support on which its authority rested, and to do so without managing to raise sufficient sums to give its ambitious foreign policy a fair chance of success.

To begin with the dangers of the situation were somewhat obscured by a number of lucky breaks. Just as the council came to power the threat of invasion disappeared and its disappearance transformed the entire military, political and diplomatic position. France was gravely weakened by its second failure to carry the war to the enemy. Not only was the failure dispiriting in itself but the political consequences were nearly disastrous. The taxes and forced loans imposed to finance the invasion had been of unprecedented severity, and their failure to produce any result whatsoever provoked correspondingly great discontent.[3] The government was deeply in debt and it was doubtful whether it dared make further demands on its subjects. At the beginning of the new year the queen of Sicily was curtly informed that the state of the king's finances made it impossible for him to assist her in Provence, let alone in Naples or Sicily; and according to Froissart no one really believed that France was capable of yet another attempt to invade England, despite her promise to do so.[4]

In addition to low morale and financial exhaustion, France was also beginning to show signs of internal dissension. Immediately after the cancellation of the invasion, the young king was at odds with his uncle Philip over his possession of Lille, Douai and Orchies.[5] This was the first sign of the breach which was to lead to Philip's dismissal some two years later, and it was particularly ominous in view of recent events on the other side of the Channel. Though the quarrel was patched up, Philip's control over the government was never again as secure as it had been in the past, and his insecurity produced an element of indecision and vacillation in French policy which had not previously been apparent. But for this development the spectacular series of events which dragged Brittany back into the war (to the detriment of France) would almost certainly never have occurred.

Finally, the military situation in the south had changed drastically on the eve of the council's appointment, and the change was entirely to its advantage. John of Gaunt's rapid conquest of Galicia, the failure of his negotiations with Castile, and his conclusion of an alliance with Portugal, had combined to make his threat to Castile far more formidable than it had appeared at the outset. So precarious did the Castilian position appear that the French council gave it priority over all other concerns. No sooner was it back from Sluys than it turned its attention to the leadership and composition of an expeditionary force to Spain, and by March 2,000 troops were on their way to King John's assistance. But with this effort the council had for the moment shot its bolt. Despite its declared intention of mounting a further invasion of England, military preparations at the beginning of 1387 aimed at nothing more ambitious than limited assistance to Castile and a defensive posture on all other fronts.[6] The initiative had passed to England.

Gloucester and Arundel set out to exploit this initiative with some energy. Within a month of the dissolution of the Wonderful parliament they had begun to assemble an expeditionary force under Arundel's command. On 10 December 1386 the earl was appointed admiral of the north and west, and six days later retained to serve the king with 2,500 men for three months from the following 1 March. By the beginning of January he had already begun to assemble his fleet.[7]

Before he sailed considerable effort was put into a diplomatic offensive designed to repair the neglect of the past three years. Spain and Gascony were ignored – these could safely be left to the king of Portugal and John of Gaunt for many months to come – and attention concentrated on Flanders and Brittany. If either of these could be lured back into the English camp, the whole complexion of the war might yet be changed.

Though ambitious, this was by no means an impossible objective. Flanders in particular seemed ripe for revolution. The ravages of the French army at the end of 1386 had provoked widespread discontent which was dangerously intensified early in the new year when Philip banned all commerce with England.[8] By endangering the livelihood of the bulk of the Flemish population this measure created a potentially in-surrectionary situation which the English government was not slow to exploit. Gloucester had in fact already opened secret negotiations for an alliance with Ghent in the previous November, and these negotiations continued steadily throughout the winter and into the spring of 1387. Unfortunately nothing is known of their nature, apart from the fact that they were intended to produce an alliance against Philip and France;[9] but since the Flemish principal was none other than Francis Ackermann, they were evidently meant in earnest. Ackermann, it will be recalled, had led the revolt against Louis de Mâle between 1379 and 1382, brought the Flemish fleet over to England after Roosebeke, led Despenser's crusade through Flanders in 1383, and seized Damme and disrupted the French invasion of England in 1385. After the peace of Tournai he had remained in Ghent, and with his record he could not afford to run foul of the Burgundian authorities: he evidently judged they could be overthrown.

Negotiations with Ghent were backed up by others with Guelders, and although these came to maturity too late to affect the situation dur-ing the first half of 1387, they deserve consideration at this point for the light they throw on the general tendencies of Gloucester's foreign policy. The duke of Guelders was certain to figure prominently in any attempt to curtail French influence in the Low Countries, and de la Pole's studious neglect of him had played an important part in his appeasement of France. Gloucester was not slow to remedy this neglect. The early stages of his negotiations with the duke are unfortunately lost to view – they were probably conducted by the agents responsible for the secret negotiations with Ghent[10] – but by the spring of 1387 they were already nearing completion. On 18 April Duke William formally empowered his ambassadors to conclude an alliance; the English proctors were appointed a month later, and the alliance was finally drawn up on 10 June. In return for an annual pension of £1,000 the duke agreed to give homage to Richard II; to serve him with 500 men, especially against the 'occupier' of France; and to defy Charles VI and Philip of Burgundy 'openly and publicly'.[11]

It is against this diplomatic background that Arundel's military strategy must be viewed, for a misunderstanding of his objectives has led to misrepresentation of his activities, which have been written off rather unfairly as a lucky naval victory followed up by some aimless plundering along the Flemish coast. Arundel wanted to attack Flanders and hoped when he did so to provoke an insurrection against Burgundian rule; but first he had to deal with the Franco-Flemish fleet which had been assembled to invade England in the previous year. After the de-mobilization of the French army the greater part of this fleet, under the Flemish admiral John Buck, had made for La Rochelle, where it refitted and loaded with the French wine harvest, whose main outlet was at La Rochelle. Thus laden, it set out in March to return to Sluys, where it was due to reassemble for another attempt to invade England later in the year. Before Flanders could be attacked this fleet had to be destroyed, and this was Arundel's first objective.

His own fleet began to assemble early in the new year at Sandwich, from where it could survey both the Channel and Flanders itself. Its concentration was followed by the French with considerable apprehension. As early as January a solitary German ship trying to enter Sluys harbour at night was taken for the vanguard of the English attack, precipitating a general panic in which several ships were badly damaged; and a month later a nervous local official in the Caux region reported that 200 ships were about to descend on upper Normandy and Flanders.[12] At this date, however, the English fleet was only thirty-six strong, and even when finally mustered it only numbered sixty ships.[13]

By 13 March the English concentration was complete. Ten days later the capture of an enemy ship provided information about the approach of the Flemish fleet and Arundel put to sea. Battle was joined on 24 March. The enemy fleet was about 250 strong, four times the size of Arundel's; but the odds were not as great as these figures suggest. Due to a quarrel between the Flemish admiral and the marshal of France, who was to have supplied men-at-arms to protect the fleet, the Flemish fleet left La Rochelle with an inadequate complement of soldiers. Moreover, when the battle began some seventy German and Dutch ships deserted the Flemings and joined Arundel, reducing the odds to 130:180. In these circumstances superior armaments and manpower were decisive and Arundel's victory was complete. The Flemish admiral and some fifty of his ships were captured and another dozen or so burnt and sunk. As one Flemish chronicler noted, this was the worst disaster suffered by Flanders at sea during the second half of the fourteenth century. In a period of Flemish history notable for its disasters, this was by no means the least of them.[14]

In England the most widely noted effect of the victory was the subsequent cheapness of wine. Between 8,000 to 9,000 tuns – almost as much as was imported in a normal year! – had been captured and it was sold off at a fraction of its normal price, much to the popularity of the council. But despite the attention it received, this was an unimportant side-effect. The real significance of the victory lay in its military and strategic consequences. By smashing the Flemish fleet it destroyed the possibility of another attempt to invade England in force, exposed Flanders itself to attack, and gave the Flemings further cause for discontent with their French prince and his French policies. It remained to be seen whether Arundel could successfully exploit these advantages.

Immediately after his victory Arundel pursued the tattered remnant of the Flemish fleet to Sluys without waiting to escort his prizes back to England. As soon as he arrived he established himself in the Zwin opposite Sluys and dispatched envoys to Ackermann in Ghent.[15] His next moves determined the outcome of the campaign.[16] At this moment his enemies were still in disarray and Sluys itself was at his mercy. Had he seized the town and castle, which were all but unguarded, he would have had the whole of west Flanders at his mercy for as long as he could keep his fleet together, and a *coup* of this importance might have brought Ghent out into the open. But though he was strenuously advised to do so by no less a person than Peter van Bos, one of the triumvirate who ruled Ghent from 1379 to 1385, Arundel chose to ignore the advice and to stay in his ships, which he used as a base from which to raid the surrounding countryside. He was not given the chance to reconsider his decision. Within days of the naval disaster Philip of Burgundy, his marshal, and his governor of Flanders had all rushed their available troops to Sluys, and they were quickly reinforced by French troops. The surrounding districts were ordered to put themselves into a state of defence, and requisitions for men, money and materials reached out as far afield as Tournai. On 31 March, only a week after Arundel's victory, the deputies of Bruges, Ypres and Ghent met to concert defensive measures.

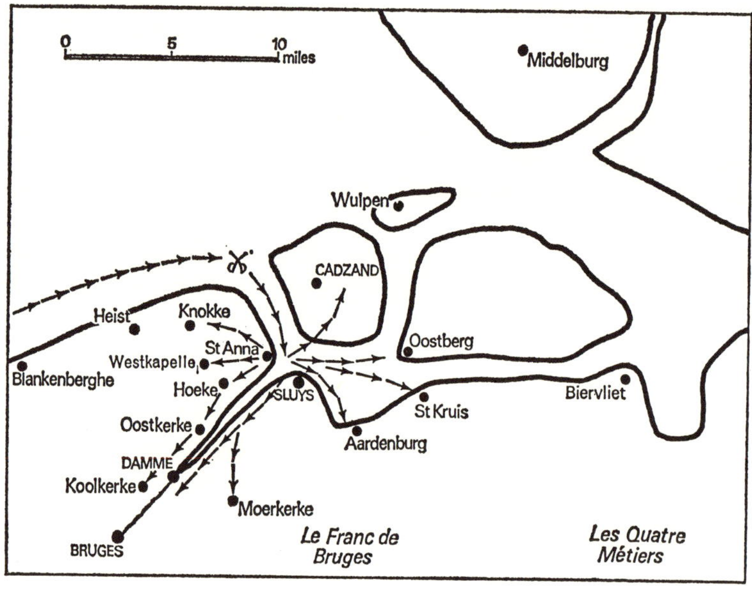

3   Arundel's expedition of 1387

This meeting showed that there would be no general rising against the French. How energetically Ghent co-operated with her neighbours it is impossible to say, but it is clear that Bruges took the lead in defence. As soon as Arundel's arrival was reported, troops were sent to defend Damme, the most likely target after Sluys itself; and at Bruges the authorities threw themselves energetically into the huge task of digging a ditch outside the perimeter of the town walls to strengthen their defences.

The rapid reaction of the Flemish and Burgundian authorities, coupled with Arundel's initial tactical mistake, confined the English successes to the accumulation of booty. For three weeks the countryside around Sluys was systematically raided, and Froissart estimated the takings at 200,000 francs, more than the cost of the expedition; but after three profitable weeks, Arundel was forced to weigh anchor and sail back to England.

By most standards Arundel's activities up to this point were a very great success. His destruction of the Flemish fleet was one of the few victories in pitched battle since the war began; and although the king's favourites derided it as a massacre of merchants, the chorus of praise in the English chronicles shows that this was by no means a popular view. Apart from soothing national pride after the reverses of recent years, it had also destroyed the threat of invasion and produced a rich haul in prizes. On land, Arundel had achieved far less; but even here he had given the Flemish government cause to fear him. Although he had failed to bring Ghent back into the war, he had come so close to doing so that Philip of Burgundy was forced to take emergency measures to combat for the future the combined threat of English aggression and domestic treason. In August he appointed his cousin, William of Namur, governor of Flanders, with special powers in military and judicial affairs. His two main tasks were to supervise the defence of Flanders – and particularly of west Flanders – and to track down and eliminate those who had been in secret correspondence with England. (As we shall see, he was eminently successful in both tasks.)[17] All this gives some measure of just how close Arundel had come to upsetting the peace of Tournai. But despite his outstanding victory at sea and his partial success on land, his campaign must be judged a failure in the context of what the council was trying to achieve. Gloucester and Arundel deliberately turned their backs on the king's efforts to secure peace with France, and in order to justify this they had to produce a significant change in the balance of military power, sufficient to enable England to continue the war on more equal terms. By these standards the campaign was a failure: Flanders remained in the French camp.

On a long view the failure of Arundel's spring campaign marked the effective end of England's hopes of challenging French predominance in the Low Countries. Admittedly the council had some bad luck later in the year. In particular, it lost the one man who might have raised Flanders against Philip of Burgundy. Shortly after Arundel left Sluys, Ackermann was murdered in Ghent.[18] Whether his murder was in any way connected with his recent dealings with England it is quite impossible to say, but it certainly ruined any remaining chance that they would be productive. Apart from a minor, and apparently unfounded scare in December, when it was believed that certain discontented elements in Ghent intended to seize the castle of Ruppelmonde and sell it to the English, Flanders remained quiet for the remainder of the year.[19]

The failure to win over Flanders ruled out the possibility of effective military co-operation with Guelders just when it was most needed. A peace conference between Guelders and Brabant was held at Bois-le-Duc in June; but with the assurance of English support, the duke refused a settlement.[20] Both sides then prepared for war, a war in which the duchess of Brabant was to be wholeheartedly supported by Philip of Burgundy. Despite the pressure of events in Spain, Brittany and England, and the challenge to his own position within France, Philip found time to visit Brussels in May and to be present at the peace conference at Bois-le-Duc in June. He solemnly swore before the French council that he would make the affairs of Brabant his own, and he backed up his oath with immediate military assistance to the duchess.[21] Despite this, Gloucester and Arundel not only failed to support their ally but deliberately set out to embroil him with France and Burgundy as well as Brabant. On 12 July they published an offensively worded defiance of Charles VI and Philip the Bold in the name of the duke of Guelders, which they somehow contrived to deliver at the French court as though it emanated from Nimwegen.[22] Whether or not the French were deceived, they seized on it as an excuse to invade Guelders in the following year, eliminating its threat to Brabant for the next decade and considerably diminishing the duke's chances of ever contesting the succession. The ultimate effect of Gloucester's policy was to consolidate the Burgundian hold on the Low Countries.

But most of this was in the future when Arundel left Sluys towards the middle of April, and his attentions were concentrated on other schemes which allowed no time to brood on his comparative failure in Flanders. After refitting and briefly resting his men at Orwell, he turned round and set sail for Brittany. There were still almost two months of his contract to run.

His departure had been preceded by considerable diplomatic activity aimed at luring de Montfort back into the English camp. Though relations with Brittany had apparently never been worse, the chances of mollifying the duke were not as slender as they appeared. He had been driven into the arms of France by the threat to release his rival: if the threat disappeared his hostility might well vanish with it. Whether it would be replaced by the co-operation which the council wanted was rather more dubious, though even this was not out of the question. Now that Philip of Burgundy's hold on the French government had been shaken, the French alliance no longer provided de Montfort with absolute security; and if the price were high enough he might well be bought for England.

The council was prepared to pay a high price. While the Wonderful parliament was still sitting, the release of John de Blois was forbidden except with the authority of parliament, and at the same time de Montfort was promised the return of the earldom of Richmond.[23] In return the council wanted an alliance and peaceful tenure of Brest. By February formal negotiations were in train, and on 26 February English commissioners were appointed to re-negotiate the tenure of Brest, to finalize the return of Richmond, and to conclude an alliance. The negotiations were conducted with unusual speed and concluded in a manner largely favourable to the duke, both measures of the council's urgency. On 1 March Richmond was restored and on 20 March de Montfort was confirmed in his possession of Castle Rising and promised that the depredations of the garrison at Brest would cease if he raised the seige of the town. The duke was not pinned down to an alliance, though arrangements were made to continue the negotiations on this point.[24]

But de Montfort was in search of domestic security, not foreign adventure, and his security was not yet entirely dependent on English support. While negotiating with Gloucester he was looking for insurance in France. On 8 May he concluded an alliance with the duke of Berry against Olivier de Clisson and John de Blois; and since Philip of Burgundy continued to block de Clisson's attempts to secure the release of de Blois, de Montfort was able to dispense with an English alliance.[25] He went even further than this in fact. Despite his recent agreement with the English government, the duke continued to besiege Brest. Instead of leading an Anglo-Breton attack on France as he had hoped, Arundel had to devote his energies to the relief of Brest when he arrived in Brittany. Even this limited objective was only partially achieved. Despite the eulogies of patriotic English chroniclers this part of Arundel's campaign was a dismal failure.[26]

By midsummer England had shot her bolt without gaining any very notable military or political advantage. Despite every effort to squeeze the last possible penny out of the grants made by the Wonderful parliament, the funds at the disposal of the council were exhausted. One of its first measures had been to cancel all assignments made on the subsidy, mainly at the expense of those who had been forced to lend money to the government in the previous autumn. Similar efforts were later made to maximize the receipts of the customs. In February the collectors were forbidden to honour *any* tallies of assignment until further notice, a prohibition repeated to local officials at London in July. Even assignments in favour of Calais were forbidden.[27] The effect of these measures was, of course, to pile up trouble for the future. Even so the government was broke by the summer, with no prospect of further funds during the remainder of its term of office. When it attempted to raise another army in August it had to scrape the barrel and exercise every ingenuity of purveyance and persuasion to collect even a tiny contingent for just a few weeks' service.[28]

The initiative therefore passed to France. Despite the destruction of the Flemish fleet, the unfavourable situation in Spain, the attack on Flanders and the possible dangers from the direction of Brittany and Guelders, the French government had not abandoned its intention to attempt another attack on England. But the financial situation made it necessary to put off the attempt until the summer, and even then lack of money and the loss of the Flemish fleet ensured that the 'fourth army of England' would be on a considerably smaller scale than its predecessors. However, a very respectable force was raised on the proceeds of the *taille* levied in March, ostensibly to pay the troops sent to Spain. By May it had begun to concentrate at Tréguier in north Brittany under the constable, de Clisson, and at Harfleur in Normandy under the admiral, John de Vienne, and the general supervision of Charles VI himself. By late June it was ready to sail.[29]

The 'fourth army' was described as a fleet in the French records and this, taken in conjunction with its reduced size, makes it unlikely that it intended to land in England in force, as was planned in 1385 and 1386. The English government evidently did not think so. Apart from special measures taken to defend Southampton at the beginning of July, its defensive preparations were confined to ordering all ships to remain in port under the protection of the local authorities.[30] It looks as if the French fleet was expected to make hit-and-run raids on English shipping and perhaps on one or two ports, rather than attempt a serious invasion.

Whatever its aims, they were unfulfilled. Like its predecessors the expeditionary force of 1387 did not even leave port. On this occasion the venture was wrecked by the duke of Brittany.

In his search for security de Montfort hit on a plan which, for its ingenuity, deserved better results than it finally achieved. Like most good plans it was very simple: the duke decided to put an end to his troubles by laying his hands on their author, the constable. De Clisson was at this time in Brittany supervising the final preparation of his half of the French fleet. As a Breton vassal he was convoked by the duke to a *parlement* at Vannes and there, on 25 June, was seized, thrown into prison, and forced to put his seal to two documents. By the first, dated at Ermine castle on 27 June, he agreed to hand over most of the strongholds in his possession. Some were his own, but the majority belonged to John de Blois. They included Josselin, Lamballe, Roche-Derrien, Chastel Guy, Guingamp, Chatelaudren, Clisson, Bron, Blain and Jugon. Jugon, le Gavre, Cesson and Enqui were ceded in perpetuity. Had these two clauses been implemented, they would have ruined the Blois party forever, and would have given the duke a stranglehold on the northern half of the duchy where his own possessions were sparse. On top of this the constable promised to renounce his position as lieutenant for John de Blois, to cease his efforts to procure de Blois's ransom, and to repudiate the projected marriage between de Blois and his own daughter, Margaret. The whole agreement was ratified by a second document dated at Moncontour on 4 July, when de Clisson was free. He subsequently claimed that the second document was also drawn up at Ermine castle while he was still under duress, and in the circumstances it is difficult to disbelieve him. Finally, he was forced to pay the duke 100,000 gold francs. In return for these concessions he was excused further punishment and released.[31]

From de Montfort's point of view the beauty of this *coup* was the number of divergent aims it could be expected to serve. It would ruin his domestic rivals by depriving them of their strongholds; satisfy the rulers of France by weakening and humiliating a potential rival; and mollify the English council by dispersing the fleet at Tréguier. Unfortunately for him, however, the last of these features gave rise to the suspicion that he had conspired with England to destroy the French fleet, and the suspicion produced a wave of revulsion which very nearly led to a French invasion of Brittany.[32]

On the surface this reaction was justified and the duke's guilt quite palpable. He himself subsequently claimed that his seizure of the constable had been designed to aid the English government. Moreover, when the *coup* took place an English ambassador was at his court for the express purpose of concluding an alliance; and immediately afterwards his proctor in these negotiations, his confessor Master Peter Adam, set out hot-foot for Westminster, where his arrival prompted the rapid organization of an expeditionary force to Brittany.[33]

Despite all this, however, it is highly improbable that de Montfort had taken the English government into his confidence. The near synchronization of events in England and Brittany really proves his innocence, rather than the reverse. Within two weeks of the constable's arrest the exchequer was paying messengers sent to scour the ports for a fleet destined for Brittany;[34] but they would surely have been dispatched sooner if the government had had prior knowledge of de Montfort's plans. As it was, despite every effort to hurry preparations, the expedition did not muster until 30 August – more than two months after de Clisson's arrest – by which date it was too late to be of any assistance to de Montfort, who had completely lost control of events in Brittany.

The composition of this expeditionary force also indicates the government's ignorance, or at least uncertainty of de Montfort's intentions. By scraping the barrel the council managed to collect a total of 932 men-at-arms and archers. Even this small body of men could be paid for only two months and the commander, Hotspur, was encouraged to finance a longer period of service out of his own pocket by the promise of all the gains of war and the free disposal of any prisoners he might take. But the most interesting feature of his contracts was the destination of his troops: seventy were to reinforce the garrison at Brest; another seventy could be used for the same purpose if Hotspur judged they were needed, and the remainder of the fleet was to be at the free disposal of its commander.[35] All this reveals a decided ambivalence. Clearly Brest was not the main object of the expedition; equally clearly Brest was still thought to be threatened. Even after they had been informed of de Montfort's *coup* the English government were still not sure if he were on their side.

Gloucester's uncertainty as to the duke's intentions is strikingly evident in his treatment of his ambassador, Peter Adam. If there had been collusion, Adam was the intermediary, since he arrived in England at the right moment and returned to Brittany with Hotspur's fleet. Yet he was handled in a way which suggests that neither he nor his master were trusted an inch. Hotspur was instructed to receive Peter Adam and his servants:[36]

> causing them to travel to Brest castle in his company . . . and to return thence to the king and his council in England and

> nowhere else, suffering them in the meantime to write naught,
> to have no speech with any man there save in the presence of the
> said Henry and his household, so that the said Henry may have
> full knowledge of their behaviour in word and deed, and may give
> the king and council information thereof.

The instruction closed with a reminder to Hotspur that in no circumstances was Peter Adam to be allowed to withdraw from his company or leave Brest castle. Whatever the reasons for this high-handed treatment of the Breton ambassador, conspiracy was surely not among them.

Finally, the fate of Hotspur's expedition is difficult to reconcile with the theory of collusion between England and Brittany; for though he met little resistance at Brest and was able to disperse the besieging force for good, Hotspur received no positive assistance from the duke and his expedition consequently achieved no further results.[37]

All this suggests that de Montfort approached England only after arresting the constable, and then only as a form of insurance. His later claim to the English council that he arrested de Clisson to destroy the French fleet proves only that he was an adroit liar, since he told an entirely different story to the French council.

Unfortunately for him, however, the superficial evdience of his guilt was persuasive enough to convince most observers, and the circumstances ensured that there would be retribution. After the successive failures of the first, second and third armies of England, a fourth failure necessitated a scapegoat, and de Montfort filled the role to perfection.

In Brittany itself sympathizers of de Clisson took to arms immediately after his release and regained much of what he had been forced to cede by treaty. By the end of September Chatelaudren, Guingamp and Lamballe had fallen and shortly afterwards Chastellin and Plessix-Bertrand also fell into their hands.[38] In France Philip of Burgundy and his brother were unable to resist pressure to intervene on the constable's behalf, however delighted they may have been at his humiliation. Three embassies were sent to Brittany in the second half of 1387 demanding de Montfort's submission to the king for the attack on one of his officers and restitution to the constable himself. As early as the end of July the duke of Berry abandoned his alliance with the duke (contracted only two months previously) and settled his differences with de Clisson. Philip was party to this agreement: the tide of opinion favouring the constable was clearly so strong that there was no choice but to swim with it. By October the French had taken over St Malo; by November

Berry and Burgundy had withdrawn their opposition to the ransom of John de Blois and headed the list of those who underwrote it; and by December the constable was at Pontorson with an army at his back.[39]

Initially de Montfort refused to accept the French terms, a decision probably influenced by the presence of Hotspur's fleet. But by the autumn, with no outside help available, he was forced to make substantial concessions. In September he allied with France against England and Navarre. But though this may have satisfied Philip it was a very long way from satisfying the constable, whose influence was increasing rather than diminishing. By the end of the year John de Blois had been released and had married de Clisson's daughter, and de Montfort's only possible allies, Gloucester and Arundel, were locked in a struggle with their sovereign whose outcome could not be predicted. If Richard II won, de Montfort would be completely at the mercy of his enemies; he had no choice but to surrender. On 31 December he submitted to the arbitration of Charles VI. Protesting that his submission was made under constraint, he delivered the disputed castles into the hands of the French ambassadors and gave his county of de Montfort as security for the 100,000 francs he had extracted from the constable. In return he was taken into royal protection, thus averting an invasion of the duchy.[40]

The terms of this agreement show quite clearly that only the threat of invasion at a time when he could expect no outside help had induced the duke to surrender, and that he was hostile to French intervention as such and apprehensive about the judgment the king was likely to give. The stage was thus set for his alliance with Gloucester and Arundel should they emerge on top in the English civil war. Paradoxically enough, the *coup* designed to destroy the constable and relieve the duke of the necessity of leaning too heavily on either England or France actually had the effect of strengthening de Clisson and pushing de Montfort into the arms of England.

NOTES

1 *Statutes of the Realm*, ii, 39–43; *RP*, iii, 220–1.
2 Knighton, *Chronicon*, ii, 218–19, which reads like a summary of an official hand-out.
3 *Chronographia regum francorum*, iii, 74, 77–8, 84; *Istore et croniques de Flandres*, ii, 392; Cochon, *Chronique normande*, 181; Le Fèvre, *Journal*, i,

335–8; Froissart, *Chroniques*, xiii, 101; Palmer, 'Prêts à la couronne', *BEC*, cxxvi, 419–25.

4 Le Fèvre, *Journal*, i, 333.

5 *Ibid.*, i, 329–30.

6 Russell, *English Intervention in Spain and Portugal*, 460, n. 1; *Annales avignonnaises*, xii, 97–9; Le Fèvre, *Journal*, i, 332, 333.

7 C 76/71, m. 18; E 364/21, m. 6v (cf. *CCR, 1385–9*, 208–9); E 403/515, m. 27.

8 *Ordonnances de Philippe le Hardi*, i, nos 134–5 (Paris, 15 January).

9 Appendix 1(e) for a discussion of the materials.

10 One of the key agents in the Anglo-Flemish negotiations took part in those between Guelders and Brabant.

11 *Foedera*, vii, 535–8 (misplaced under 1386 and misdated 10 July).

12 *Hansisches Urkundenbuch*, iv, 370–1; Froissart, *Chroniques*, xiii, xlix, n. 2.

13 E 364/21, m. 6v; E 403/515, m. 25.

14 *Croniques de Tournai*, 310–15 (the best account); Froissart, *Chroniques*, xiii, 136–46; *Higden*, ix, 91–2; Knighton, *Chronicon*, ii, 234–5; Walsingham, *Historia Anglicana*, ii, 155–6; *Hanserecesse*, iii, 207.

15 Cartellieri, *Philipp der Kühne*, 130.

16 In addition to the sources cited in n. 14 see, Froissart, *Chroniques*, xiii, li, n. 4; *Inventaire . . . Bruges*, iii, 96–101; *Rekeningen der stad Gent*, i, 377; *Handelingen van . . . Vlaanderen*, no. 34.

17 ADN B 1271/11671 (powers); B 1281/15761 (instructions, *c*. September 1387, though endorsed 'environ 1440').

18 Appendix 1(f) for the date of Ackermann's murder.

19 ADN B 18822/23461, letter of 23 December 1387.

20 Laurent and Quicke, *Origines de l'état bourguignon*, 197–206 for the general background.

21 ACO B 1467, fos 24, 25v, 36; Petit, *Ducs de Bourgogne*, i, 463; Froissart, *Chroniques*, xiv, 180–3.

22 Appendix I (g) for a discussion of this episode.

23 *PPC*, i, 47–8; *RP*, iii, 232, 279.

24 *Foedera*, vii, 553–4; *CChR, 1341–1417*, 307; C 76/71, mm. 8, 6.

25 *Mémoires . . . Bretagne*, ii, 534; Le Fèvre, *Journal*, i, 330ff.

26 Knighton, *Chronicon*, ii, 234–5; Walsingham, *Historia Anglicana*, ii, 155–6; *Higden*, ix, 93, 98; Froissart, *Oeuvres*, xi, 331–7; De la Borderie, 'Le siège de Brest en 1387', *Revue de Bretagne, Vendée et d'Anjou*, ii, 202–3.

27 E 403/515, m. 16; *CCR, 1385–9*, 211, 341–2. These measures left their mark on the receipt roll (Steel, *Receipt of the Exchequer*, 57).

28 Below, 100.

29 Cochon, *Chronique normande*, 181; *Chronographia regum francorum*, iii, 86; *St Denys*, i, 480: *Croniques de Tournai*, 317–18; Froissart, *Chroniques*, xiii, lxviii, n. 3; Lehoux, *Jean de Berri*, ii, 200–1.

30 *CCR, 1385–9,* 327, 329.

31 *Mémoires . . . Bretagne,* ii, 540–2, 552–5.

32 *St Denys,* i, 480–2; Froissart, *Chroniques,* xiii, 282.

33 BM, Cotton Julius B VI, no. 55 (see appendix 1(l) for further information); E 101/319, m. 26; C 76/71, m. 6; C 76/72, m. 22.

34 E 403/517, mm. 12, 13.

35 E 101/68/11/253–4; E 364/25, m. 5; E 159/166, *Brevia baronibus,* Easter term, m. 14; E 403/517, mm. 13, 17. The force was so poorly equipped that the king's favourites were accused of sabotage (Walsingham, *Historia Anglicana,* ii, 156–7).

36 *CCR, 1385–9,* 344 (20 August).

37 *Higden,* ix, 98; E 159/166, *Brevia baronibus,* Michaelmas term, m. 31v; E 403/518, m. 2.

38 *Mémoires . . . Bretagne,* ii, 546; Lefranc, *Olivier de Clisson,* 314.

39 ACO B 1467, fo 25; *Mémoires . . . Bretagne,* ii, 529, 543–7; Froissart, *Chroniques,* xiii, lxxviii, n. 4; Lefranc, *Olivier de Clisson,* 313–19.

40 *Mémoires . . . Bretagne,* ii, 543–7.

Chapter Six

The King's Peace
1387

For the greater part of 1387 the king and his advisers were the helpless spectators of the activities of the council. Ever since it had dictated the rejection of the French peace offer at the end of 1386, English foreign policy had been the foreign policy of Gloucester and Arundel. The king's actions were subject to their scrutiny, his agents to their interrogation, his writs to neglect.[1] Walsingham may have been correct in his belief that Richard and his advisers sought to belittle, and refused to support the military efforts of Arundel and Hotspur;[2] but they were powerless to do anything to deflect or to impede the Flemish and Breton expeditions. But though they were temporarily forced to acquiesce in the council's aggressive policies, they could and did plan to reverse them in the near future. The power of the council was due to expire on 19 November and that of the king to recommence on the following day. On that very day the king planned to reinstate his own policy with three acts which would wipe the slate clean; on 20 November John de Blois was to be ransomed; on 20 November an Anglo-Flemish peace conference would open at Calais; and, finally, on 20 November Richard intended to meet Charles VI in Picardy to conclude peace with France. These arrangements demonstrate to perfection the king's determination to adhere to the foreign policy elaborated by his chancellor while underlining its importance in his struggle with the baronial opposition.

In the middle of 1387 the main obstacle in the king's path was removed by the termination of the war in Castile.[3] The Anglo-Portuguese invasion of Leon in March, coming on top of the Lancastrian occupation of Galicia in the previous autumn, finally convinced the Castilian king that he must buy off John of Gaunt in order to isolate his real enemy, Portugal. Secret negotiations had begun by the beginning of May, while the Anglo-Portuguese campaign was still in full swing. By the end of the month an understanding had been reached, for on 1 June John of Gaunt abandoned his Portuguese ally and disbanded his own army. Both steps presuppose the existence of a firm agreement with Castile, which subsequent events confirm.

With the dispersal of the Lancastrian army the situation in Castile not only ceased to be an obstacle to an Anglo-French peace but actually became a further incentive to conclude it. By the terms of his alliance with the English government John of Gaunt was obliged to detach Castile from her French alliance, a condition which King John could not possibly accept. The only way out of this impasse was the conclusion of a general settlement, which would minimize the importance of the Franco-Castilian alliance. John of Gaunt and John of Castile were thus converted by their own private interests into strenuous advocates of an Anglo-French peace. On 20 July, at the end of preliminary discussions with Gaunt, the Castilian king commissioned his ambassadors to attend a general peace conference. Their powers were astonishingly wide. They could treat anywhere at any time for either peace or truce between Castile and any of her allies and her enemies and any of their allies. They could also treat on any subject which involved Castile, whether as principal or ally: in other words, they could participate in an Anglo-French peace conference.[4]

John of Gaunt's conversion greatly strengthened the position of his nephew and the viability of his policy. Up to this point the king and his advisers had struggled to implement an unpopular policy in the face of strong opposition from the magnates, not one of whom is known to have supported the king. His policy could all too easily be misrepresented as that of an idle and selfish court party which was too spineless to play its allotted role in society. This was the view purveyed by Walsingham,[5] and almost certainly shared by large numbers of his contemporaries. Once the most respectable and powerful of the king's uncles had been brought to share his views, however, they could not so easily be misrepresented. The baronial party was greatly weakened by Gaunt's conversion and made strenuous efforts to win him back to their side.

Finally, the end of the war in Castile meant that France had no further reason to continue the struggle with England. She had established her predominance in the Low Countries, kept England out of Brittany, and now seen Gaunt retire from Spain. She was unlikely to improve on this and the situation might very easily deteriorate. The attitude of the duke of Brittany was dangerously ambivalent; the settlement in Castile was not yet final; and the Flemings were clamouring for a separate peace with England. These circumstances ensured that the French would lend a favourable ear to Richard's overtures, which were all the more welcome in view of the aggressive attitude of his council.

By the end of April the king was once again in contact with the industrious king of Armenia;[6] and although the nature of their business is unknown, it was almost certainly concerned with the renewal of the negotiations broken off by the council in the previous November. By this date it appears that tentative arrangements had already been made for a conference in Picardy on 1 August, through the mediation of Albert of Bavaria, ruler of Holland, Zeeland and Hainault. The date and place had, however, proved inconvenient and Albert wrote to suggest a later date and a different venue. In his reply[7] Richard agreed to a postponement, insisted that the meeting take place in or near Calais, and rejected the proposal for a long general truce.

By the time Albert received this reply Richard had established direct contact with the French court. At the end of May he bypassed the mediator and sent a personal agent, Simon Shiringham, to Charles VI;[8] and although Shiringham's business is unknown, it was sufficiently important to earn him the hatred of Gloucester and Arundel, who excluded him from the general pardon granted to most of their enemies at the end of the Merciless parliament in the following year. In all probability he was instructed to explore the possibility of an interview between the two kings. The idea was already in the air at this date, for when King John of Castile appointed ambassadors to attend an Anglo-French peace conference two months later, he authorized them to treat 'even with those of royal dignity'.[9] This was such an unusual provision that it must have been inspired by foreknowledge of Richard's intentions.

Shiringham was apparently well received. Favourable developments in Spain allowed Charles VI to take a more encouraging view of his relations with England and on 5 July he replied with an embassy of his own. His ambassadors were personally insignificant – an imposing delegation would probably not have been allowed access to the king – but their business was sufficiently important to require the sanction of the dukes of Berry and Burgundy.[10] The ensuing negotiations cannot unfortunately be followed in detail. The king's enemies subsequently claimed that he conducted them through persons of low estate,[11] evidently in an attempt to escape their surveillance. However, the identity of particular agents and knowledge of their comings and goings is only of peripheral interest, and it is sufficient to note here that the key embassy of the series was that of Sir John Golofre, one of Richard's more trusted chamber knights, who was sent to France at the end of September. According to one chronicler he was commissioned to make the final arrangements for the meeting of the two kings; and since the council ordered his arrest if he returned to England, this was probably no more than the truth.[12]

In reply to Golofre's mission Charles VI wrote from Gisors on 5 October agreeing to a personal interview with his rival, offering to come to Boulogne as soon as Richard signified his readiness to cross to Calais, and promising to bring with him 'the greatest persons of our blood'. Perhaps significantly, he did not ask Richard to follow suit.[13]

As soon as Charles's reply was received practical arrangements were put in hand. The offer was accepted, a date fixed, and certain preliminary documents exchanged. Safe-conducts for the king, Robert de Vere and a few others were brought from France by one James Lustrak, but unfortunately fell into the hands of the duke of Gloucester.[14] (For his pains Lustrak was excluded from the pardon issued at the end of the Merciless parliament; but he was luckier than most of those outlawed in this way since he managed to escape to Rome, armed with a letter of introduction to the pope thoughtfully provided by the king.)[15]

The precise date of the interview is unknown, but all the evidence indicates that it was to have taken place immediately after the king's resumption of power at the end of November. Safe-conducts had been issued to the king before 13 November, when the revolt of Gloucester and his allies forced him to change his plans; and according to Walsingham the king was actually on his way to Calais when the rising of 13 November forced him to turn back. A letter written from Aragon on 2 January 1388 requesting information about the result of the meeting implies that it had been arranged to take place shortly before the new year. Taken together these three pieces of information suggest a date towards the end of November, or possibly early in December; and since two other closely related events – an Anglo-Flemish conference and the release of John de Blois – were scheduled for 20 November, this was in all probability the notional date for the beginning of the Anglo-French conference.[16]

The king's domestic opponents were later to represent this conference as a conspiratorial gathering of the two kings for the purpose of murdering the leaders of the English council. The truth of these charges will be examined below, but it is necessary to note here that the implication that it was to have been a hole-and-corner affair is very far from the truth. Despite the secrecy with which it was arranged, it was never intended to restrict the conference to a furtive interview between the two kings, for it was designed to secure a settlement not only between England and France but also in Castile, Flanders, Brittany and Scotland. The king of Castile had appointed his ambassadors in July; and since the king of Scotland had signified his intention of doing so at an earlier date, it is likely that he too was to have been represented.[17] The Flemish deputies were at Calais at the end of November, when the duke of Burgundy was due to arrive with his nephew. Many of the Breton notables were also present, though it is not known whether de Montfort had accredited representatives. Finally, Richard II tried to raise the conference to a level of European significance by securing the attendance of the emperor, Wenzel,[18] who was unfortunately too busy securing the throne of Hungary for his brother. Even so, the conference would have been as imposing as that of 1396 had it met.

But it was not allowed to meet. The rebellion of Gloucester, Arundel, Warwick, Nottingham and Derby forced the king to face his domestic enemies and in the ensuing struggle foreign affairs naturally took second place. It is probable, however, that as soon as the crisis broke Richard sent his most trusted adviser, Michael de la Pole, to explain the situation to Charles VI, postpone the conference, and seek a temporary truce which would leave his hands free to deal with his domestic enemies. This at least is the most likely construction which can be placed upon two apparently unrelated incidents connected with the flight of the king's favourites and advisers.

The first of these incidents is the alleged 'first escape' of Michael de la Pole, which is described in more or less detail in all the English chronicles. According to their account de la Pole fled to Calais disguised as a merchant soon after he was appealed of treason on 17 November. In one version of the story the 'merchant' was picturesquely transformed into a disreputable Flemish poulterer, head and beard shaven, clothes rumpled and torn, clutching a string of birds in one hand. Since his first act on arriving at Calais was to seek an interview with his brother Edmund, captain of Calais castle, the disguise was scarcely well chosen and may have contributed to the unbrotherly welcome he is said to have received. For Edmund immediately handed him over to the captain of the town, William de Beauchamp, with the remark – if we choose to believe Walsingham – that since he had fled from England he had evidently committed a very grave crime against the kingdom. Beauchamp apparently took a similar view since he arrested de la Pole and sent him straight back to England. But as soon as he arrived the king released him and he escaped again, this time to the Continent – but not Calais – via Hull.[19]

This story was evidently circulated by the Appellants to ridicule de la Pole. It is so full of improbabilities that it is astonishing that it was ever believed. The merchant disguise, even without its elaborations, arouses immediate suspicion since it is an obvious gibe at de la Pole's ancestry. The timing of the escape is even more suspicious. The king did not throw in the towel after the appeal of 17 November, and his remaining advisers stood by him. Robert de Vere raised an army in Cheshire and north Wales, Simon de Burley tried to raise 5,000 archers from the Cinque ports, and Tresilian and Brembre attempted to win London to the king's side. No one in fact deserted the king until after de Vere's defeat at Radcot Bridge on 20 December, and even then Burley, Brembre and Tresilian left it too late to save their own skins. In these circumstances it is incredible that de la Pole turned tail several weeks previously.

Not only is it unlikely that he tried to escape so early in the proceedings, but it is in the highest degree improbable that he would have gone to Calais had he wished to do so. When he escaped a second time he made for France, a more sensible choice. On that occasion he also remembered to make a long detour via Hull, his home town, in order to pick up a ship-load of valuables which he had apparently forgotten in the heat of his first escape.[20]

Even if all these objections are disregarded and it is accepted that de la Pole acted the coward and fled to such an improbable place in such an improbable disguise, forgetting his private fortune in his desperation to escape, it remains impossible to reconcile the story with what is known of its two other characters, Edmund de la Pole and William de Beauchamp. For if Edmund played the popular role assigned to him he received no thanks from the Appellants, who removed him from office shortly after they seized power; and if de Beauchamp acted as he is reported to have done, then this was his sole action which favoured the king's enemies in any way. Despite their known attitudes towards France, Brittany and Flanders, de Beauchamp allowed the release of John de Blois, arranged peace talks with Flanders, and presumably raised no objection to receiving the king and his entourage for the interview with Charles VI. Even after the king's defeat he did not throw in his lot with the Appellants. When they sent an agent to Calais to arrest some of de Vere's servants and to impound the ransom money received for the release of John de Blois, de Beauchamp threw the agent into prison and allowed the servants to leave with the money.[21]

It is clear that scarcely a detail of the story can be trusted. But like most successful slander it had a basis in fact: de la Pole did go to Calais at this time. The other elements of the story were not easily checked, but if this had been untrue too many people would have been aware of the fact. It is in any case substantiated by two pieces of circumstantial evidence. In Walsingham's version of the story there appears the significant addition that de la Pole was taken to Calais by a certain William de Hoo, a professional soldier and captain of Oye Castle in the Calais march. Hoo's family were important tenants of St Albans, Walsingham's monastery; and since this detail is peculiar to his chronicle it would appear that he got the essential facts from Hoo or his family. The subsequent fate of William de Hoo himself confirms that he played the dangerous role assigned to him. Just before he took de la Pole to Calais he was granted royal licence to go on a pilgrimage to Jerusalem. If this were coincidence, what happened to him in his absence certainly was not: despite royal permission to appoint a deputy, he was deprived of his post by the Appellants.[22]

There is no direct evidence as to why de la Pole went to Calais at this critical juncture but the circumstances limit the possibilities very considerably. Only the gravest of reasons would have taken him away from England when the country was teetering on the brink of a civil war in which his personal and political fortunes hung in the balance. Almost certainly his main object was to raise troops. The garrison at Calais, over 1,000 strong, was the nearest thing to a standing army the Crown possessed, and its seasoned troops could very easily decide the outcome of the civil war. If they were the object of de la Pole's visit then the Appellants' failure to make political capital out of the episode in parliament becomes understandable, for they would not have wanted to drive William de Beauchamp into open opposition by accusing him of conspiring with traitors. Hence the story of the 'first escape', which not only ridiculed de la Pole but exculpated de Beauchamp.[23]

But Calais could not be stripped of an important part of its garrison without endangering its security, and it is probable that de la Pole sought to get round this difficulty by asking Charles VI to agree to a short local truce. The evidence is slight but in its context persuasive. The French historiographer-royal states that after the flight of his friends and advisers Richard was so overjoyed at the reception they were accorded in Paris that he sent ambassadors to Charles to conclude a short truce until March 1388.[24] There is something wrong with this story, however, since after the flight of his friends at the end of December Richard was virtually a prisoner. He had no power to conclude a truce, and in the circumstances it may be reasonably doubted whether he would have wanted to do so. On the other hand the truce cannot have been the work of the Appellants since – as will be seen – they haughtily rejected the French overtures for a truce. The chronicler's chronology must be wrong, if only slightly so. The embassy must have preceded the flight ot the king's friends, arriving in France at the end of November rather than a month later; and in all probability de la Pole himself was the ambassador. He no doubt took the opportunity to explain the situation to Charles and to postpone the peace conference. It was certainly at this point that Charles realized that the conference would have to be cancelled; for after hovering along the borders of Picardy for the past three months, he turned his back on Calais and returned to Paris after the middle of December.[25]

Though the outbreak of civil war in England made it necessary to cancel the meeting of the two kings, it did not disrupt the other arrangements scheduled to take place at Calais on 20 November. On that date the negotiations for the release of John de Blois were finally brought to a successful conclusion. John de Blois himself had been entrusted to the safe-keeping of the captain of Calais earlier in the year and negotiations for his release had continued uninterruptedly ever since. The ransom was eventually set at 120,000 francs (about £20,000), half of which was paid over to de Vere's proctors, the other half being underwritten by an impressive list of French peers headed by the dukes of Berry and Burgundy. On 20 November the proctors issued a general quittance for the full sum and de Blois was almost certainly released at the same moment (his sister received the good news at Avignon on 16 December). He immediately confirmed John de Montfort's gloomiest forebodings by marrying the constable's daughter, a marriage properly solemnized – the bride was not present on the first occasion – some weeks later on 20 January. Thus the last important tie between England and Brittany was finally cut and the duke left in dangerous isolation. Immediately after this he submitted to Charles VI.[26]

On 20 November peace negotiations with Flanders were also due to open at Calais under the supervision of William de Beauchamp. These too had been under discussion for some time, the initiative apparently coming from the Flemings, and more particularly from Bruges. As early as 6 June an ambassador of the Hanseatic League wrote from Antwerp that the deputies of Bruges, Ghent and Ypres had been meeting frequently to discuss the need for commercial freedom and had made representations to the duke of Burgundy to allow them to trade with England and Spain (i.e. Portugal). He thought the deputation had been given a friendly reception though he was uncertain as to the duke's final answer. As far as England was concerned the answer was very largely negative, but with regard to Portugal Philip made an important concession which reveals something of the pressure he was under. The Portuguese trade had been affected by the Anglo-Portuguese alliance, and more particularly by that between John of Gaunt and John of Portugal in November 1386. On 15 January – two months after the treaty of Ponte do Mouro and the very day on which he banned commerce with England – Philip had forbidden his subjects to have any dealings with Portuguese who subsequently traded with England. He now withdrew this prohibition, and on 29 July not only restored complete freedom of trade with Portugal but even promised to give three months' notice before interfering with it again. This was one of the first fruits of John of Gaunt's withdrawal from Castile and one of the first signs of Philip's difficulties in trying to restrain his subjects' desire for a separate peace with England.[27]

Naturally enough the Flemings were not satisfied by Philip's concession. Their subsequent attempts to secure free trade with England are fully, if somewhat ambiguously described in two indentures between them and William de Beauchamp, dated 22 October and 28 November respectively.[28] They tell a very bizarre story. Negotiations began at an unspecified date in the middle of the year accidentally – so it was claimed – when one Lubrecht Scutaeller, a merchant of Bruges on business at Calais, delivered an eloquent peroration before the marshal of the town on the need for free trade between Flanders and England. Not unreasonably, the marshal asked Scutaeller if he were empowered to open negotiations, and the merchant was obliged to confess that he was not – indeed, he went to considerable trouble to stress that he was acting as a private person. However he promised that he would seek the necessary powers and return at the head of a substantial delegation. Twice he returned to Calais empty-handed to ask for more time, and finally reappeared for a third time on 19 October accompanied by three other 'sufficient persons and men of estate', but no powers. Despite this he pleaded with de Beauchamp to allow the discussions to continue and asked him to request royal permission for them to be conducted at a formal, official level. In return he promised to do all in his power to secure the backing of the duke of Burgundy and Charles VI. De Beauchamp evidently concurred, for the proceedings to this point were then recorded in an indenture. At a subsequent date, after the two parties had referred back to their principals, it was agreed that an official conference should open on 20 November.

With remarkable promptitude for a medieval diplomatic gathering the conference opened only one day late, on 21 November. On the English side de Beauchamp was assisted by the notables of the Calais garrison. For his part Scutaeller had by now enlisted the support of the main Flemish towns and *le Franc*, and the Flemish delegation consisted of fifteen deputies, four from Ghent, five from Bruges, three from Ypres and three from *le Franc*. But though he was now backed by the Estates of Flanders he still had no authority – or if he had he chose not to reveal it – from the duke of Burgundy.

The subsequent talks were naturally inconclusive though the two sides did agree on certain recommendations to their rulers. In return for commercial freedom both sides offered certain guarantees and concessions. For their part the English were required to promise that they would not bear arms in Flanders, would not wage war against her, and would refrain from forming alliances *within* Flanders against its ruler and Charles VI. In return the Flemings promised to try to persuade Philip to offer guarantees that his new castle at Sluys and the fortress at Gravelines (near Calais) would cease to damage England either by land or by sea.

These two indentures raise a number of interesting points, not the least of which is their exact purpose. In all probability they were drawn up to indemnify William de Beauchamp. Again and again they emphasize his passive role, representing him as a benevolent hearer of Flemish petitions rather than an active negotiator; and they repeatedly draw attention to the informal and unofficial nature of the talks *up to 20 November*, when the power of the English council expired. Both features are consistent with the view that de Beauchamp was secretly acting on the king's behalf – he never revealed the source of his authority – but was anxious to insure himself, and both are difficult to explain on any other hypothesis.

Whatever their bias these documents reveal very clearly the Flemish desire for a separate peace with England. Whether or not the negotiations started as accidentally as they are said to have done, by the autumn Scutaeller was backed by the entire *pays* of Flanders, despite Philip's refusal to licence the negotiations. This put considerable pressure on him. In return for freedom to trade with England his subjects promised not to ally or conspire with her, a promise which implied a very obvious threat as to what would happen if he withheld his consent. But to Philip the prospect of an Anglo-Flemish truce was almost as worrying as an Anglo-Flemish alliance, since it would undoubtedly weaken his hold on the French government, which had already been badly shaken by recent events in Brittany Only a general peace offered a satisfactory way out of this dilemma. Like John of Gaunt, Philip found that his separatist interests which a few years previously dictated war with England, now dictated peace with equal if not greater urgency.

Unfortunately for both of them events in England destroyed any immediate hope of a settlement. De la Pole's mission to Calais had no effect on the course of events in England which went badly against the king. By the latter part of December his cause was on the decline; and when his favourite, Robert de Vere, was defeated by the combined forces of the Appellants in a skirmish near Radcot Bridge on 20 December, it was lost. De la Pole was now obliged to escape in earnest. The five Appellants – Gloucester, Arundel, Warwick, Nottingham and Derby – assumed *de facto* control of the government. By the new year their authority was complete and their opponents in hiding, in exile or in prison.

One of their first acts was to put a stop to the king's activities abroad and to institute an investigation into the precise scope of his policy. On 14 January the ports were sealed and the constable of Dover ordered to collect 'all writs, writings, orders and commands from 20 November 1386 until 14 January 1388 . . . on behalf of the king . . . for passage for all who have passed from the realm over the sea for whatsoever cause'.[29] The information thus acquired was put to effective use in the parliament – deservedly known as the Merciless parliament – which met on 3 February 1388 to try the king's friends, advisers and agents.

Prominent among the charges then made against them was a group of articles which accused them of treasonable dealings with France. They have never been taken seriously enough to be examined with any thoroughness; but since they can tell us a lot about the Appellants' attitude to the king's foreign policy, and also supply a number of indispensable clues as to the intended basis of the abortive conference between the two kings, they deserve more attention than they have so far received.

The charges against the king's five main advisers – Robert de Vere, Michael de la Pole, Archbishop Alexander Neville, Sir Nicholas Brembre and Sir Robert Tresilian – fall into two groups, those classified as treason and those as lesser crimes.[30] The second, consisting of only one article, may be quickly dismissed. It charged them with ransoming the 'heir to Brittany', John de Blois, thereby 'greatly fortifying the king's adversary of France and greatly weakening the king and kingdom, and contrary to the ordinances and statutes made in the last parliament'. They were found guilty, a manifest piece of chicanery since John de Blois was released only on 20 November, when the statutes and ordinances made in the Wonderful parliament had expired.

The second group of charges, comprising five articles, were more serious. According to these the king had been persuaded by his advisers to buy the support of the king of France against his domestic enemies by selling him the fortresses of Calais, Cherbourg and Brest. On the pretext of concluding a five year truce with France, they planned to lure Gloucester, Arundel and Warwick to Calais where, with the assistance of Charles VI, they were to have been seized and executed.

None of this is very credible. Richard may well have intended to seize and execute his enemies, but he would scarcely have set about it in this manner. In another article of the appeal the Appellants outlined a different, and far more credible version of how they were to have been dispatched, which suggests that they themselves did not find the story of a French conspiracy very convincing. They offered to produce the safe-conducts granted to the king for his meeting with Charles VI as evidence of their charge, thereby as good as confessing that they had no shred of proof that de la Pole and his colleagues had done anything more culpable than arrange the meeting itself. Finally, it is of course inconceivable that Charles VI and Philip of Burgundy would have lent themselves to such a scheme even if Richard had asked them to do so.

It might fairly be asked why Gloucester made such an implausible allegation. In part the explanation may simply be that he was throwing as much mud as he could, hoping that most of it would stick. After all, though he might not be able to prove that his enemies had conspired his death in this particular manner, neither in the nature of things could they prove that they had not. But there must be more to it than this because the whole group of articles relating to the king's dealing with France centred around this one point. Perhaps this provides the clue to its purpose. Shorn of the conspiracy charge what is left scarcely amounts to treason. The king's advisers were accused with arranging a meeting between the two kings, planning to conclude a five year truce, and formulating peace proposals which involved certain territorial concessions. As will be seen, this was a fairly accurate statement of royal policy, a policy which could reasonably be defended. By presenting it as a conspiracy whose sole purpose was to destroy the council, the Appellants secured its condemnation as treason. This was almost certainly their objective. These particular charges were designed to damn the king's foreign policy rather than his domestic advisers.[31]

There can be little doubt that the substance of these charges was accurate enough. We have already seen that Richard had arranged to meet his rival and it is certain that the first item on their agenda was the conclusion of a long truce, as alleged by the Appellants. For within a few weeks of the cancellation of the royal interview Philip of Burgundy wrote to Gloucester to inquire whether he intended to continue the negotiations for a four- or five-year truce between the two sides and their allies. These negotiations had evidently been in train for some time since Charles VI had already given his consent to the truce in principle.[32]

The accuracy of the indictment on these two points lends a certain credence to the third and more serious charge. There is no direct evidence as to the basis of the projected peace talks but one circumstantial detail tends to corroborate Gloucester's allegations. It can be shown that in or immediately after 1387 the French raised their minimum requirements for a peace settlement suddenly and drastically. According to an official memorandum drawn up in 1390, in '1388 or thereabouts' the French council added the return of Calais, Cherbourg and Brest, and the retention of Rouergue to its previous minimum demands. It is quite likely that behind this reference to '1388 or thereabouts' there lies a document prepared for the abortive conference.[33] But in any case, if not in 1387, then very shortly afterwards Charles VI raised his terms for peace to include precisely those fortresses which Richard's advisers had reputedly offered to sell him at the end of 1387. It looks as if Gloucester was telling no more than the truth.

Before leaving this group of charges one interesting omission deserves attention. Though they did not hesitate to accuse their enemies of intent to murder, conspiracy with a foreign power, and treacherous betrayal of English interests abroad; and though in another article (8) they charged them with appointing unsuitable captains in return for bribes, so that important castles were lost to the enemy, the Appellants made no reference to their plans for the duchy of Aquitaine. Curious in itself, this omission is all the stranger in view of the fact that the main English chronicles, summarizing what is evidently Appellant propaganda, say that the king's advisers persuaded him to offer homage to Charles VI for Aquitaine.[34] The Appellants were determined to make political capital out of this yet unwilling to make it the basis of a formal charge, for reasons which presumably have something in common with their failure to accuse de la Pole of attempting to subvert the garrison of Calais. The only person who was likely to be offended if Aquitaine were made the subject of a charge of treason was John of Gaunt, and then only if the proposal to confer the duchy on him was still in the air. The Appellants' reticence suggests that it was.

The Appellants' intense dislike of the king's foreign policy affected not only the nature of their appeal against his main political advisers but also the punishments they meted out to their lesser victims. In general those who suffered worst, and those who suffered in the greatest numbers, were those who were implicated in the exchanges with France.

The two principal groups of victims – those appealed by the Lords on the one hand and those impeached by the Commons on the other – were, of course, found guilty on a variety of charges and the punishment for each was not specified. It is remarkable, however, that of the six of these nine men who were actually caught and executed only one, Sir John Salesbury, was dispatched with the full barbarity of the judgment passed on him, and this was due to the fact that he was guilty of treason both within *and without* the kingdom, as one chronicler phrased it. Salesbury was one of the three men known to have been given a safe-conduct to accompany the king at his interview with Charles VI – the other two, Robert de Vere and Sir John Lancaster, escaped the clutches of the Appellants.[35]

The remainder of those involved in the king's dealings with France managed to get away, and the high proportion of escapes is eloquent testimony of the known dangers of being implicated in the king's foreign policy. These royal agents figure prominently in the list of eighteen persons excluded from the general pardon issued at the end of the Merciless parliament: Sir John Lancaster, who was to have accompanied the king to Calais; Nicholas Southwell, Simon Shiringham and James Lustrak, who were involved in the negotiations which led to the agreement for the interview between the two kings; Henry de Ferrers, who had a hand in the negotiations which led to the release of John de Blois; and Henry Bowet, who probably carried the invitation to Wenzel to attend the Anglo-French peace conference. It is also possible that some of the remaining men on this list of eighteen were also excluded from the pardon because of their involvement in the king's dealings with France, for they are sufficiently obscure to fall into the category 'people of small estate', denounced by the Appellants as the king's intermediaries with France.

In addition to those actually listed by name the Appellants also excluded from the general pardon all those who had escaped overseas with traitors and all those who had 'adhered' to the king's enemies of France and Scotland. These were probably a fair-sized group, most of whom had exiled themselves because they had been implicated in the king's foreign policy and were aware of the likely consequences. We have already seen that William de Hoo, who took de la Pole to Calais, betook himself on a pilgrimage to Jerusalem and was deprived of his castle in his absence; and that Sir John Golofre, who arranged the meeting between the two kings, thought it prudent to remain abroad. Golofre's prudence was almost certainly imitated by Sir John Newton and Sir William de Benjugeon, both of whom were involved in the negotiations for the release of John de Blois.[36]

Finally, those who held the castles promised to the French came under suspicion. The captain of Calais castle, Edmund de la Pole, was removed when the Appellants seized power, as was the captain of Brest, Sir John des Roches. Sir William de Hoo, captain of Oye, was deprived of his charge, while two other captains in the Calais march, Sir John Atherstone, captain of Poyl, and Sir John Drayton, captain of Guines, were charged with treason.[37]

These measures wound up the attack on the king's servants and the policy they represented. When it was over the policy appeared to be damned for ever. It remained to be seen what the Appellants would put in its place.

NOTES

1 Favent, *Historia mirabilis parliamenti*, 8.
2 *Historia Anglicana*, ii, 156–7.
3 Russell, *English Intervention in Spain and Portugal*, chapter 18 for what follows.
4 *Foedera*, vii, 624–6.
5 *Historia Anglicana*, ii, 141–2, 156–7, 164.

6 E 403/517, m. 1.

7 E 28/6, no. 9, an undated signet letter; calendared and dated *c.* May 1387 in *DC*, no. 78 and note. Though the evidence for this date looks convincing, I am a little uneasy about it; the letter would make more sense in the context of the events of 1385.

8 Edinburgh University MS. 183, fo. 84v–5, signet letter – and therefore from the king, not his council – ordering letters of protection for Shiringham (cf. C 76/71, m. 5 for these letters).

9 *Foedera*, vii, 625.

10 Edinburgh University MS. 183, fo. 66av, safe-conducts endorsed by the two dukes.

11 *RP*, iii, 234.

12 Favent, *Historia Mirabilis Parliamenti*, 6; Knighton, *Chronicon*, ii, 243, 256, 296; *CCR, 1385–9*, 394. Golofre had been granted letters of protection on 29 September (C 76/72, m. 23).

13 *DC*, no. 126n. For date see appendix 1 (h).

14 Walsingham, *Historia Anglicana*, ii, 170 (cf. *RP*, iii, 234–5).

15 *RP*, iii, 248; *DC*, no. 248, undated; but all the letters in this quire (Edinburgh University MS. 183, fos 105–12) which can be dated belong to the year 1387.

16 Walsingham, *Historia Anglicana*, ii, 170; Mirot and Vielliard, 'Inventaire des lettres des rois d'Aragon à Charles VI', *BEC*, ciii, 108.

17 *Foedera*, vii, 526–7.

18 Edinburgh University MS. 183, fo. 116, Wenzel's reply to the invitation, partly printed in *DC*, no. 99n, with the incorrect date of 2 December 1389: the year should be 1387.

19 *Higden*, ix, 108; Knighton, *Chronicon*, ii, 250–1; Walsingham, *Historia Anglicana*, ii, 169.

20 E 403/518, *sub dat.* 16 December 1387.

21 *Foedera*, vii, 565; C 76/72, mm. 8, 17; *Mémoires . . . Bretagne*, ii, 529.

22 *Foedera*, vii, 563–4; C 76/74, m. 13 (cf. C 76/69, m. 25).

23 It is perhaps idle to speculate whether de la Pole obtained any troops from de Beauchamp; but it may be remarked that if he did, then the subsequent silence of the Appellants and their treatment of the Calais garrison (see below) become even more comprehensible.

24 *St Denys*, i, 498.

25 *Séjours de Charles VI*, 437–8.

26 Le Fèvre, *Journal*, i, 340, 411, 417, 468, 469, 478–9; *Mémoires . . . Bretagne*, ii, 528–9; C 76/72, m. 10; *St Denys*, i, 498.

27 *Hanserecesse*, ii, no. 216; *Ordonnances de Philippe le Hardi*, i, nos 135, 158.

28 Appendix 4 (indenture of 22 October); Söchting, 'Die Beziehungen zwischen Flandern und England am Ende des 14. Jahrhunderts', *Historische Vierteljahrschrift*, xxiv, 193–6 (indenture of 28 November).

29 *CCR, 1385–9*, 388.
30 *RP*, iii, 232–5, arts 23, 28–32, and 243, art. 16.
31 When the duke of Gloucester was forced to negotiate with France himself later in the year he took the precaution of securing an indemnity from the king and a substantial baronial council (*CPR, 1385–9*, 502–3).
32 *CPR, 1385–9*, 502–3.
33 AN MS. Francais 15490, fo. 26; see appendix 1 (i) for the date.
34 *Higden*, ix, 103; Walsingham, *Historia Anglicana*, ii, 170.
35 *Higden*, ix, 178; *RP*, iii, 235.
36 For Shiringham, Lustrak, de Hoo and Golofre see above; for Southwell and Lancaster, *RP*, iii, 232–5; and for Ferrers, Newton (cf. C 76/72, m. 8) and Benjugeon, *Mémoires . . . Bretagne*, ii, 529.
37 For de la Pole see C 76/72, m. 5; for des Roches *RP*, iii, 293; for de Hoo C 76/74, m. 13; for Atherstone *CPR, 1385–9*, 495, 522 (cf. E 101/183/12, m. 4); and for Drayton *CPR, 1385–9*, 416, 427.

Chapter Seven

The End of the War
1388

With power once more in their hands Gloucester and Arundel re-sumed their aggressive foreign policy of 1387 with only changes of detail and emphasis. Negotiations with France were immediately terminated by the simple expedient of ignoring all communications from the French court. When the duke of Burgundy wrote to Gloucester from Compiègne on 17 December inquiring whether he intended to continue the negotiations for a four- or five-year truce, Gloucester did not deign to reply. The letter was consigned to oblivion for six months.[1]

That Philip should have written to Gloucester at all at this date was a measure of his anxiety for a settlement, for in the middle of December the ascendency of the Appellants was by no means assured – Radcot Bridge had yet to be fought. However much he wanted peace, however, Philip could expect and had to be prepared for war. Two days after putting out feelers for a long truce he ordered the levy of yet another war tax on the overburdened French population.[2] This same ambi-valence characterizes the instructions issued to an embassy sent to Castile at this time. Its main task was to seek Castilian naval aid against a fleet which England was said to be preparing for a renewed attack on either France or Castile in the new year; but the ambassadors were also told to make provision for the allocation of costs if the Castilian galleys, once prepared, were not required.[3] Philip was evidently not quite sure that the English fleet would sail; if it did not, there would be no war: he was now determined on peace.

Gloucester's ultimate objectives remained the same as before, but he was forced by changed circumstances to modify his diplomatic and military strategy. Though the destruction of the Flemish fleet, the end of the siege of Brest, and the complete passivity of France after the invasion fiascos of 1385, 1386 and 1387 appeared to allow him far more freedom than he had previously enjoyed, this appearance was very largely misleading; for the unfavourable turn of events in both Flanders and Spain deprived him of two of the three allies on whose support he had counted. Given his own limited resources these allies were indispensable. Without them his chances of producing a significant alteration in the balance of military and political power was minimal. Despite the apparent hopelessness of the attempt, therefore, he made an effort, though necessarily a forlorn one, to bring both Flanders and Castile back into the war.

In Flanders he never looked like succeeding. The failure to raise the county in the spring of 1387, followed by the death of Francis Ackermann, had all but extinguished the last flickering hope of an alliance with the towns against their ruler. In the latter half of 1387 the whole county had followed the lead of Bruges when it sought a separate settlement with England, thereby demonstrating its desire to avoid extreme courses. This new note of caution and moderation even affected the leaders of Ghent, on whom Gloucester had throughout placed his main hopes. Early in the new year they were given new reasons to steer clear of all taint of seditious activity. At the very beginning of the year a certain Clay Delit, one of the minor figures in the conspiracy of 1387, was arrested by Burgundian officials, threatening to bring the whole conspiracy out into the open with unpleasant consequences for all concerned. Philip tried to keep the arrest secret while he squeezed a confession out of the prisoner at his leisure. But the authorities in Ghent were immediately aware of the situation and set up such an outcry against what they alleged to be a breach of their jurisdiction that after only a few days the prisoner was returned to them by nervous ducal officials. Hastily examined, he was quickly found guilty of treason, condemned to fifty years' exile and packed off to safety beyond the duke's reach, much to his displeasure. While he was briefly in their hands the authorities in Ghent learnt that Delit had not only failed to implicate anyone of substance in the city, but had actually assigned sole responsibility for the conspiracy to the dead Francis Ackermann. They had, therefore, every reason to hope that they would not be further troubled for their past activities, a hope confirmed by the conciliatory attitude of ducal officials in returning the prisoner to them.

At the same time they had received a sharp reminder of the dangers of their intrigues. During their hasty interrogation of Delit the Burgundian officials, in their attempts to break him down, had revealed that some of the agents involved in the negotiations between England and

Ghent had been captured and that the Flemish government had managed to infiltrate the network with a double-agent. Although this agent had failed to learn the identity of the principals, he had compiled a complete dossier on all their agents. The conspiracy had evidently come very close to complete disaster, and those involved can scarcely have felt inclined to rebuild their network and re-establish contact with England. There is certainly no sign they tried to do so during the course of 1388.[4]

The prospect of an alliance with Flanders was therefore minimal and Gloucester's attempts to secure one were rather half-hearted. No military effort was made against the county, and since the English fleet was ordered to concentrate at Southampton as soon as a campaign was planned, it is evident that none was ever contemplated. Gloucester did, however, make an effort to turn the Anglo-Flemish negotiations at Calais to his own advantage. According to the English chronicler Knighton, he offered the Flemings a separate peace in return for the destruction of Gravelines – a thorn in the side of the Calais garrison – and the expulsion of all Frenchmen from Flanders. Knighton relates that the Flemings accepted these terms, rose against the French (killing 16,000 in Ghent, Ypres and Antwerp alone), and were only prevented from destroying Gravelines by the staunch resistance of its garrison.[5]

It is difficult to believe this. No Flemish chronicler mentions the rising, which also appears to have left no trace in the Burgundian accounts. On the other hand there is plentiful evidence of close co-operation between the Burgundian authorities and their Flemish subjects. Far from almost losing Gravelines the Flemings actually took Poyl, one of the castles in the Calais 'pale', towards the end of March. They also combined with ducal officials to resist an expected English invasion during the summer, and the governor and towns of Flanders met in conference in Ghent of all places to concert defensive measures.[6] If there were risings they were therefore too insignificant to be widely reported and so could scarcely have been the work of the Estates of Flanders.

Nevertheless the Anglo-Flemish negotiations did take place without ducal licence, revealing the continued pressure on Philip to extricate his subjects from the war. At the same time they also reveal a considerable weakening of Gloucester's position. In allowing them to be held at all he showed that he was resigned to the fact that he could no longer hope to dispute possession of Flanders with Philip. Even if Knighton's account of the terms he offered the Flemings is accurate – which may reasonably be doubted – the most he expected from them was the expulsion of the French element within Flanders rather than an alliance against France.

The deterioration of the situation in Flanders ensured that the duke of Guelders would be given no more support than he had received in the previous year. Throughout the summer of 1388 he was at war with the duchess of Brabant, who was reinforced with Burgundian troops; and in the autumn he had to face a major French invasion. In neither case did he receive any effective assistance. In July the English council debated whether to send a small contingent of 200 archers,[7] but if it did so this was its only contribution. Though English troops played a role in the defence of Grave – the main military event of the summer – they were otherwise conspicuous by their absence, as remarked by the most important of the Flemish chroniclers.[8] This situation did nothing at all to improve English prestige abroad and spelt its total demise in the Low Countries.

In this area Gloucester had never perhaps had very much chance of success and he had accordingly given it only a fraction of his attention. His hopes of bringing Castile – or rather his brother – back into the war were marginally higher and he made a very considerable effort to bribe, cajole and pressurize John of Gaunt into joining him. For one brief moment it appeared he might be successful.

Gaunt of course had no wish to become involved. When the Appellants' seizure of power rendered the prospect of a general peace remote, he at once resumed his negotiations for a unilateral settlement with Castile, despite his obligation to detach her from her alliance with France. In February he reached a provisional agreement with King John which completely ignored the existence of the Franco-Castilian alliance. This silence was not accidental, for in the same month King John reaffirmed his commitments to France, obliging himself to provide naval assistance against England that very summer.[9] Whether Gaunt himself expected the English government to accept this situation as a *pis aller* is not clear (though very likely); but in any case, in the following month he sent his son-in-law, Sir John Holand, to Westminster to obtain formal authorization for the conclusion of a unilateral settlement with Castile.[10]

Permission was refused. The Appellants had already shown their disapproval of Gaunt's entire policy by confirming the Anglo-Portuguese alliance. In response to Holand's embassy they went even further, explicitly condemning the very basis of the Lancastrian negotiations with Castile. On 1 June powers were issued to Gaunt to treat with Castile. In them, he was still designated 'king of Castile and Leon', and they gave him no authority to conclude a private peace with his Castilian rival. On the contrary, they reiterated his obligation to arrange peace, truce or an alliance between Castile *and England*, clearly implying that Castile must be induced to abandon her French alliance before Gaunt resigned his claim to the throne. It was not until six months after his return to England, and almost a year after he had actually concluded his unilateral treaty with Castile, that John of Gaunt was released from the obligations imposed on him in 1387.[11] By that time, the war with France was over.

The Appellants knew, of course, that they could not bully Gaunt into relinquishing the fruits of his invasion of Castile, and they dangled a carrot while they wielded the stick. To compensate for his losses in foregoing a settlement with Castile, they offered him the prospect of gains in France. In May he was appointed lieutenant in Aquitaine, and at the same time a considerable army of 2,000 men was placed at his disposal. Part of this force was raised immediately by Sir Thomas Percy (150), a further 800 troops were to be recruited in Aquitaine, and the remainder were to be sent from England as soon as possible. To facilitate recruitment the English troops were offered a double bonus. Accompanied by the first draft, and with more than £2,000 in hand, Sir Thomas Percy left for Aquitaine on 10 June, escorted on his way by a major English fleet commanded by the earl of Arundel.[12] Shortly before their departure, the Appellants made one final effort to sweeten their relations with John of Gaunt. Though they had responded unfavourably to his demands, they proceeded to load his ambassador and son-in-law with wealth and honours. Despite a desperate financial situation and a recent parliamentary ban on grants from the Crown lands, Holand was created earl of Huntingdon and endowed with quite exceptional liberality. By these means the Appellants hoped to ensure Gaunt's support for their attack on France.

The attentions showered on John of Gaunt were surpassed by those lavished on John de Montfort, understandably so since Gloucester's hopes of an alliance with Brittany were rather better founded than his expectation of co-operation from his brother. With his rival free, married to the constable's daughter and backed by the French government, de Montfort was virtually forced into Gloucester's arms. At the end of 1387 when an English alliance had not been available, he had agreed to appear before Charles VI and submit to his judgment in Orleans at Easter. Now he performed a rapid volte-face.

At the end of January, a few weeks after the Appellants had seized power, an embassy had been sent to Vannes[13] which evidently negotiated an alliance with the duke, for de Montfort failed to make his promised appearance at Orleans. Charles VI waited there in vain for over a fortnight, from 11 to 27 April.[14] His feelings can be imagined. Kings of France were not wont to be treated in this manner, and de Montfort would not have dared to offer him such a personal affront unless he were very sure indeed of his English ally and had been guaranteed support commensurate with the dangers which threatened him.

Though the Anglo-Breton treaty has not survived and only an informed guess can be made as to its date, its main provisions may be deduced with reasonable assurance from the contents of a second treaty proposed later in the year (which refers to this earlier agreement) and from the powers given to the earl of Arundel shortly before he set sail for Brittany in June.[15] From these it appears that de Montfort was promised the support of a large army at an early date. When the earl of Arundel contracted to command this expedition in March his indenture specified that he have a force of 3,500 men – 1,500 men-at-arms and 2,000 archers – ready by 11 May, and it seems fair to assume that de Montfort was promised no less an army at no later a date. When it arrived, this army was to be entrusted with a number of Breton strongholds, presumably as pledges of the duke's good faith. De Montfort himself was to provide a substantial military force, and the two armies would join hands first against John de Blois and then in an invasion of France. According to Froissart, the invasion of France was the main object of the alliance and his statement is partially corroborated by de Montfort himself, who subsequently declared that its object was 'to advance the quarrel of the king' as much as to maintain his own position. The Anglo-Breton alliance was capped by an agreement between Brittany and Navarre, which also implies that a campaign outside the confines of the duchy was planned.[16]

Between them the armies of the earl of Arundel and John of Gaunt were to have numbered 5,500 combatants. There is no evidence as to the size of the contingent promised by de Montfort, and it is not known whether the king of Navarre had obliged himself to provide any troops at all. But on the lowest possible assessment of their contributions the grand total of the allied armies was to have been at least 6,000, and probably nearer 7,000 men. No larger army had been sent to France since the war began in 1369.[17]

Gloucester's strategy was as ambitious as the size of his armies and was clearly based on that of the Crécy and Poitiers campaigns. The Anglo-Breton and Anglo-Gascon forces were to operate independently but simultaneously north and south of the Loire, dividing and distracting the French and so giving one of the two armies the chance of delivering a crushing blow. Charles VI had good reason to justify yet another tax on his war-weary subjects in May on the grounds that it was necessitated by the two-pronged threat from 'the great army' being mustered by Arundel in England and the Anglo-Gascon army in Aquitaine.[18] On paper Gloucester's plans for 1388 represented the most serious threat to France since the war began in 1369. Yet so insignificant were their results that the plans themselves have since been buried in almost total oblivion.

The first and in many ways the most important cause of this fiasco was the attitude of the duke of Lancaster. He refused to accept his younger brother's lead and steadfastly pursued his own ends. Although the French government believed, or affected to believe that he posed a serious military threat, there is no sign that he set out or even intended to set out on campaign, and much to prove the contrary. He made no use of the 2,000 men offered him by the council, and he was subsequently discharged of his obligations in this respect after his return to England.[19] Far from preparing a campaign, in fact, he continued to devote himself to the problems of peace. Despite the prohibition of the council, he not only continued his unilateral negotiations with the king of Castile but actually brought them to a successful conclusion. On 8 July the treaty of Bayonne was finally sealed. It was a 'Lancastrian' settlement, which left the problem of relations between England and Castile on the one hand, and between France and Castile on the other in virtually the same state as it had existed on the eve of Gaunt's Castilian expedition. Its only concession to the demands of the English council was that Castilian naval aid to France was to be limited to what had already been promised her.[20]

Pride of place in the treaty was given to a pledge that both parties would exert all their influence to ensure that the kings of England and France 'be friends'. This was no empty formula, and Gaunt in particular had already expended considerable energy in an effort to limit, if not to end the Anglo-French war. During April and May there were discussions for a marriage alliance between one of his daughters and the

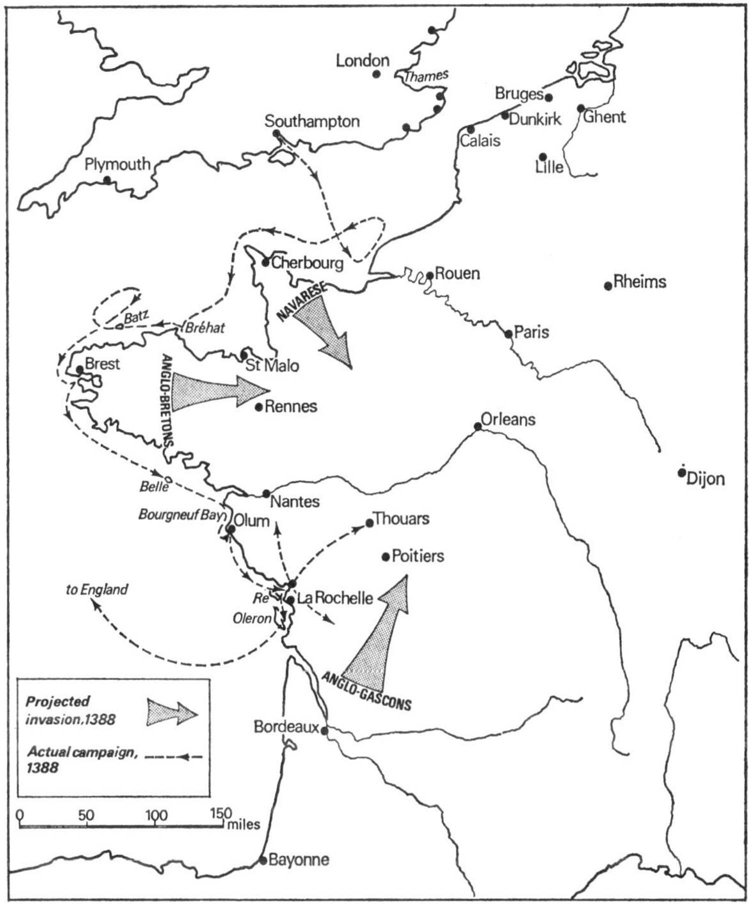

4   The campaign against France in 1388

duke of Berry, who had recently been widowed;[21] and although nothing came of them, they were the prelude to a suspension of hostilities
throughout southern France. Negotiations for a truce appear to have
begun in the later spring; for the details had been thrashed out before
the end of July, and the truce itself was published at Blaye on 18 August.
It took effect eight days later and covered all the territories south of the
Loire.[22] It therefore appears that from the very moment he was
created lieutenant in Aquitaine – if not sooner – Gaunt had set himself

to minimize the scope of the Anglo-French war. His brother, who had given him his powers to widen the scope of the conflict, had miscalculated badly.

John of Gaunt's defection effectively sabotaged the plans of the English council. Not only did it lop off the southern prong of the projected attack on France but it also contributed in no small measure to the failure of the campaign in the north. For Gaunt's defection was almost immediately followed by that of de Montfort, whose withdrawal was determined – according to Froissart – by Gaunt's conduct.[23] Nothing is more likely. Without the distraction of a diversionary campaign in the south the French army could give Brittany its undivided attention. Even with the support of an English army de Montfort could not have relished this prospect, given his recent reverses in the duchy. Even so, he might possibly have persisted in his original intentions had it not been for the time factor: Arundel arrived too late.

Arundel's preparations had begun in good time, early in March. On 12 March he was again given command of the English forces; on 23 March he contracted to serve for three months with 3,500 men, and a fortnight later he was appointed captain of Brest. The army was ordered to muster at Southampton on 11 May. All these provisions clearly envisaged a campaign in Brittany, the focus of Arundel's attentions from the very first. To hurry matters along parliament took the unusual step of granting a subsidy before the end of the session, and during the Easter recess Arundel brought his preparations to completion. His forces began to assemble at the beginning of April and were ready to embark by 5 May, a week before they were due to leave port.[24]

The advantages of this most unusual efficiency were, however, dissipated by the complications of domestic politics. Though the army and fleet was ready to sail Arundel was unable to join them. Both he and Gloucester had under-estimated the force of the opposition within the Merciless parliament and so misjudged the time they would require to wind up its business. Parliament reconvened after the Easter recess on 13 April, which left almost a month before Arundel was due to sail to dispose of its outstanding problems. But owing to the obstinate opposition of the king, variously supported by the duke of York, the earl of Derby and an anonymous but obviously important section of the Lords, this period was almost entirely consumed by the trial of Sir Simon Burley. Desperate for time, Gloucester and Arundel decided to postpone the retribution they intended to visit on their lesser victims,

1. The Crown of Thorns between the Crowns of England and France
(1395): an allegorical representation of Anglo-French harmony (Reproduced
by courtesy of the Trustees, The British Museum, London)

2. The Wilton Diptych (c. 1395), left panel (Reproduced by courtesy of the Trustees, The National Gallery, London)

3. The Wilton Diptych (c. 1395), right panel (Reproduced by courtesy of
the Trustees, The National Gallery, London)

who were bound over to appear before another parliament in the autumn. Even so it was almost two months before the Merciless parliament itself could be brought to a close, and in the face of stiff opposition Arundel dared not leave Gloucester's side until it had completed its business. The departure of the fleet had to be postponed for a month. The delay proved disastrous.

At almost precisely the moment that Arundel was due to leave Southampton the French royal council met in Paris to discuss the Breton situation, probably on 12 May.[25] This was the day after Arundel was due to set sail and only a fortnight since de Montfort had failed to make his appearance at Orleans: the French council had not been laggard. It was, however, divided over what course to take. The constable naturally favoured force, Philip equally naturally favoured diplomacy and soft words. Philip had more than usually good reasons for his stand. If de Montfort were forced into the arms of England – or rather, if he were not lured out of them – the war would certainly continue for some time to come and it would centre on Brittany. Neither result would do him anything but harm and both would enhance the authority of the constable, who would be on home ground and fighting for his own ends under a plausible patriotic pretext. This was the role Philip had monopolized for himself over the past half-dozen years and he was anxious to retain it while he still had unfinished business with the duke of Guelders, the one surviving threat to his complete dominance in the Low Countries. The duke's defiance of Charles VI in the previous summer was all the excuse Philip needed to lead a French army into Guelders, but if it were committed first to Brittany he might never extricate it in time for a campaign in the north. He therefore exerted all his influence to secure a peaceful settlement with John de Montfort, and the council agreed with him, at least to the extent of dispatching another embassy to Brittany. According to Froissart Philip personally instructed the Lord Couci and the admiral, John de Vienne, the leaders of this embassy, to be as amiable to the duke as circumstances permitted. If they could not persuade him to come to Paris, they should at least get him to agree to meet the royal uncles at Blois. In either case, of course, his complete submission was still required, for on this matter no concessions were offered him as appeared in the sequel.

This should have ensured de Montfort's continued resistance. It would probably have done so but for Gaunt's desertion and, more immediately, Arundel's tardiness. The French embassy arrived at

Vannes within a day or two on either side of 20 May. At this date Arundel was already overdue; there was no sign that he would move for some time, and de Montfort had to make his decision on the spot: he chose to submit. Since there had been no significant change in the terms offered him by the French court since his failure to appear at Orleans in the previous month, his decision to turn his back on the English alliance was evidently due to a reassessment of its value, a reassessment prompted by the activities of John of Gaunt and the non-appearance of the English fleet at the crucial moment. Reluctantly, de Montfort made his way to Blois to meet the dukes of Berry and Burgundy and from thence in their company to Paris, where the party arrived on 7 June.

A major war in Brittany was thus averted by a hair's breadth. The French ensured that the danger would not reappear that year. Though de Montfort was warmly received and magnificently entertained in Paris – to the considerable astonishment of some onlookers – negotiations on the terms of his submission were dragged out in order to keep him in quarantine while Arundel was at large. It was not until after 20 August that he was finally allowed to leave for Brittany.[26] By that date Arundel had been at sea for over two months and was nearing the end of his term of service. The prospects of an Anglo-Breton campaign in 1388 were virtually non-existent.

From de Montfort's point of view his journey to Paris was a disaster. Not only had he antagonized the English council but he had done so to no good effect, since the terms of Charles VI's award on 20 July were almost entirely unfavourable to him.[27] He was ordered to return to the constable the 100,000 francs and the castles of Josselin, Blain, Bron, Jugon, Gavre and Guillac. In return he was promised the reversion of Jugon, a miserable concession since Jugon belonged to him in any case, being held by de Clisson only for the term of his life. All de Montfort's earlier gains were thus obliterated; and although Charles's retention of Guingamp, Lamballe, Roche-Derrien and Chatelaudren 'pending further inquiry' might seem to offer the possibility of concessions in the future, the more immediate effect was to place a chain of strongholds in north Brittany in the hands of the French, rendering more remote than ever the chance of recovering his position through an alliance with England. The duke's feelings can well be imagined. No sooner was he back in Brittany than he was once again intriguing with the English government.

But this was in the future: Gloucester and Arundel were as yet unaware that the present alliance had collapsed. On 2 June, the very day that de Montfort joined the dukes of Berry and Burgundy at Blois, the town, county and honour of Richmond were solemnly confirmed to him in full parliament, and on the same day Arundel was commissioned as royal ambassador to Brittany.[28] The terms of his commission reveal that he had no suspicion that the duke had deserted him. He was empowered to negotiate a final peace or an alliance and 'to receive, retain, occupy, possess and fully and freely dispose of. . .all. . .cities, towns, lordships, castles, fortresses, lands, tenements and rents', and to receive in the king's name all manner of homages and obedience from the duke's subjects. Armed with these extensive powers, Arundel made haste to put to sea. On the previous day his expedition had been blessed by a great banquet at Westminster; on 2 June itself, without waiting for the closing ceremonies of parliament, he left for Southampton whence he set sail on 10 June.[29]

Only at this point did he become aware of his isolation. Arriving at Bréhat off the north coast of Brittany, he discovered that de Montfort was already in Paris and had made no provision to receive him. He could not accept that he had been finally and irretrievably deserted and hung around the north coast of Brittany for about month, waiting for the duke to reappear. His anxiety is understandable, for with his ally he had lost all mobility on land: de Montfort was to have supplied him with horses. When it became apparent that the duke was not going to appear, or if he did so would be too late to participate in a campaign, Arundel moved south towards Aunis, Saintonge and La Rochelle, perhaps hoping to effect a junction with the duke of Lancaster. If so he was disappointed for the second time. But he stuck grimly to his task. Ignoring an order for his recall from Westminster, he led his forces on a series of plundering expeditions around La Rochelle and the adjacent islands (penetration inland was impossible due to lack of horses), possibly a profitable, but certainly a militarily ineffective exercise.[30] No English army of comparable size had achieved such insignificant results for a very long time. Its ineffectiveness sealed the fate of Gloucester's policies and rendered his domestic position untenable.

Arundel could not have failed to be aware of the magnitude of his failure and its likely consequences, and it was no doubt this awareness which prompted him to ignore his recall to England in the latter half of July in order to make one last effort to concert an attack on France with the duke of Brittany. De Montfort reached his duchy towards the end of August. Between that date and his return to England on 3 September

Arundel established contact with him through his lieutenant at Brest, Sir Edward Dalingrigg, and agreed on the outlines of a new alliance and a new campaign.[31] Despite his apparently weak and dependent position de Montfort's terms were high, a measure of his assessment of Gloucester and Arundel's desperation. In return for military co-operation he demanded an alliance which would guarantee both himself and his heir – if he should have one – against French aggression, and England was to accept no settlement with France which did not accord recognition to the duke and his heir as true dukes of Brittany. If he himself chose to retire from the fray, moreover, England was to defend his rights until he died. Meanwhile he was to be restored to all his properties in England and given an additional pension of £10,000, to last for his own lifetime and that of his heir. In return he offered to bequeath his duchy to the king if he should die without a son and – more immediately and practically – to receive an English army in Brittany. Once it had landed, however, it was not to withdraw without his consent, and the government was not to conclude either peace or truce – even a short truce – without his express approval.

The general outlines of a campaign were also mapped out. A small fleet carrying 1,000 or 1,200 troops was to be sent to the duchy as soon and as secretly as possible and be given control of a number of key towns and fortresses. Once installed, it was to be reinforced with all possible speed by a second contingent of similar size from England and by all the troops the duke could muster. The insistence on speed and secrecy suggests that the campaign was to be timed to coincide with the French attack on Guelders, thus allowing the allied armies the maximum possible time to develop their attack against minimum resistance. On paper it looked very plausible, but unfortunately for Arundel it was also completely unrealistic. The situation in England precluded further military efforts on the Continent.

The dismal failure of Arundel's summer expedition was one of the factors which shaped the situation in England, but there were others equally if not more important. The most serious was undoubtedly the financial situation.

In 1388 parliament had again voted only a meagre half-subsidy, repeating its parsimony of the previous year. Between October 1386 and October 1388, therefore, Gloucester and Arundel received only one full subsidy – about £34,000 – in direct taxation. This was the price they paid for the political support of the Commons. At no period of the war had taxation been lower: even in the two years after the Peasants'

Revolt the level had been as high. Yet with these minimal sums Gloucester and Arundel had tried to intensify the war. To do this they had to
resort to every dubious financial device which occurred to them. All the
tricks of 1387 were repeated in 1388. Once again the government refused
to honour its own or its predecessors' drafts on the revenue, thereby
plunging the Crown even deeper into debt.[32] But these measures were
no longer sufficient in 1388 and the Appellants embarked on more
desperate courses. The Merciless parliament was induced to assent to a
number of radical provisions designed to finance the war at the king's
personal expense. The council was empowered to sell the forfeited
estates of those condemned of treason and devote the proceeds to the
cost of government. At the same time the king was deprived of his
control over the Crown lands and his feudal rights by a statute which
enacted that all 'lands and tenements, escheats, forfeitures, wardships,
marriages and other profits which be or shall come into the king's hands'
should remain there for the duration of the war. In other words, while
the war lasted the king was forbidden to make any grants out of his
hereditary resources.[33] No measure could more clearly illustrate the
close relationship between war finance and domestic unrest, and it would
scarcely be overstating the case to say that this was the most revolutionary act of the Merciless parliament. Indeed it is difficult to think of
any previous parliamentary measure which had limited the royal pre-
rogative more drastically or in a more humiliating manner.

By these and lesser measures of a similar kind the Appellants proposed to finance the war with the minimum of assistance from the
Commons. It was a hopeless task. The sale of forfeited lands was a once-
and-for-all boost to the exchequer, and since the bulk of the lands were
sold to the political allies of the Appellants, or to the Appellants themselves, it may reasonably be suspected that the receipts were not all
that they should have been. However great the savings made from the
Crown lands and feudal resources, they could never make more than a
marginal difference to the financial health of the government. Even if
receipts from this source doubled they would still scarcely pay for the
maintenance of Calais, let alone a continued escalation of the war effort.
In any case these savings were quite negligible by comparison with the
huge and rapidly mounting burden of debt, which could not be ignored
for very much longer.

It is unfortunately impossible to estimate the exact extent of the
Crown's indebtedness; but if, as I have suggested elsewhere,[34] it stood
at £120,000 at the end of 1385, then in all probability it had doubled,

even possibly reached a quarter of a million by the autumn of 1388. In the last year of the war alone defence expenditure totalled some £63,000, and to this must be added the cost of Arundel's expedition, the war expenses of the dukes of Guelders and Lancaster and the extraordinary grant made to the Appellants themselves (£57,000): in all some £100,000 *more than* the revenue from direct taxation. The situation in 1387 could not have been much different.[35]

By 1388 the government had not only accumulated an enormous burden of debt but had also exhausted its credit. The inevitable result of refusing to honour past commitments was the disappearance of willing lenders. Without the collateral of a large parliamentary subsidy Gloucester and Arundel approached their creditors empty-handed and returned in a similar condition.

With all possible sources of cash receipts already exploited to the full, credit drying up, a crippling burden of debt and no prospect of any fundamental change in the situation, the government's ability to wage war, let alone expand its war effort was very near its end by the autumn of 1388. A really spectacular military victory might just conceivably have induced the Commons to be vastly more generous than they had so far shown themselves (though this is very doubtful). But the fiasco of Arundel's expedition confirmed them in their reluctance to vote large subsidies and so doomed the earl's plans for continuing the war.

An additional incentive to end the war was provided by the growing tension between the Commons and the government as a result of its continued demands for money. Despite the reduction in the level of their contributions the Commons were very far from being satisfied. They wanted an end to taxation, not merely temporary relief. The more acute members of the Commons, moreover, could scarcely have been unaware that even this momentary alleviation was procured by methods which were likely to increase the burden on them in the future. Someone would have to foot the bill in the end, and the longer the war continued the larger it would be.

These considerations prompted the Commons to put forward their own remedies in a petition to the Merciless parliament which was so little to the Appellants' taste that it found no place in their record of its proceedings.[36] Drawn up some time in May during the second session of the assembly, it reveals a highly critical attitude towards the administration both in parliament and in the country at large. Discontent among the taxpayers had apparently reached such proportions that the Commons were acutely nervous of the possibility of another Peasants'

Revolt. There were risings in Kent and other southern counties in the spring, and the Commons feared that further demands for taxation would be sufficient to turn these sporadic outbreaks into a general conflagration.[37] They proposed three radical remedies: that taxation cease altogether; that the king's wars be 'straitly examined' – presumably with a view to ending them;[38] and that a small council of six or eight be appointed to introduce sweeping financial reforms. It is perhaps significant that when a council of five was nominated towards the end of parliament, the only one of the Appellants to find a place on it was the earl of Warwick, who had taken no active part in the government's foreign policy.[39] Disenchantment with the Appellants and their policies was evidently complete: the reformers were being asked to reform themselves.

There was good reason why they should be asked to do so, quite apart from the expense of their foreign policy. During their two years in power Gloucester and his associates plundered the revenues to enrich themselves. Gloucester's very first act on seizing power in 1386 had been to have the terms of his peerage redefined in a manner highly advantageous to himself.[40] He followed this up by quietly helping himself to £1,600 from the exchequer for 'old debts'. Arundel meanwhile voted himself a bonus of 1,000 marks for his services; doubled his fee as captain of Brest (though this had been reduced only two years previously at the behest of the Commons); and took an enormous profit from his 1388 expedition: though he served for only three of the four months stipulated in his indenture and failed to take his full complement of troops, he insisted on payment in full. This meant in effect that he made a profit of at least £7,000, possibly more. Finally, in the Merciless parliament itself the Appellants voted themselves £20,000 'for their labours' and conferred the earldom of Huntingdon on Sir John Holand with an annuity of 2,000 marks 'to support his estate' which set a record in such grants. Between them the Appellants pocketed all the money voted in direct taxation between October 1386 and October 1388, while the annuity given to Holand made it unlikely that significant savings would be made from the recent parliamentary ban on royal grants.

In these circumstances it is scarcely surprising that disenchantment soon gave way to positive hostility. In the Cambridge parliament of September 1388 the Commons turned on the 'reformers', and it is probably not fortuitous that the records of this assembly have failed to survive. Arundel's servants were called to account for the monies he had received and spent on his summer campaign, and although he was vindicated – or at least, not punished — this was an omen which boded nothing but ill for him and his colleagues. This same assembly also refused to vote further monies for a Continental campaign, earmarking its subsidy for defence against the Scots.[41]

The Scots were the final element in the complex of causes which forced the government to abandon its aggressive foreign policy. They refused to renew the truce and prepared to invade in force. According to the Westminster chronicler the invasion which began on 29 June was the most formidable for over a century. The Appellants evidently took a similar view. The northern earls were called out in force and in the middle of July Arundel was ordered to return immediately and join the earl of Northumberland and the northern magnates with his fleet.[42] As we have seen, he ignored his recall. On 5 August the English forces were decisively beaten at Otterburn – the only major Scottish victory on English soil during the entire war – and the northern counties severely ravaged. The situation appeared so grave that the king himself prepared to lead an army northwards.[43] But the withdrawal of the Scots made unnecessary what financial stringency rendered very difficult, and the campaign was postponed until parliament could vote the funds for a defensive war in the north.

The threat from Scotland, and more specifically the decision to recall Arundel, marks the moment when the government finally accepted that it was over-extended and must seek an accommodation with France. A few weeks previously, on 12 June, the duke of Gloucester tentatively reopened the negotiations which his accession to power had so brusquely terminated. He did so only with the greatest reluctance, as the manner of his approach and the tone of his correspondence clearly reveal. Unwilling to assume the initiative himself, he retrieved a French offer made six months previously and, after excusing his belated reply on the grounds that he had been occupied with other important business, accepted its proposal for a long truce. If he were still interested, the duke of Burgundy was advised to contact the captain of Calais, suggesting a date and a place for a meeting. If it could be arranged, he might then receive a favourable reply.[44]

It is not quite clear what happened next. Negotiations for a truce did in fact begin at the very end of the year, and then continued without serious interruption for the next five years. But what exactly occurred between Gloucester's original letter and the first meeting is uncertain. In all probability the French accepted the English offer but played for time. All the cards were now in their hands. Spain was quiet; Brittany was quiet; Flanders was quiet. Scotland on the other hand was very far from being quiet and promised to occupy England to the exclusion of all else. The opportunity to put French ascendency in the Low Countries beyond challenge was too good to be missed and Philip seized it. Though his October campaign against Guelders produced no resounding military victories, it effectively warned the duke off Brabant, strengthened the Burgundian claim to succeed to the duchy, and inflicted a further humiliation on England, who made no move to aid her ally.

The Guelders campaign was the last of the war. It is not difficult to see why. In itself it opened no new area of conflict, merely confirming a French supremacy in the Low Countries which was already apparent in 1385 and which had been accepted in England (however reluctantly) by the end of 1387. The Castilian problem had been solved even more definitively by the treaty of Bayonne. And if the Breton dispute were still alive, there were powerful parties within both England and France who were determined that it should not become over-active. But the most important contribution to peace was the utter discredit of those who favoured war, particularly in England. In November Philip of Burgundy was replaced by his rival, the constable, amid public declarations in favour of peace and lighter taxation;[45] but this was rather symptomatic of the desire for peace than a step towards its realization, since Philip himself had long since been in favour of a settlement. The really important change took place in England. Only the determination of Gloucester and Arundel to keep the war going had prevented a solution once the Castilian problem was settled. When they admitted their defeat, therefore, the war ended abruptly and decisively: all other parties had long since been converted.

It would seem that they prolonged the war to no useful purpose. But they did perform one important (if unintentional) service. By showing that even its most ardent advocates could not prosecute the war with any hope of success in the existing conditions, they converted all parties to peace. It has been remarked that Richard II's foreign policy was one of the most unpopular features of his reign and one of the major causes of his downfall. Applied (as it invariably is) to the last years of the reign this judgment is wide of the mark. The struggle over foreign policy was fought out between 1383 and 1388, and the king's policy won though the king himself was defeated. The realities of power forced the aristocratic opposition to recognize the validity of de la Pole's analysis of the situation and to take the first steps towards peace themselves. In so doing they cut the ground from under their own feet. After 1388 opposition to peace with France was factitious and clearly recognizable as such. Though there might be individual outbursts (from Gloucester and Arundel) against the perfidious French there was no war party in England after 1388: it had been destroyed in the two previous years.

NOTES

1 *CPR, 1385–9*, 502–3.
2 BM, Additional Charter 3360.
3 Terrier de Loray, *Jean de Vienne*, appendices 126–7.
4 Cartellieri, *Philipp der Kühne*, appendix 4; ADN, B 18822/23464. See appendix 1(e) for a description of these materials.
5 *Chronicon*, ii, 270–1 (cf. Walsingham, *Historia Anglicana*, ii, 175). Other materials for the negotiations in *Higden*, ix, 176; C 76/72, m. 13; E 364/22, mm. lv, 8; *Foedera*, vii, 581–2; *Handelingen van . . . Vlaanderen*, 425–7.
6 *Higden*, ix, 172, and E 101/183/12, m. 4 for Poylle; *Ordonnances de Philippe le Hardi*, i, nos 188–9, *Inventaire . . . Bruges*, iii, 115, and *Handelingen van . . . Vlaanderen*, no. 55 for defensive measures.
7 E 403/519, m. 19.
8 *Croniques de Tournai*, 328. See Laurent and Quicke, *Origines de l'état bourguignon*, 211ff. for the campaign and its circumstances.
9 Perroy, *L'Angleterre et le grand Schisme*, appendix 11; Terrier de Loray, *Jean de Vienne*, appendices 126–7.
10 *Higden*, ix, 172.
11 C 76/72, mm. 12–11; *Foedera*, vii, 587–8, 679–80 (for a different interpretation see Russell, *English Intervention in Spain and Portugal*, 504–5).
12 *Foedera*, vii, 583–5 (commission); E 159/166, *Brevia baronibus*, Trinity term m. 16v (indenture); E 403/519, mm. 8, 12, 23 (payments to Percy).
13 E 101/319/33.
14 *Séjours de Charles VI*, 439.
15 BM, Cotton Julius B VI, no. 55 (to be published by Dr M. Jones in a forthcoming book on John de Montfort); *Foedera*, vii, 586–7 (cf. below, 133).
16 *Oeuvres*, xiii, 100, 105.
17 Cf. Sherborne, 'Indentured Retinues and English Expeditions to France, 1369–80', *EHR*, lxxix, 718–46.
18 *Ordonnances des rois de France*, vii, 188.
19 *Antient Kalendars and Inventories of H M Exchequer*, ii, 35.
20 I hope to publish a text of the treaty shortly.
21 See appendix 1(j) for a discussion of this point.
22 *Foedera*, vii, 595–6.
23 *Oeuvres*, xiii, 117–19.
24 C 76/72, mm. 10, 11; E 101/40/40; E 364/24, m. 5; *Foedera*, vii, 578; *RP*, iii, 244–5.

25 Froissart, *Oeuvres*, xiii, 100ff; *St Denys*, i, 508–10; Le Fèvre, *Journal*, i, 523–9 for what follows, and appendix 1(k) for its chronology.
26 Froissart, *Oeuvres*, xiii, 185 (cf. *Séjours de Charles VI*, 440).
27 *Mémoires . . . Bretagne*, ii, 552–5.
28 *CChR, 1341–1417*, 309 (Richmond); *Foedera*, vii, 586–7 (commission).
29 *Higden*, ix, 182.
30 Froissart, *Oeuvres*, xiii, 146–7; *Higden*, ix, 187–8; Walsingham, *Historia Anglicana*, ii, 175; *Recueil des documents concernant le Poitou*, vi (*AHP*), 201.
31 BM, Cotton Julius B VI, no. 55 (cf. n. 15); for date see appendix 1 (l).
32 *CCR, 1385–9*, 379–80.
33 *RP*, iii, 244–6; *Statutes of the Realm*, ii, 52.
34 Palmer, 'The Parliament of 1385 and the Constitutional Crisis of 1386', *Speculum*, xlvi, 477–90.
35 Ramsay, *Genesis of Lancaster*, ii, 386 (defence); E 101/40/40, and E 364/24, m. 5 (Arundel); *RP*, iii, 245 (Appellants).
36 Knighton, *Chronicon*, ii, 265–70; for date see appendix 1(m).
37 *Ibid.* ii, 266, 267; cf. Favent, *Historia mirabilis parliamenti*, 21.
38 Though this might be a hint that corruption and peculation were suspected (see below, pp. 137–8).
39 *Higden*, ix, 178.
40 *CPR, 1385–9*, 233 (cf. SC 8/215/10707, Gloucester's petition). For what follows see E 403/518, *sub dat.* 16 December; E 403/519, mm. 4, 8, 20, 22; E 403/521, mm. 16, 19 (Gloucester); E 101/40/40; E 364/24, m. 5; E 364/27, m. 4v (Arundel); *RP*, iii, 245 (Appellants); 250–1 (Holand).
41 E 159/167, *Brevia baronibus*, St Michael term m. 51 (Arundel's servants); *CFR, 1383–91*, 265, and Knighton, *Chronicon*, ii, 298 (subsidy). cf. Tuck, 'The Cambridge Parliament, 1388', *EHR*, lxxxiv, 225–43 for further evidence of hostility between the Appellants and the Commons.
42 *Higden*, ix, 184, 187; E 403/519, m. 19.
43 *CCR, 1385–9*, 606; *Foedera*, vii, 594.
44 *CPR, 1385–9*, 502–3.
45 *St Denys*, i, 568–70; *Higden*, ix, 200.

Chapter Eight

Towards Peace
1389–94

The increasing disrepute of the baronial administration and the humiliations of the summer and autumn of 1388 vindicated the king's policy and paved the way for his return to power. He could probably have resumed control of the government at any time after the Cambridge parliament in September; but he bided his time, allowing the Appellants to assume responsibility for the truce negotiations and so publicly acknowledge the error of their own policies. But though they did the work the Appellants were not allowed to take the credit. When the negotiations neared completion the king took control. On 3 May 1389 he dismissed his baronial counsellors; on 5 May he renewed the safe-conducts for the French ambassadors; and on 14 May he issued the commission to conclude the truce which was finally sealed on 18 June.[1]

His resumption of power was evidently timed to coincide with the conclusion of the truce. His first important political act was to claim the credit for its benefits. Less than two weeks after dismissing his counsellors he announced to his over-taxed subjects in a public manifesto for which he took sole personal responsibility that he intended to dispense with the subsidy voted in the Cambridge parliament if the truce were concluded. He went on to criticize the heavy war taxation imposed during his minority and ended with a pledge to reduce the burden if peace could be secured.[2] He had learnt a lesson from the events of the past five years. Though his policy remained essentially unchanged he was now determined to stress its more positive (and popular) aspects. He was also determined to avoid de la Pole's mistake of appeasing France; there were to be no further one-sided concessions to her.

The truce, published on 8 July, was to last until August 1392. It was expressly designed to facilitate the conclusion of a peace. In April 1392 it was extended to September 1393, and in April 1393 until September 1394.[3] The entire period from 1389 to 1394 was one of uninterrupted peace and almost continuous negotiations. There were of course some strains and stresses, particularly in the early years. No sooner was the truce sealed than the French were looking for an outlet for their energies in Italy. Their ambitions there culminated in a grandiose plan to invade Italy in the spring of 1391. A huge army led by Charles VI, his brother and uncles was to install the king's brother in the Romagna, expel Boniface IX from Rome, and consolidate the Angevin hold on Naples. It may even have been intended to crown the whole enterprise with Charles VI's coronation as Holy Roman Emperor. The English government reacted forcefully against this threat to the 'true' pope and the balance of power and there ensued a diplomatic duel which brought the two countries to the verge of war in the winter of 1390–1. War was averted only when the French agreed to abandon their plans. The crisis was a salutary one. It taught the French that the days of appeasement were over and so paved the way for the genuine peace and real co-operation which was to be the hallmark of the mid-1390s.

The only other episode to mar the good relations between the two countries was the brief crisis occasioned by Charles VI's threatened invasion of Brittany in August 1392. But this was the product of a combination of circumstances which was never likely to recur – the attempted assassination of the French constable and the near insanity of the French king – and in no way the result of the settled policies of either government. It was an aberration which was swiftly corrected and never repeated. Its effect on the long-term relations of the two countries was barely discernible but – such as it was – it was to the good. Philip of Burgundy seized the opportunity afforded by the illness of Charles VI and the reckless opportunism of the constable to resume control of the French government, and with de Clisson's disgrace the faint chance that the Breton civil war would engulf England and France disappeared for good. But war over Brittany had never been very likely. By the summer of 1391, when the Italian crisis had been resolved, the pattern of good relations was already solidly established.[4]

The changing political situation naturally affected the development of the peace negotiations. Before 1391 only one important conference was held (May to July 1390). It was not conducted at the highest level and it ended in deadlock on a procedural point. Arrangements made to follow it up came to nothing. By contrast the conferences after 1391 were more frequent, they were at a higher level, and they all produced definite progress towards a final settlement. There is good reason to suppose that they issued in a secret agreement in 1394. Nevertheless the

May conference of 1390 cannot be written off as a complete failure, if only because it implicitly reaffirmed that the negotiations would be taken up again at the point they had reached in the 1380s, not begun from scratch. This immediately defined the framework and much of the content of succeeding conferences.

On the very eve of the first meeting John of Gaunt, who had recently returned to England, was created duke of Aquitaine.[5] In the circumstances this could only be taken as a declaration of intent, signifying that Richard II intended to adhere to the essential feature of the earlier negotiations, the separation of England and Aquitaine.

Within this framework the conference of 1390 also defined the major issues which later conferences were called on to resolve. The instructions given to the bishop of St Davids, the head of the English delegation, show that English territorial ambitions were limited to the duchy of Aquitaine, Calais and Ponthieu, and that the king was prepared to recognize French sovereignty in principle. On both subjects further concessions were envisaged if the French earned them. Territorial sacrifices were implied rather than stated, but on the more important issue of sovereignty the bishop was empowered to offer simple homage and 'services', though these were to be performed by the duke of Aquitaine (i.e. John of Gaunt), not the king of England. At a pinch he could concede that the king's successors would do homage in person.[6]

All this was very moderate as a beginning, and although the conference ended in deadlock the official text recording this fact implies that the French position was no more extreme.[7] Reading between the lines, it is possible to see that they had committed themselves in principle to some (as yet unspecified) territorial concessions and to modifications to their exercise of sovereignty. Questions of principle had been resolved and the horse-trading could begin. Despite their inability to agree as to who should make the first formal offer, therefore, the two sides had gone a long way towards a solution when they separated in July 1390.

At this point the negotiations were interrupted by the Italian crisis which was only resolved in the following February, when Charles VI agreed to abandon his invasion of Italy in favour of an interview with Richard II at Calais. The royal interview, scheduled for the end of June, was intended to save the face of the French by diverting attention from their diplomatic defeat over Italy. The arrangement was clearly made in too much of a hurry and it was quickly discovered that there was insufficient time to complete the necessary groundwork. It was therefore postponed in favour of preliminary meetings of the princes of the Blood. The decision was only reached after much expenditure of time and interchange of embassies; but finally by October 1391, it had been definitely arranged that the royal uncles should meet at Amiens in the following spring under the aegis of Charles VI himself.[8]

At Amiens the English delegation led by John of Gaunt laid down three major conditions for peace: the king was to retain Calais and its march; he was to be paid the balance of King John's ransom; and he was to be given the whole of Aquitaine, including Poitou. In return he would renounce his claim to Ponthieu, recognize French sovereignty over Aquitaine, and allow the duke of Berry to hold Poitou for life. The question of French sovereignty over Calais was to be reserved for the decision of the two kings.

For the French the duke of Burgundy reiterated his government's basic condition: all English territories in France were to be held in liege homage, subject to the sovereignty and *ressort* of the French Crown. Further, the allies of France were to be included in any treaty according to the tenor of their alliances with her; and England must abandon her claim to Ponthieu, surrender Calais and return Cherbourg. If these conditions were met he offered modifications to the exercise of French sovereignty, 1,200,000 francs for the balance of King John's ransom, and substantial territorial concessions in Aquitaine: the Agenais, Périgord, Saintonge south of the Charente, Angoulême, Rouergue, Quercy (except for Montauban and the lands between the Aveyron and the Tarn), and Bigorre. In other words, the duchy of 1360 less Poitou, Saintonge north of the Charente, Aunis and Limousin.[9]

The gap between the two sides was narrowed considerably by these offers. It was closed even further by the duke of Burgundy who, at the end of the Amiens conference, promised John of Gaunt that if he maintained his position England would be allowed to retain Calais, one of the crucial points at issue.[10] The Breton crisis which followed hard on the heels of the Amiens meeting caused only a very temporary interruption in the negotiations and was ultimately beneficial since it placed Philip in a position to honour this promise.

This he did, as the instructions issued to the French ambassadors in March 1393 reveal. Though they were to offer very considerable incentives to the English to abandon Calais, the ambassadors were not to break off negotiations if they persisted in their refusal to leave. They were also to offer further territorial concessions or up to two million francs as a monetary equivalent – a huge sum (*c.* £330,000).

The English delegation led by John of Gaunt and the duke of Gloucester came armed with equally generous concessions. Until 1393 England had rejected the French demand for the inclusion of allies in a final settlement, presumably because she wanted a free hand in Scotland. Though the embassies of 1390 and 1392 had been armed with powers to negotiate either a general or a unilateral peace, they had apparently made use of only the latter set.[11] But in 1393 the English delegation was no longer instructed to press for a unilateral settlement; in fact, it was not even issued with powers to conclude a separate Anglo-French peace. This was a major concession. So too was the promise to return Cherbourg sealed on 1 March, just before the English embassy left Westminster.[12]

The conference of March 1393 thus opened auspiciously. Both delegations were headed by the royal uncles, and the two kings held themselves in the vicinity. After protracted discussions and the brief return of the English delegation to England in May, the negotiations neared their end early in the following month. On Wednesday 4 June one of the English delegation reported to the king that certain 'writings' had been drafted which

> were not yet conceived or ordained quite in accordance with the intentions of the said (French) deputies and of ourselves, although, thank God, there is no variance, difficulty or disagreement in any actual thing or point, but that wherever there has been challenge, everything with little correction combines well and graciously to the good accomplishment of the business, with God's help.

The ambassadors, he continued, were due to meet again in three day's time and he anticipated 'a certain conclusion' to their business.[13]

He was not unduly optimistic. On 16 June 1393 the dukes of Berry, Burgundy, Lancaster and Gloucester set their seals to a provisional treaty which, if ratified, would have settled most of the outstanding problems.[14] The allies of each side were included; the territorial limits of Aquitaine defined; the homage for the duchy agreed to be liege, not simple; and Calais and its march assigned to England. Three issues remained: the amount of King John's ransom, England's war indemnity; the nature of the tenure of Calais and La Rochelle; and the details of modifications to French sovereignty. The first two were left to the decision of the kings and the third was to be thrashed out by a conference of legal experts.

The territorial settlement was definitive. Here the French made notable concessions. Calais remained English, with the boundaries assigned to it in 1360. Aquitaine itself was to comprise Saintonge south of the Charente, Agenais, Périgord, Limousin, Quercy, Angoumois, Rouergue, Tarbes, Bigorre and Gaure, together with the homage of the counts of Armagnac, Foix and Périgord and of the *vicomte* of Limoges. A glance at the map will reveal that this was a very substantial part of the duchy as constituted by the treaty of Brétigny, and considerably larger than its extent at any time during the century after the treaty of Paris of 1259. Of the territories granted to Edward III only Aunis, Poitou and northern Saintonge were relinquished,[15] and these losses

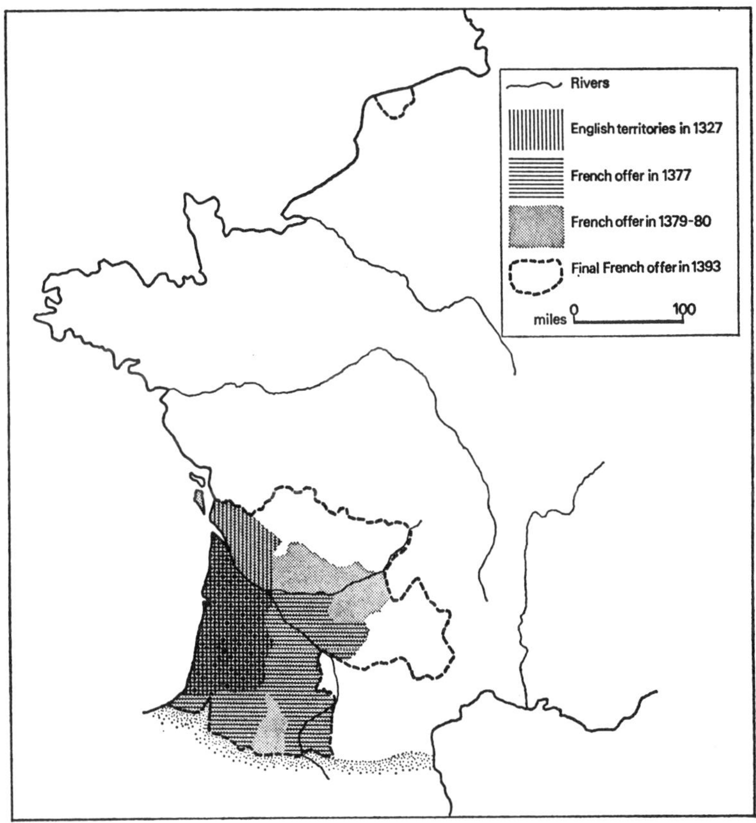

5 France: projected territorial settlements, 1377–93

were to a certain extent compensated for by the large war indemnity promised to Richard II. The war had evidently not gone so badly against England as is commonly supposed.

The major English concession was, of course, the recognition of French sovereignty, even though its exercise was to be subject to certain limitations. Now that the duchy was to be held by John of Gaunt and his heirs the problem of sovereignty was no longer as intractable as it had been in the past and the four dukes did not anticipate any serious difficulty in devising satisfactory modifications. On the very day they sealed the provisional treaty they laid down a timetable for the final stages of the negotiations which allocated only a few weeks for the discussion of modifications and left them in the hands of low-ranking experts, presided over by a mere bishop.[16]

By contrast, the precise nature of French sovereignty over Calais and La Rochelle was reserved for the decision of the two kings, presumably because Richard II intended to retain them himself. Calais had been reserved for this special treatment at earlier conferences, not surprisingly since the king had no intention of granting it to his uncle with Aquitaine. But the addition of La Rochelle is of a quite different order of interest. For if Richard intended to detach the town from the duchy and join it to his Crown, then he was still thinking along the lines of his grandfather, Edward III, who had been prepared to alienate Aquitaine but had wanted to retain Bordeaux, Bayonne and Dax as the bastions of English defence. Richard had simply replaced these three by La Rochelle, to the advantage both of John of Gaunt and the English Crown.[17]

Although it represented a considerable advance towards a final settlement the provisional treaty of 16 June was only a part of what the two sides had hoped to achieve in the summer of 1393. The original plan had been to crown the meeting of the four dukes with an interview between the two kings, and so presumably to convert the provisional treaty into a final peace. The imminence of a treaty which was thought to involve the sacrifice of Aquitaine to John of Gaunt provoked a rebellion in the north of England during May, causing Gaunt and his brother to return in a hurry. But the revolt was quickly suppressed and caused no change of plan. There was not even any serious loss of time, since the opportunity was taken to refer the progress so far made to the two kings.[18] This was judged to be so encouraging that preparations were now made for the royal interview. Charles VI was already at Abbeville within reach of the negotiations at Leulingham. When John of Gaunt and his brother returned to France they were accompanied by the king as far as Canterbury, where he remained for the next fortnight preparing to cross to Calais.[19] Then suddenly the entire programme was revised. The king returned to Westminster, preparations at Calais were suspended, and the royal interview was replaced by a provisional treaty which was to be completed and ratified in three further stages. It was agreed that legal experts should meet in mid-August to thrash out the details of modifications to French sovereignty, that the royal uncles should reconvene on 29 September, and that the royal interview be deferred until the following February. The reason for this drastic change of plan was the serious recurrence of Charles's mental instability.[20]

The same cause prevented the new schedule from being fulfilled. The legal experts met as arranged, and their work would seem to have been successfully accomplished since commissions were issued in September for the next stage in the proceedings, the conference between the four dukes.[21] But before they could meet it had become apparent that the continued insanity of the French king would necessitate a further delay, and so their conference was postponed until the end of February 1394.[22] Shortly before this Charles finally recovered his senses after an illness lasting six months or more. Although his incapacity had prevented any progress for the better part of a year, his return to normality seemed certain to produce the settlement which had been imminent when he fell ill. The original programme was resumed from the point it had then reached. Towards the end of March the dukes of Berry, Burgundy, Lancaster and York met at Leulingham, remaining in conference until the end of May or the beginning of June;[23] and when they met it was still intended to crown their labours with a personal interview between Charles VI and Richard II.[24] But during the final meeting of the four dukes the plan was abandoned. Indeed not only was the royal interview indefinitely postponed but no provision was made for any further meetings at all. This was manifest in the subsequent activities of the two royal families. Richard II and the duke of Gloucester went to Ireland; John of Gaunt to Aquitaine; Orleans, Berry and Burgundy to Avignon. The two key figures, John of Gaunt and Philip of Burgundy, planned to lead a crusade to the Balkans in 1395 which would take them away from the centre of affairs for a long time to come. The negotiations had evidently been broken off. Why?

The natural assumption is that they had broken down. But this is very hard to believe. Relations between the two countries were never more cordial than in the six months or so which followed the end of the final conference. During this period Philip and Gaunt completed their preparations for a crusade, the duke of Gloucester planned to send his only son on a tour of Philip's dominions, and Richard II corresponded with him on unusually warm, even intimate terms.[25] None of this is easy to reconcile with the view that the negotiations had broken down, and there is a reasonable amount of more positive evidence to show that they had not. During the final meeting between the royal uncles the existing truces were extended for four years in order – so it was said – to allow time to complete the peace negotiations. This may have been merely a pretext; but the best informed of the English chroniclers suspected otherwise and expressed his surprise when no further agreement was published. John of Gaunt himself referred to the probability of a 'final' peace in grants made to the three Estates of Aquitaine and to one of his principal Gascon vassals in the spring of 1395. Finally Froissart, who attended the final conference, was convinced that a secret treaty was concluded there. He was not, it is true, in anyone's confidence and so he could not vouch for the existence of this pact. He could only guess at its contents and he had no ideas at all as to why it was necessary. Nevertheless the atmosphere of the negotiations had convinced him and all other bystanders that an agreement had been reached, and since none was published it was *ipso facto* a secret one.[26]

A secret treaty would, of course, explain the situation in the summer and autumn of 1394 to perfection, and it is difficult to think of any other which would do so. It would explain the extreme friendliness of the two sides; it would explain their co-operative plans; and it would explain why the negotiations had been broken off when they had patently not broken down. But if an understanding had been reached, why was it necessary to keep it secret and why was it never converted into a public treaty? To answer these questions it is necessary to take a close look at some relatively unknown events which took place in Aquitaine while the peace negotiations were in progress.

NOTES

1 *Foedera*, vii, 614, 616–17, 622–30, 636–8.
2 *Ibid.*, vii, 620–1 (16 May).
3 *Ibid.*, vii, 623, 633–4, 719, 748.
4 Palmer, 'English Foreign Policy, 1388–1399', *The Reign of Richard II*, 75–107, for these crises.
5 *RP*, iii, 263–4 (2 March 1390); cf. chapter 2.
6 *PPC*, i, 19–23 (April 1390).

7 Moranvillé, 'Conférences entre la France et l'Angleterre, 1388–1393', *BEC*, l, 367–9. Moranvillé's collection of documents is indispensable for this period (cf. n.9).

8 *Ibid.*, 369–71; *DC*, nos 132, 135 and notes.

9 Moranvillé, *BEC*, l, 371–3. A better manuscript of these documents than that used by Moranvillé – BN, Nouvelle Acquisition Française 6215, fo. 48 –contains the English offer to recognize French sovereignty over Aquitaine.

10 Moranvillé, *BEC*, l, 377. *Ibid.*, 373–80 and *DC*, no. 150 for what follows.

11 C 76/77, m. 8: 1393 (cf. *Foedera*, vii, 668–9: 1390; and C 76/76, mm. 7–6: 1392).

12 E 30/316.

13 *Anglo-Norman Letters*, no. 133 (editor's translation).

14 Palmer, 'Articles for a Final Peace between England and France, 16 June 1393', *BIHR*, xxxix, 182–5.

15 Outside the duchy England was to renounce Thouars, Belleville, St Sauveur-le-vicomte and Ponthieu.

16 E 36/188, fo. 42.

17 For Edward's plans see chapter 2. Richard's surrender of Cherbourg and Brest might seem to controvert the point made in the text, but it should be remembered that he was under solemn treaty obligations to give them up.

18 *St Denys*, ii, 78–82; *Annales avignonnaises*, xiii, 75; *Chronique des quatre premiers Valois*, 331; Walsingham, *Annales*, 159–62 (cf. *Foedera*, vii, 746–7).

19 BM, Additional MS 24512, fo. 89, and Thorne, *Chronica*, col. 2197 (Richard's itinerary); C 76/78, m. 18.

20 E 36/188, fo. 42; *St Denys*, ii, 80–2; *Annales avignonnaises*, xiii, 75; *Chronique des quatre premiers Valois*, 331.

21 C 76/78, m. 15; E 364/27; m. 2v; *Foedera*, vii, 753.

22 *DC*, no. 197.

23 *St Denys*, ii, 86–8; *Chronographia regum francorum*, iii, 110 for Charles's illness, and *Foedera*, vii, 770; E 364/27, mm. 5v, 8; *Itinéraires de Philippe le Hardi*, 235–6 (cf. Petit, *Ducs de Bourgogne*, i, 484); Lehoux, *Jean de Berri*, ii, 311 and nn. for conference.

24 *Anglo-Norman Letters*, no. 106.

25 *Documents pour servir à l'histoire de la maison de Bourgogne*, nos 28–30; *Anglo-Norman Letters*, no. 3.

26 *Foedera*, vii, 769; *Higden*, ix, 282; *Livre des Bouillons*, 265; C 61/106, m. 2; Froissart, *Oeuvres*, xv, 108–27.

Chapter Nine

The Gascon Revolt
1394–5

The turbulent society of south-west France had a vested interest in war
and much to lose by peace. Throughout the last decade of the century
there were constant infractions of the truces along the borders of
Aquitaine. The Gascons did not hesitate to incite England to renew the
war, and even the great trading city of Bordeaux tried to embroil her
with France when an opportunity arose.[1] The Gascons had good reason
for their aggression; for if peace itself held few attractions for them, the
particular form of peace projected by Richard II was anathema. The
establishment of an English prince in Gascony would entail an immediate restriction of their freedom, and a corresponding decline in their
prestige. In the long run separation from the English Crown might
have even more baneful effects, for it would expose them to the en-
croachments of the French court and involve the attenuation, if not
the loss of valuable privileges, particularly those associated with the
wine trade, the basis of the wealth of the region. From whatever point
of view they were examined the Anglo-French peace proposals boded
ill for Gascony.

They threatened to be equally damaging to her immediate neighbours, the two houses of Foix and Armagnac. In fact if not in theory, the
counts of Foix and Armagnac were virtually sovereign rulers. So marked
was their independence, so great their predominance, and so fixed their
rivalry that Philip de Mézières could list them with Guelf and Ghibel-
line, English and French, Portuguese and Spanish, as the supreme
examples of warring states known to his day.[2] But their independence
would be eroded, if not terminated by the creation of a Lancastrian
dynasty in Aquitaine, for both were due to become its vassals and to
surrender to it valuable territories. It is therefore scarcely surprising
that both were hostile to the Anglo-French proposals.

The counts of Armagnac had the most to lose and the better opportunity to resist. The appeal of John I (1319-73) against the taxation of the Black Prince in 1368 had given Charles V his excuse and his opportunity to tear up the treaty of Brétigny, and in return he had promised Armagnac the counties of Bigorre and Gaure and had sworn that in no circumstances would he or his successors renounce their sovereignty over Aquitaine without his express consent. Despite the fact that the peace proposals of the 1380s and 1390s would have entailed the surrender of Bigorre and Gaure and the modification of French sovereignty, none of the Armagnacs was consulted. They were not slow to react. On one occasion when a final settlement seemed imminent, the count went to the extreme lengths of summoning on his own initiative the three Estates of Rouergue, the Agenais, Quercy and Bigorre to protest against the projected settlement. He urged the assembled deputies to send a delegation to Charles VI to remind him of his obligations, to ask that they be taken into his confidence, and to demand assurances that he would neither relinquish his sovereignty nor surrender them to the duke of Aquitaine. All of this, of course, amounted to a demand to reject the English peace terms.[3] On another occasion there were even hints of a possible rebellion if peace were concluded on unfavourable terms. On the eve of the summit conference of 1384, Arnaud-Amanieu of Albret (1358-1401) – another of the Appellants of 1368 – informed his cousin Armagnac that if peace were concluded 'you and I and all our country down there will be given to the duke of Lancaster, who is to be our duke'. The prospect evidently did not please him, and he was confident that his feelings would be shared by Armagnac whom he advised – rather ingenuously – 'not to fail to guard your country with care and better than ever before, for truly there will be greater need of this than there ever was previously'.[4] Whether Armagnac took the hint cannot be known; but the marked deterioration in his and his brother's relations with Paris in the 1390s may well have been the effect of the continued French pursuit of a *rapprochement* with England.

Unlike the Armagnacs the count of Foix had not appealed to Charles V in 1368, but he had almost as much to lose from a resident English duke. He would be forced to surrender Bigorre and to give homage to John of Gaunt, and his territories would be dwarfed by the reconstituted duchy of Aquitaine.[5] Like Armagnac he was therefore prepared to resist John of Gaunt, and an ideal opportunity to do so occurred in 1394, when the Gascons themselves rebelled against him. On 6 April 1394 the Gascons renounced their allegiance. They knew that Gaunt was collecting an army to discipline them and they looked around for military support. On 11 May Nompar, Lord of Caumont, one of the principal Gascon rebels, allied with Matthew, count of Foix, who promised to aid him against 'all men in the world who might wish him harm' except his own natural lord. Nompar himself reserved his allegiance only to his sovereign lord, Richard II, not John of Gaunt. A little later, on 26 August, the three greatest Gascon nobles, the Lords of Duras, Lesparre and Montferrand contracted a similar alliance with Archambaud de Grailly, who had just returned from England. An important Gascon noble in his own right, de Grailly was also heir-apparent to Foix, and the link between these two alliances.[6] Both were clearly directed against John of Gaunt.

Elements outside Gascony therefore played a part in the eventual defeat of the Anglo-French peace proposals.[7] But the hard core of the opposition came from the Gascons themselves, and their opposition is fortunately well-documented. When, after a prolonged struggle, John of Gaunt and his subjects reached a compromise in 1395, they recorded the main facts of their dispute in a notarial deed for the guidance of Richard II, to whom they agreed to leave the final judgment. The deed has survived, and with its aid the struggle can be followed in some detail.[8]

Initially the Gascons received the news of Gaunt's appointment as their duke with reserve but without any sign they would eventually refuse to recognize him. On 14 September 1390, some six months after he was created duke, the three Estates 'at present in the obedience of the king of England and France, our most sovereign lord' met at Bordeaux in order to present a formal reply to Sir William le Scrope 'claiming himself to be seneschal of Aquitaine for the most excellent lord, John, Duke of Aquitaine and Lancaster'. They began with a protestation of loyalty which augured well for an eventual settlement. 'By nothing that they said or did', they protested, 'was it their intention to conspire or plot against the king our said lord, or against his Crown, or against the said lord the duke, in any manner'. But they had certain objections to the grant which they must raise in order to preserve their liberties and privileges. If these were met, their privileges safe-guarded and their allegiance to the king reserved, they declared themselves 'ready and prepared to obey the mandates of our lord the king'.

But first, lest their objections be misunderstood, they put on record once and for all their pleasure at the honour conferred on them and the duke:

since it pleases and has pleased the king and his honoured council
to give the duchy of Aquitaine to the most excellent lord the duke
of Lancaster, it pleases us – provided always that our faith and
allegiance are retained by and reserved to our lord the king. And
we have great pleasure and joy that his royal majesty has deigned
to provide us with such a lord as he: of royal blood and very close
to the lineage of our said lord the king, full of great nobility, of
noble prudence and wisdom, gifted by nature and fortune and
blessed with great spiritual and temporal virtues, and many others
which would take too long to describe. And therefore he pleases
us more as our lord than any other person in this world after the
person of our said lord the king.

This clarified, they then turned to their objections, which arose for
the most part out of the ambiguities of the grant. As it stood it threatened their liberties and they asked that these be guaranteed. Above all,
they demanded assurances that the grant would not constitute a precedent which could lead to their separation from the English Crown. To
obviate this risk they stipulated that the duke and his seneschal should
tender an oath in writing to observe their liberties, and that the king
himself should give a similar promise with a special clause specifying
that they would not be alienated from the English Crown. Finally they
demanded that all grants of rents, lands or castles made by Richard II
or his predecessors be ratified. They asked that these requests be fulfilled by 12 March 1391. In order not to prejudice their position in the
meantime they refused to accept le Scrope as seneschal for the duke,
but they permitted him to 'govern the office of the seneschalcy' in the
name of the king and by reason of the powers vested in him as con-
servator of the truces in Aquitaine. But once their demands were conceded:

the said lords of the three Estates offer to receive the said lord of
Lancaster as duke of Aquitaine, and to do for him what we are
bound or accustomed to do, saving our allegiance to our said lord
the king, sovereign duke of Aquitaine. And we make this reply
to our said lord the king and to the said lord of Lancaster with all
the reverence and honour that we ought or are able. And we have
very great joy and pleasure at the said grant because of the great
nobility, prudence, discretion, wisdom and righteousness of the
said lord of Lancaster, and because of his very great and most
noble rank.

The final demand made by the Estates was quickly settled to their satisfaction. Unlike their other requests this did not arise out of the grant of Aquitaine itself, but out of a separate instrument by which the king revoked all previous grants on the lands and revenues of the duchy in order to disencumber them for the benefit of his uncle. Gaunt now agreed to forgo this favour. The revocation of March 1390 was itself revoked in November. The issue did not arise again.[9]

To understand the other objections raised by the Estates it is necessary to appreciate the nature of their 'liberties', especially that of being attached to the English Crown. By virtue of a series of grants made by earlier kings of England, Aquitaine itself, most of its towns and a number of the lay lords were privileged to be annexed to the Crown, from which they could only be separated as a temporary apanage for the king's eldest son.[10] The Gascons therefore had unimpeachable grounds for challenging the validity of the grant to John of Gaunt. It is all the more important to stress that they did not do so. Time and again they reiterated their readiness to accept him as their duke for his lifetime. But his grant was ambiguous and could lead to their permanent separation from the Crown under a Lancastrian dynasty. This they were not prepared to accept: hence their repeated demand that his title be 'defined'.

Their first attempt to secure a definition was not a success. On 23 November 1390 the king replied to their objections. He reaffirmed that the grant to his uncle was for life only, underlined the fact that sovereignty was reserved to himself, and promised that the duchy would return to the Crown after Gaunt's death. This would appear to have satisfied all the Gascons' requirements, and it would have done so but for the saving clause: the king reserved sovereignty to himself 'according to the force and effect of our said letters of donation' – that is, as 'king of France', not of England. In other words he merely reiterated the terms of his earlier grant, complete with its ambiguities. He did not even promise that the grant would not be treated as a precedent.

When the Estates met in March 1391 as previously arranged, therefore, they were in something of a dilemma, for they had received none of the assurances they required. On the other hand the king had made no overt move to bring about the final separation between England and Aquitaine, and negotiations with France had apparently broken down: indeed, the two countries appeared to be on the verge of war over the French plans to invade Italy. Comforted by this, the Estates decided not to press matters for the moment. They accepted Gaunt as their duke on terms as ambiguous as those on which he had been appointed.

The seneschal William le Scrope was prevailed upon to swear an oath to obey their liberties. He then promised to obtain a similar pledge from Gaunt himself. To prevent further misunderstanding the Estates themselves drafted the letter they wished the duke to send them, and le Scrope guaranteed to deposit a properly sealed original dated 12 March 1391 in the hands of the Gascons by November. If he failed to do so, the reception of duke and seneschal was to be 'as though not made nor conceded, null and of no value'. Provisionally, therefore, le Scrope was received as sensechal and John of Gaunt as duke of Aquitaine on 12 March 1391. The Estates then took an oath to their lord to be good, loyal and obedient subjects during his lifetime; to give him faith and good and true counsel; to guard his secrets, work for his well-being and honour, eschew all that might redound to his harm or injury, serve him with life and limb, and 'stand with him against all who might live or die'. All these things they swore with one reservation: 'saving and reserving always the sovereignty due to our lord, the *king of England*'.

On 4 September 1391 John of Gaunt granted the letter required by his subjects and só no impediment arose to his original reception.[11] From 12 March 1391 he was recognized as duke, and his seneschal exercised his jurisdiction 'peacefully and quietly' until 18 August 1392 when, according to their own account, the mayor and jurats of Bordeaux 'claiming and alleging that the said seneschal had not observed those things promised and sworn to by him', ordered that no one should obey him until he had made amends. Le Scrope's crime was not specified. Whatever it was neither he nor his successor, Hotspur,[12] saw fit to rectify it. But this did not prevent either from exercising their office outside Bordeaux, nor did it affect the position of the duke himself or of his other officials anywhere in the duchy. At the very moment they challenged the authority of his seneschal, the major and jurats of Bordeaux wrote to John of Gaunt to protest their loyalty, declaring that those who had questioned the validity of the king's grant were troublemakers who deserved no credence. As soon as he had guaranteed their liberties they and the barons of Bordelais had accepted him as duke, and they would continue to do so.[13] They honoured this promise for a further twenty months. Until April 1394 Gaunt was recognized as duke 'both in secret and in public' by Bordeaux and the three Estates of the duchy.

In that month, however, his status was challenged openly and unambiguously for the first time. On 6 April 1394 the archbishop of Bordeaux and four other ecclesiastics, fifteen barons, a representative of the gentry, the mayor, under-mayor and eleven jurats of Bordeaux, and fully accredited delegates of the towns of Bayonne and St Sêurin met in the cathedral church of Bordeaux to examine the credence and listen to the message of Sir Peter Arnald of Béarn, sent to them by the king. As a result of what they saw and heard, the Estates swore henceforth and for ever to be governed only by the king and his Crown. They pledged loyalty and aid to each other and exchanged promises to stand firm against all who might procure them harm because of their oath to be ruled only by the king. This last step, clearly implying the use of force against John of Gaunt, apparently troubled ecclesiastical consciences. The notary remarked at this point that he had left out the record of an altercation between Bordeaux and the archbishop.

As we have seen, the Gascon lords did make serious preparations to resist Gaunt if need arose. In the meantime the Estates drew up a justification of the 'Union', as they chose to name their rebellion. The 'Instrument of Union' once again traversed all the ground surveyed at the time of le Scrope's reception in 1390. This time, however, it came to a very different conclusion. The Estates refused to accept Gaunt as their duke on four grounds: first, his appointment 'did not please the king and was not made by his will'; second, 'the duchy is, and should be, annexed to the Crown of England'; third, the king himself had sworn not to alienate it; and finally, if the grant to Gaunt were allowed to stand the duchy 'could in the future be completely separated from the Crown of England'. To prevent this the Estates reversed their previous decision. Henceforth Gaunt's officers had no authority in the duchy and Hotspur, his seneschal, was recognized by the Gascons only as the king's representative.[14] Their work completed, the Estates dispersed. Their acts were endorsed on 6 June by the *captal* de Buch, the lord of Duras, and the *vicomte* of Orthe, all of whom had been in England at the time of the 'Union'.

All this had been provoked by the oral message which Sir Peter Arnald of Béarn had been empowered to deliver on behalf of the king. It is unfortunate therefore that its contents can never be known with absolute certainty. The Estates found them so little to their taste that they instructed the notary to omit even the formal credence from his record. They asserted elsewhere that they knew that the grant to Gaunt had been made against the will of the king 'because of the credence'. But if this were in fact the subject of that document it is difficult to see why they deliberately excluded it from their justification and quite impossible to understand why they should have found it necessary to resort to rebellion.

Fortunately the general tenor of Arnald's message may be deduced from another source. In the summer of 1395 the chronicler Sir John Froissart visited England and attached himself to the court. He found the king and his entourage preoccupied by the Gascon problem and sought an explanation of what it was all about. He had the good fortune to come across an old acquaintance, Sir Richard Stury, who was now a member of the royal council, and asked for enlightenment. Stury, who had just emerged from a long debate in council on this very problem, hesitated at first, but then with the remark that everyone would know about it sooner or later, plunged into a narrative which Froissart purports to record verbatim.[15]

The origin of the present trouble, he said, was a grant made by the king to his uncle in the previous year. By this the king had conferred Aquitaine on John of Gaunt 'purely and absolutely, to him and his heirs in perpetuity'. He had then commanded the Gascons to accept Gaunt as their 'sovereign lord' and to give him the faith and homage they had previously rendered to the king of England. But on receiving this command the cities, barons, knights and gentlemen of Aquitaine had bound themselves to resist the duke and to reject his rule. Since Gaunt had been unable to coerce his subjects to recognize him, the entire affair had been remitted to the king and his council for their decision.

If Froissart is right, then the Gascon revolt was provoked by the king's attempt to convert his uncle's life tenure of Aquitaine into a grant in perpetuity. There are good reasons for preferring this version of events to that given by the Gascons. Sir Richard Stury had no reason to dissimulate. The Gascons, on the other hand, were deliberately evasive about the contents of Sir Peter Arnald's message. They implied that they were rebelling against Gaunt because they had learnt that the king himself did not wish his uncle to be their duke. But this was manifestly absurd, as they themselves had recognized at an earlier date.[16] It was a pretext not a reason.

Froissart's story explains certain features of the revolt which are incomprehensible in the light of the Gascons' own account. First and foremost it explains why they should have revolted at all after accepting Gaunt as their duke for three years. Secondly, it explains why the Gascons repeatedly stressed their willingness to have Gaunt as their duke for life if the king retained his sovereignty. They could, after all, have taken their stand on their legal privileges and refused to accept him as duke for any period, under any conditions. Finally, it explains the timing of the revolt. For if the king ever revealed to the Gascons his ultimate intentions, then the moment he would have chosen to do so was precisely the moment the revolt actually occurred: on the eve of a settlement with France. The revolt broke out just as the final peace conference convened.

Its immediate effect was to wreck the conference. Until Gaunt's position in Aquitaine were assured, no treaty based on his tenure of the duchy was worth the parchment on which it was written. Hence the fate which overtook the peace negotiations in the summer of 1394: they were indefinitely suspended, a projected meeting between the two kings abandoned, and a secret treaty – or at least an understanding — concluded.[17]

The fate of the negotiations now depended on Gaunt's ability to bring his subjects to heel. After his return from Leulingham in June he began collecting troops, and he finally set sail for Aquitaine in November with an army some 1,500 strong.[18]

His arrival had been preceded by a diplomatic battle between the king and the Estates. After their declaration of 'Union' on 6 April the Estates had written to the king to ask him to make arrangements for the government of the duchy during the interregnum and to provide them with safe-conducts for the ambassadors whom they wished to send to explain their actions. According to their own account neither request was fulfilled. The king would not receive an embassy from rebels. Instead he commanded them on 22 June to send representatives to appear before him at Waterford on 6 October when, he promised, he would put an end to the debates and dissensions in Aquitaine. The promise was taken as a threat. When they replied – rather belatedly – on 26 August the Estates refused to send representatives and reaffirmed their solidarity. The king, they said, was badly informed if he believed there were any dissensions within the duchy. On the contrary, the Estates were of one will and mind, determined to be ruled only by the king himself. They would never obey anyone else, and in this resolve they would live and die: nothing would persuade them to change it. As for sending representatives, this was impossible. They were not accustomed to be summoned outside the duchy, and in any case they were needed for the defence of its borders: they could serve the king better in Aquitaine than in England.

The king's reply was evidently not pacific for the Estates decided to omit it from their record. In the meantime Richard had written to them again from Cardiff on 8 and 10 September to reaffirm his grant and to deny rumours that it had ever been made against his will. He absolved the Estates from their oath of 'Union' and ordered them to obey Gaunt and render him homage. They remained quite unmoved.

This was the position when Gaunt arrived in Gascony at the end of the year. Unfortunately the events of the next three months are almost completely hidden from view. According to the Gascons, Gaunt threatened to use force if he were not recognized as duke, but whether or not he did so is uncertain. Bordeaux at least resisted his progress, since he had to petition for admittance to the city when the two sides finally agreed to negotiate; but whether the resistance was more than passive it is again impossible to say.[19]

On the other hand there is abundant evidence that Gaunt tried to buy off the opposition. On 12 January 1395 he offered confirmation of all their grants and concessions to those who would recognize his authority, and in the weeks which followed he evidently negotiated a large number of private deals behind the scenes, for his settlement with the Estates in March was accompanied by a spate of grants and charters. The earliest of these, conceded to Lord Mussidan on 13 March, was the model of many that were to follow.[20] Mussidan was forgiven his opposition, guaranteed against reprisals, and promised that any past denial of justice by ducal officials would be made good. All his grants and concessions were ratified, together with his liberties and privileges, even though these had been abused or fallen into disuse. He was assured that no taxation would be imposed without the assent of the Estates. If the duchy were enlarged and its new subjects refused to obey the duke, then he was not to be compelled to fight them. In return for these and some lesser concessions, Mussidan gave his consent to Gaunt's recognition as duke. On 22 March substantially similar terms were granted to the three Estates of the duchy for a similar price, and in the days which followed further special concessions were showered on the city of Bordeaux and the more important Gascon lords. Gaunt was ready to pay dearly for his recognition and his subjects were apparently willing to sell it to him.

On 13 March, the date of his grant to Mussidan, Gaunt was permitted to enter Bordeaux, an event which may be taken to mark the end of the revolt. Formal negotiations with the three Estates began on 16 March and ended five days later in an agreement which appeared to give Gaunt all that he wanted. The Estates agreed to remit the whole dispute to the king and this time to abide by his decision. Pending his judgment Gaunt could rule the duchy, though not as duke; and once his title had been 'defined' he would be recognized by his subjects as 'true duke'. But this appearance of victory is misleading. Behind the formal agreement of 21 March there was evidently an informal understanding as to what would constitute an acceptable 'definition' of Gaunt's title, and on this point – the crux of the entire debate – he was defeated, as subsequent events were to reveal. When they abandoned their revolt the Gascons did not surrender to Gaunt, they merely retreated to the position they had occupied in 1390.

For the fourth time in as many years the dispute was thus remitted to the king to ascertain – so it was said – whether the grant of 1390 was 'against his will'. On 22 and 23 July 1395 a great council was held at Eltham to review the entire problem. Both John of Gaunt and the three Estates were represented. According to a surviving fragment of its minutes, the council was preoccupied by the legal question of whether Bordeaux's privilege of being annexed to the Crown could be reconciled with the king's grant to his uncle. The legal officers of the Crown advised that it could not, and that the grant should be revoked. The majority of the council were prepared to accept this advice; and although the duke of Gloucester demanded further investigation of Bordeaux's privilege, and the earl of Derby another hearing for his father's case, no one stood out against the majority view. But though the final recommendation of the council was made on purely legal grounds, the debate which preceded it was dominated by political considerations. According to Froissart – or rather, according to Sir Richard Stury – the crux of the Gascon case was that the grant was a standing threat to the security of England and to the independence of Aquitaine. However close the relationship between the king and his uncle, the passage of time would inevitably erode personal bonds. The duke, and more especially his heirs, would marry into the houses of Anjou, Maine, Brittany, Berry, Foix or Armagnac, establishing new relationships which would be more important than existing ties between England and Aquitaine. The links between them would become strained, then broken, and the duchy would be absorbed into the kingdom of France.[21]

Despite the agreement of an overwhelming majority on the council no decision was taken. On the following day the Gascon delegation was granted safe-conducts to remain in England for as long as they pleased, and the mayor and jurats of Bordeaux were permitted to visit England during the next four years at their pleasure.[22] Evidently a final decision was not to be made for some considerable time. In fact the king did not announce his decision until 6 July 1397, and even then it proved not to be final. But in the meantime a working compromise was patched up. On 14 September Hotspur and Sir Ralph Selby were sent to confer with the Estates, and on 8 November they solemnly published in a full and public court in Bordeaux a whole series of charters and past agreements relating to the special relationship between England and Aquitaine. All the documents which had figured in the dispute between Gaunt and his subjects since 1390 were among them, together with a letter from Henry III dated 8 June 1252 informing the mayor and jurats of Bordeaux that he had granted Aquitaine to his eldest son and his heirs on condition that it was never alienated from the Crown of England, and Bordeaux's own charter annexing it to the Crown. Two days later an identical privilege enjoyed by Bourg was also published.[23]

None of this defined Gaunt's title with any precision. But it did at least give the Gascons some assurance of their ultimate attachment to the English Crown, and so they allowed the whole affair to simmer down, even though Gaunt retained his status as duke of Aquitaine. This tranquillity was threatened in the summer of 1397, when the king announced that he had decided in favour of his uncle and ordered the Gascons to obey him as 'true duke'. But the announcement apparently had no repercussions. It was almost certainly prompted by a domestic crisis in England rather than renewed determination to force the Gascons to submit, and it was not followed up.[24] The entire project was apparently abandoned in the following autumn when John of Gaunt ceased to use his title. His place was taken by his eldest illegitimate son, John Beaufort, marquis of Dorset, who was appointed king's lieutenant in Aquitaine for the next seven years on 2 September 1398.[25]

The success of the Gascon revolt wrecked the secret understanding between England and France. The foundations on which the peace negotiations of the past twenty years had been based were demolished, and when the two sides came together again they began building from scratch. They never looked like succeeding. Within a very short time of the resumption of the peace talks a twenty-eight-year truce was signed, thereby acknowledging just how remote the prospect of a final peace had become. For this the Gascons were largely, if not exclusively, responsible.

NOTES

1 Moranvillé, 'Conférences entre la France et l'Angleterre, 1388–93', *BEC*, l, 380; C 61/103, mm. 2–1; *Anglo-Norman Letters*, no. 150.

2 *Le songe du vieil pèlerin*, i, 294. For the history of Foix and Armagnac in this period see Lehoux, *Jean de Berri*.

3 BN, Collection Doat vol. 194, fos 294–301: for date see appendix 1 (n).

4 *Histoire de Languedoc*, x, 1691–2: for date see appendix 1 (c).

5 The count had been granted Bigorre in 1390 on condition that he return it to Charles VI if it had to be restored to England (Lehoux, *Jean de Berri*, ii, 259, n. 3). The provisional treaty of 1393 stipulated its return.

6 Lewis, 'Decayed and Non-Feudalism in Later Medieval France', *BIHR*, xxxvii, 167, 182.

7 The duke of Berri had most to lose by the Anglo-French proposals but there appears to be no evidence that he sought to upset them (Lehoux, *passim*).

8 E 30/1232. Unless otherwise noted all information and quotations in the remainder of this chapter are taken from this source.

9 *Foedera*, vii, 662, 687–8.

10 Le Patourel, 'The Plantagenet Dominions', *History*, l, 301–2; *Lettres des rois*, i, 415–16; *Gascon Rolls, 1307–17*, nos 1595, 1626, 1637, 1787, 1797; *Foedera*, iv, 552–3; v. 221, 222, 252–3, 260, 263–4, 301, 318 *etc.*; Boutruche, *Crise d'une société*, 203.

11 *Livre des Bouillons*, 293–4.

12 Hotspur succeeded le Scrope in May (E 403/543, mm. 8, 9, 19).

13 *Anglo-Norman Letters*, no. 150 (cf. *Foedera*, vii, 728).

14 C 61/104, m. 10 (cf. E 403/549, m. 11; E 403/551, m. 13). The Gascons claimed they obeyed other ducal officials until 24 May and the constable of Bordeaux until September.

15 *Oeuvres*, xv, 157–9.

16 *Anglo-Norman Letters*, no. 150.

17 The four dukes were kept informed of events in Aquitaine during the peace conference (E 403/548, m. 7).

18 Froissart, *Oeuvres*, xv, 135. Froissart's figure is circumstantially corroborated by the large number of attorneys granted to Gaunt's retinue (C 61/104, mm. 9–1) and by a story told by Walsingham (*Annales Ricardi Secundi*, 159–61).

19 *Livre des Bouillons*, 257–8.

20 *Ibid.*, 244–5; BN, Collection Duchesne vol. 108, fos 17–19 (Mussidan); *Livre des Bouillons*, 259–67 (Estates), 269–72 (Bordeaux); C 61/107, mm. 28–6, 23, 20, 16, 13, 5; C 61/108, mm. 25, 7; c 61/109, mm. 11–9 etc.

21 Baldwin, *The King's Council*, 504–5; Froissart, *Oeuvres*, xv, 157–9.

22 C 61/104, m. 5.

23 E 364/29, mm. 3v, 4; E 30/1234; E 30/324; E 30/295.
24 C 61/104, m. 2; C 61/105, m. 12, both issued immediately after the arrest of Gloucester, Arundel and Warwick.
25 C 61/105, m. 9. It is possible that Beaufort's appointment represents a change of tactics tather than of strategy, since he may well have been designated as his father's heir in Gascony from the first. But there is no way in which this can be tested.

Chapter Ten

Final Settlement
1395–6

When negotiations with France were suspended in the summer of 1394 in order to allow John of Gaunt to bring his rebellious subjects to heel, Richard II himself made use of the interlude to begin the reconquest of Ireland, a project which had occupied his thoughts for several years. Just before Gaunt set sail for Aquitaine his nephew embarked for Ireland, where he enjoyed rather more success than his uncle. He had intended to consolidate his initial gains during the course of 1395; but in April, on the eve of a new campaigning season, he abruptly cashiered his army and hurried back to England. The reason for this precipitate change of plan was the sudden deterioration in the prospects of a stable peace with France.

This deterioration was brought about by two independent but con-current events. The first of these was of course his uncle's failure to win over the Gascons, for the success of their revolt destroyed the very basis of all the progress which had hitherto been made in the peace negotiations. Serious though this was, however, it need not have disturbed relations with France nor have called for prompt action but for the concurrence of a second and more immediately disturbing prob-lem, the crisis precipitated by the king's search for a wife.[1]

His first wife, Anne of Bohemia, had died on 7 June 1394, on the eve of the Irish expedition. Despite his intense grief he did not wait many months before looking for a second wife. He badly needed an heir to strengthen his domestic position and he was politician enough to put reason of state before his personal feelings. By the winter of 1394 – if not earlier – he had made a firm decision, and in March 1395 an embassy was dispatched to Barcelona to ask for the hand of Yolande of Aragon.

The choice of Yolande was largely, if not exclusively dictated by the diplomatic situation in Europe, and more particularly by the need to strengthen the English position *vis-à-vis* France. The end of the war had inevitably led to a resurgence of French power and the task of containing French expansionist tendencies had preoccupied the English government throughout the early 1390s. On the whole it had been successfully accomplished; but by 1394 the very imminence of a final settlement made it increasingly difficult to maintain the requisite diplomatic pressure, and so more necessary than ever to find reliable allies. There were two areas in which they were most needed and could most profitably be sought: in north-west Germany and in Spain. The rapid expansion of Burgundian power in the Low Countries was easily the most alarming change in the balance of power since the beginning of the century, and although it was too late to challenge it, it might still be contained. There were two natural allies for this task, the duke of Guelders and Rupert of Bavaria, count palatine of the Rhine, who was rapidly assuming the part which should by rights have been played by the emperor. England was already allied to Guelders, and Richard opened negotiations for an alliance with Rupert during the summer of 1394. It is possible – even probable – that he proposed a marriage alliance with the Wittlesbachs at the same time.[2] But if so nothing came of it. Within a few months he had turned his attentions to Spain.

In Spain England had a head start in the rivalry for power and influence. The kings of Portugal and Castile were already married to daughters of John of Gaunt, and their father was due to become ruler of an enlarged duchy of Aquitaine which would lie athwart communications between France and the peninsula. In these circumstances a marriage between the king and an Aragonese princess would clinch English predominance and nullify the effects of the Franco-Castilian alliance, a consummation devoutly to be wished in view of the support which France had received from Spain since 1369. It would also bring certain negative advantages in Italy, where French expansionist tendencies were most in evidence. Yolande of Aragon was engaged to Louis II of Anjou, titular king of Naples, who hoped to secure with his fiancée Aragonese support in south Italy. Richard's marriage to Yolande would not only frustrate these ambitions but might conceivably encourage the Aragonese – who had claims on Naples dating from the end of the thirteenth century – to oppose the Angevins. Perhaps Richard was not so sanguine as to count on this; but in any case he could expect his marriage to Yolande to check French expansion in Italy and consolidate English influence in Spain, two very desirable results.

But in laying these plans the king over-reached himself and provoked a vigorous reaction from Paris. The French court might have been prepared to stomach his marriage to Yolande if it had threatened them with no more than the loss of important diplomatic advantages. But it was feared that it would result in the union of the Crowns of England and Aragon. Yolande had no brothers and her only sister had renounced her claim to the throne on her marriage to the count of Foix. She therefore had a plausible claim to succeed her father. It is highly improbable that Richard had designs on the Aragonese throne, and in any case King John intended his brother Martin to succeed him (as happened in 1396). But in view of the recent English claims to the French and Castilian thrones, Charles VI's alarm is understandable. Even if Richard himself could be trusted his successor's attitude could not be guaranteed. Hence the vigour of the French reaction.

When the crisis broke the English ambassadors were travelling overland through France to Spain. They were induced to delay their journey to allow time for Charles to contact Richard in Ireland. A French embassy was then dispatched post-haste to Dublin to offer three of Charles's cousins as alternatives to Yolande. In the meantime diplomatic pressure was put on Aragon to refuse an English alliance, and Charles followed this up with an urgent personal appeal to Richard to abandon his marriage plans in the interest of peace between their two countries. He finally capped these efforts by offering his six-year-old daughter Isabel as Richard's bride.

This was the situation which brought the king hurrying back from Ireland. The Gascon problem had been referred to him at the end of March and the French ambassadors arrived in Dublin early in April: the two crises had merged, threatening to undo the patient labour of half a decade. The situation might still be saved, however, by accepting the French proposals, which would not only resolve the immediate crisis but might also provide an alternative basis for the settlement which the Gascon revolt appeared to have wrecked. This would mean sacrificing the diplomatic advantages which would have gone with the Aragonese marriage of course; but since these had never been more than ancillary to the main objective – a stable peace – it was a sacrifice which had to be borne. But in any case the issues involved were too important to be left to underlings and had to be given precedence over Irish affairs. On 21 April, within a few days of the arrival of the embassy from France (and probably also from Gascony), Richard cashiered his army. By 1 May he was on board ship ready to return to England. No sooner was he back than a whole series of councils were held to discuss the two related problems of the Gascon revolt and the king's marriage.[3]

As we have seen, no immediate decision was made on the Gascon problem, for reasons which will become clear later on. As far as the king's marriage was concerned, however, the crucial decisions had already been taken on 8 July, when formal powers and instructions were issued to the archbishop of Dublin, the bishop of St Davids, the earls of Rutland and Nottingham, Lord Beaumont and Sir William le Scrope. Both documents appear straightforward and have often been analysed.[4] The ambassadors were empowered to contract either an engagement or a marriage with Isabel, to negotiate the size of her dowry and dower and the terms of payment, and to settle a number of comparatively minor matters relating for the most part to her expenses and the date of her delivery to her husband. They were instructed to demand initially two million gold francs (£333,333 6s 8d) for the dowry, a sum which could be progressively reduced until they reached a million, where they were to hold firm. Since this point was to be reached after only four days of bargaining, the king evidently expected no more, and was probably prepared to settle for rather less than a million. If this figure were agreed, he wanted a downpayment of 400,000 francs (£66,666 13s 4d) and the balance in three annual instalments of 200,000 francs. He also required that Isabel be brought to Calais at her father's expense, and that he be given an indemnity of three million francs if she subsequently broke the contract or engagement. For his part he offered to endow Isabel with lands worth £6,666 13s 4d a year, and to take another of her father's close relatives in marriage if she died before she was thirteen. Finally, he instructed his ambassadors to negotiate a second marriage, between Isabel's sister Joan and the earl of Rutland. After asking for a dowry of 220,000 francs, they could settle for 160,000, payable in two equal instalments, in return for an annual income of £1,333 6s 8d for Joan. But if the French showed any reluctance, Rutland's marriage should be dropped before it prejudiced that of the king.

On the same day that they received these powers and instructions, the English ambassadors were authorized to conclude a final peace and issued with a second set of instructions – also dated 8 July – which can only be described as breathtaking:[5] After making the customary protestations (clause 1) they were to demand:

(2) the duchy of Aquitaine as granted to Edward III by the treaty of Calais (October 1360), without homage;

(3) Calais, Mark, Guines and Ponthieu as granted by the same treaty, also without homage;

(4) the king's retention of his present armorial bearings;

(5) the arrears of King John's ransom, plus reparations for the damage done to England since the war began;

(6) the inclusion of Boniface IX in the treaty;

(7) the duchy of Normandy and the counties of Anjou and Maine for the king's eldest son by Isabel 'as entirely and completely as any king of England had ever held them';

(8) Normandy for the eldest son and Anjou and Maine for the second child, if there were more than one;

(9) French assistance for the conquest of Scotland if it were agreed that it belonged to the English Crown and the king decided to give it to another son by Isabel.

Not even Edward III and Henry V had the effrontery to ask for the Angevin Empire, Scotland, and French military support against her ex-ally.

At first sight these demands represent a total break with the policy hitherto pursued by the king. At no previous date is he known to have asked for more than a return to the treaty of Brétigny and a war indemnity. Only two years previously he had been prepared to settle for Aquitaine, shorn of Poitou, Aunis and Saintonge and subject to the sovereignty of the French Crown. What prompted him to raise his terms so drastically in 1395?

In part, the explanation may lie in the circumstances in which the marriage was proposed. Since Charles VI used his daughter as a bait to lure his rival away from a dangerous liaison with Aragon, Richard was able to pitch his terms high – high enough to compensate for the advantages he would lose in Spain and Italy. But though this might account for the apparent extravagance of the demands for a sovereign Aquitaine and recognition of English claims on Scotland, it scarcely explains the inordinate pretensions to Normandy, Anjou, Maine and French military support in the north. Almost certainly these were never meant in earnest. Unlike the others they were not made as of right and as the price of peace, but on behalf of Isabel's children and as the price of her marriage. In effect Normandy, Anjou, Maine, and her father's military assistance in Scotland would constitute her dowry. But Richard also asked for a dowry in money. However sanguine he could not have expected a million francs *and* half the Angevin Empire with his wife, and of the two demands there can scarcely be any doubt as to which was the real and which the bogus one. The very extravagance of the territorial claims shows that they were made to force up the price of a cash settlement. Their unrealistic nature points to the same conclusion. Given Isabel's youth, it would be more than a decade before any of them could be implemented. In practical political terms such an arrangement was simply not on.

If these instructions do not seriously envisage the resurrection of the Angevin Empire, neither is there any reason to believe that they represent a departure from the policy of separating England and Aquitaine. In themselves they are uninformative on this subject, but, the circumstances in which they were drafted indicate that the king still had some hope of implementing his original plan. Despite considerable pressure, he not only refrained from 'defining' his uncle's title but refused to make any concessions to the Gascons. He persisted in this refusal until the negotiations for peace had broken down, and then immediately gave way. His ambassadors returned from France at the beginning of September and – as will be seen – they returned empty-handed: the French rejected Richard's terms completely and demanded a long truce rather than a peace settlement. A few days later, on 14 September, Hotspur and Ralph Selby were sent to Bordeaux to publish the various charters and grants which guaranteed the attachment of the duchy to the English Crown. Though this did not quite amount to an express rejection of the policy of alienating Aquitaine to John of Gaunt, who still retained his title, it was nevertheless the least ambiguous concession which had been made to the Gascons since the entire controversy began. It had evidently been prompted by the failure of the peace negotiations.

In all probability this failure was itself partly due to the Gascon revolt. By jeopardizing the establishment of a Lancastrian dynasty it made the French considerably less willing to contemplate important territorial concessions in Aquitaine. Their reluctance to do so was, however, substantially reinforced by the high price the English were now asking for peace. Even if the pretensions to Normandy, Anjou and Maine were disregarded and the demand for the restoration of the treaty of Brétigny taken simply as a point of departure, the additional claim on Scotland made these terms more exorbitant than any the king had previously offered. The French consequently rejected them in favour of a long truce. When the English ambassadors returned to Paris in October[6] they were empowered to extend the existing truce for a further five years. Since it still had three years to run, its extension until 29 September 1403 was evidently proposed as an alternative to peace, not a necessary condition for it. But even this did not satisfy the French, who demanded an even longer truce. When the English ambassadors returned to France for the third and final time in January 1396, they were armed with powers to conclude a twenty-eight year truce.[7]

The twenty-eight year truce was duly sealed in Paris on 9 March 1396. It was to run from the end of the existing truce and so would last until 29 September 1426. Allies could be included if they so wished. In general its effect was to freeze matters as they stood. No new castles were to be built along the frontiers and no old ones reinforced; *patiz* (ransoms) were to remain in force at their present rate; the territorial position was stabilized. There was one important exception to this general standstill. In some areas *patiz* were so excessive that they were ruining the peasantry. To ameliorate their condition a bipartite commission was established to make inquiries and reduce *patiz* where necessary. Its terms of reference were set out in a separate document[8] which laid down that the two sides were to send their commissioners to Paris by 1 May, whence they would set out for Aquitaine. If their work were not completed by 29 September they were to return to Calais, where the royal uncles would make the final decisions. Other disputed questions were to come before the conservators who were appointed throughout France to ensure that the truce was properly observed and enforced. It was stipulated that it should remain in force for the full twenty-eight years, irrespective of whether the marriage of Richard and Isabel were dissolved or otherwise prevented and irrespective of individual breaches. When these occurred they were to be promptly rectified and were not to constitute, nor to condone war between the two countries. Finally, two omissions deserve notice. No reference was made to sovereignty over Aquitaine or to Richard's title as 'king of France', which presumably meant that he was to continue to enjoy the use of both.

The truce was supplemented by two further agreements, also dated 9 March 1396. By the first of these the English ambassadors promised in their own names to induce their king to nominate different conservators from those appointed to safeguard the previous truce, since they had proved themselves unreliable; and by the second Richard himself swore not to give aid or favour to those allies who did not respect the truce.[9] Charles VI presumably gave a similar undertaking.

A long truce was probably not as advantageous to England as a final settlement, if only because treaty obligations towards Navarre and Brittany made it necessary to return first Cherbourg (1393), then Brest (1397).[10] But the details of the twenty-eight-year truce were with few exceptions favourable. If it is compared with the projected forty year truce of 1376, for example, it will be seen that the provisions relating to *patiz*, and the crucial silence over French sovereignty and the title to the French throne were substantial gains.[11] Though England would rule over a rump Aquitaine, she would at least rule over it absolutely. France gained no comparable advantages, though the inclusion of the king of Scotland can perhaps be seen as an important, if inevitable concession to her. Of all the allies Scotland was the only one on which either king had unresolved claims.

The marriage negotiations were also successfully consummated on 9 March 1396. It is evident from the instructions issued to the English ambassadors for their final trip to Paris in January that by this date only matters of detail remained to be settled.[12] The size and nature of Isabel's dowry and the renunciations required of her – the two principal features of the marriage contract – had already been agreed, and it only remained to settle the terms of payment and the problems which would arise in the event of the premature death of bride or groom. One of these details, however, deserves a close scrutiny since it has attracted a disproportionate amount of attention and has been the source of considerable confusion. In a clause devoted to the terms of the payment of the dowry the ambassadors were instructed to require that the king of France should aid and sustain his son-in-law against his subjects and all 'who should in any way obey him'. This has been seized upon as proof of the king's despotic intentions, and it has even been argued that the entire object of the marriage alliance was to obtain French aid against his domestic opponents.[13] But it has not been observed that Richard placed a price on this French aid, and it was a decidedly low price. The French had offered a dowry of 800,000 francs (£133,333 6s 8d), 200,000 on the wedding day and the balance in annual instalments of 100,000. Richard accepted the first and last of these three offers but objected to the second and put forward three counter-proposals. In order of preference they were:

(1) a deposit of 300,000 francs;

(2) a deposit of 200,000 francs as suggested by the French, but with a further 100,000 made available whenever he should require it;

(3) a deposit of 200,000 francs and aid against his subjects if he needed it.

The third alternative was therefore the least desirable. Moreover, it did not entail financial sacrifices as is usually stated. Whatever method were adopted Richard would still receive 800,000 francs in the end: in the event of his third proposal being preferred, he would simply have to wait an extra year for the final instalment.

The French accepted Richard's first proposal, and in the marriage contract the dowry was fixed at 800,000 francs, 300,000 to be paid on the wedding day and the balance in annual instalments of 100,000. Predictably, Isabel's descendants were denied any right to the succession to the French Crown, though Richard's existing claims were safeguarded and Isabel's slim chance to succeed to the duchy of Bavaria was recognized. If the king died childless before her twelfth birthday, Isabel was to have 500,000 francs of her dowry for her own disposal; if she died childless, the king could retain 400,000. If on the other hand she died leaving daughters, then they were to be adequately endowed, the king retaining the entire 800,000 francs for this purpose. Isabel's dower was fixed at 10,000 marks ($£6,666·66$), and it was specified that she was to continue to enjoy it until her death, even though she might return to France and the two countries be at war. If she refused to consent to her marriage on arriving at her twelfth birthday, then the king could console himself with the whole of her dowry; but if he rejected her when she reached the age of consent, then he was not only to return the dowry but add another 800,000 francs of his own as compensation. In the event of the king's death Isabel was to be be free to return to France with her jewellery and free of all obligations, and the king's relatives were to give written obligations on this point. She was to be escorted as far as Calais at her father's expense, honourably arrayed.

The most important clauses of the contract were devoted to a rejection of the territorial demands made by the English at the outset of the negotiations. It was stipulated that the dowry was given not only for Isabel herself but for her children and their descendants as well, 'for, and in lieu of all allotments, apanages, successions of mother and father, and all other rights whatever that she, her children, their descendants . . . (etc.) . . . could demand'. It was further specified that as soon as she reached her twelfth birthday Isabel was to renounce any claims she or her children might conceivably have to apanages or possessions in France. The king himself was to authorize this renunciation, and the ambassadors gave a personal pledge that he would do so in the most secure manner which could be devised. Isabel's children would have to be content with their share of 800,000 francs and English peerages: Normandy, Anjou and Maine were implicitly denied them.

The summer months of 1396 were taken up with the formal ratifications of the marriage contract and the truce, with preparations for the wedding and a meeting between the two kings at Calais,[14] and with the work of the bipartite commission on *patiz*. All went off reasonably smoothly. Despite later complaints about the regulation of *patiz*,[15] the commission appears to have performed its task adequately. It set out for Aquitaine fairly promptly and was back at Calais by 29 September as stipulated, remaining in session there until early December. Charles VI was positively effusive about part of its work, and none of its failures were sufficiently important to figure in the fairly extensive diplomatic correspondence between the two courts at this period. On the basis of its findings the two kings agreed on 5 November to reduce all *patiz* by 25 per cent and to abolish new impositions altogether until another peace conference could meet in April 1397.

The only other important political business of the summer months was the discussion for a double marriage between Charles VI's two other daughters, Joan (b. 1391) and Michelle (b. 1395), and the earl of Rutland and the future Henry V (b. 1387).[16] Henry's suit was apparently quickly dropped since nothing is heard of it after July, but Rutland's seemed at first to have been assured of success. His marriage to Joan had been proposed at about the same time as that of Richard and Isabel. When the first formal embassy was sent to negotiate these two marriages in July 1395 the king had instructed his ambassadors not to press Rutland's suit if the French appeared unwilling to entertain it. Since it was still under consideration a year later it would appear that Charles had been encouraging. After this date, however, considerable confusion set in and it is difficult to make sense of what followed. Since 1392 Joan had been contracted to the heir to the duchy of Brittany, Peter, Count of Mont-fort (b. 1389). On 19 September 1396 they were married. Despite this, Rutland's suit was not dropped, and when the two kings met at Calais a little over a month later Charles gave his personal assurance that his marriage to Joan would be finalized. Yet only a few weeks later, on 2 December, Joan was once again vowed to the count of Montfort who was solemnly rebaptized, changing his name from Peter to John. As though this were not baffling enough, Charles protested in the following April that he intended to honour the pledge he had given at Calais. Not only did he fail to do so, however, but three months later, on 30 July 1397, Joan was married to John de Montfort for the second time, an irregularity having been discovered in the dispensations for the first marriage. Nothing further is heard of Rutland's suit after this date. Not many months later he found an English heiress for himself.

Whatever the explanation of this startling discrepancy between the words and actions of the French king, its effect was to deprive Richard II of considerable diplomatic advantages. The marriage of Rutland and Joan would have strengthened the ties between the two royal houses but it would also have broken those between France and Brittany, an equally important consideration. They had already been weakened by Richard's own marriage to Isabel, for to marry him she had had to break her engagement to John (b. 1385), heir to the count of Alençon and Perché, who had promptly married Mary (b. 1391), daughter of the duke of Brittany, in July 1396. (Mary herself had been contracted to Henry of Lancaster (b. 1387), who abandoned his suit to make a bid for the hand of Isabel's youngest sister, Michelle of France.) The effect of this marital reshuffle was to strengthen the duke of Brittany. Alençon and Perché was an important border lordship between Normandy and Brittany, and Isabel's marriage to the heir had almost certainly been arranged to control and contain him. As it was, the weapon intended to control him was now placed in his own hands.[17]

Apart from the agreement on Rutland's marriage and the solemnization of Richard's own marriage to Isabel, the meeting between the two royal houses at Calais produced two other acts of political importance. By an act dated 28 October 1396, at Ardres outside Calais, Richard swore to aid his father-in-law against all men, and he promised that neither he nor his relatives would bear arms against Charles VI or his relatives during the lifetime of the twenty-eighty-year truce. If serious disputes arose they were to be settled by consultation between the two royal families. Meanwhile he would work for the rapid conclusion of 'a good, final peace'.[18]

The second of the two acts was rather more important. At the end of a week of banquets and conferences Richard married Isabel on 4 November. On the evening of the following day the final meeting between the two kings and their uncles took place under the walls of Calais, and there the two sides issued a joint *communiqué*.[19] It pledged common action on two problems. In return for the continuation of the peace negotiations, Richard promised his assistance to end the Schism. A peace conference between the royal uncles was arranged for 1 April 1397, and at the same time a joint Anglo-French delegation was to set out for Rome and Avignon to demand the resignation of the two popes and the unanimous election of a third by 29 September (a date subsequently deferred until 2 February 1398). The support of the king of the Romans was to be solicited by both parties. It appears from a later document that the two kings agreed to withdraw their obedience if the popes did not satisfy their demands.[20]

Only part of this programme was put into effect. Both kings wrote to Wenzel, and the joint Anglo-French embassy did proceed to Rome and Avignon to lay their demands before the two popes. But at this point Charles VI began to make difficulties over the peace conference arranged for the spring of 1397. First of all a projected Italian expedition was used as an excuse to postpone it, then Charles pleaded 'other important business' and the absence of the duke of Berry as reasons for further delay. He caused one postponement, made difficulties about a new date, and finally returned an extremely evasive answer to his son-in-law's demand for the immediate convocation of the conference. Not surprisingly, it never met.[21]

In the face of Charles's reluctance to keep *his* promise, Richard became hesitant about his own. After his direct request that the conference be convened immediately had been evaded, he began to put mild but firm diplomatic pressure on the French court. He let it be known that he might have scruples about the use of force against the two popes; he informed French diplomats that he could see no end to the Schism before peace was concluded, a view reiterated by his uncle, John of Gaunt; he delayed publication of the twenty-eight-year truce until the last possible moment; and finally, when asked by Charles in the summer of 1398 to follow his example and withdraw obedience from Boniface IX, he adopted delaying tactics by referring the request to the clergy and the universities, whose views were perfectly well known to him. A few months later he lost his throne, before his final decision had been made known.

Ultimately therefore the Anglo-French plans to end the Schism came to nothing, and for this the French were largely to blame. Just why they had become so reluctant to pursue the peace negotiations must be a matter of surmise. They may have been affected by the uneasy situation in England; they may equally have been affected by domestic rivalries in France; and the combination of internal difficulties in both countries can scarcely have facilitated matters. But in all probability this did no more than exacerbate an already intractable problem. After the summer of 1394 the French lost all enthusiasm for a final settlement. Whenever the subject arose after that date the king and his uncles hedged. First they secured the separation of the peace and marriage negotiations; then the substitution of a long truce for a definitive treaty; then the postponement of a summit conference; and finally the complete cessation of the peace negotiations. The success of the Gascon revolt had made final peace less attractive. A treaty based upon the separation of England and Aquitaine had been highly desirable, as the French ambassadors had made clear when it was first suggested in 1375. Once this possibility had been ruled out, Charles VI and his uncles lost interest in the negotiations and pressed for an interim settlement which would secure good relations with England without sacrificing territory or sovereignty to her. The success of the Gascon revolt doomed the peace negotiations to the failure which quickly overtook them.

NOTES

1 Palmer, 'The Background to Richard II's Marriage to Isabel of France, 1396', *BIHR*, 75–107 and Palmer, 'English Foreign Policy, 1389–99', *The Reign of Richard II*, xliv, 1–17.

2 *Foedera*, vii, 785; Palmer, *BIHR*, xliv, 3n. 2.

3 E 101/402/20 for army; Tout, *Chapters in the Administrative History of Medieval England*, iii, 495 for itinerary; Froissart, *Oeuvres*, xv, 142ff. for councils.

4 *Foedera*, vii, 802–5; analyses in Mirot, 'Isabelle de France, reine d'Angleterre, 1389–1409', *RHD*, xviii, 561ff.; Ramsay, *Genesis of Lancaster*, ii, 305–6; Tout, *Chapters*, iv, 1–2; Calmette and Déprez, *La France et l'Angleterre en conflit*, 260–2.

5 C 76/80, m. 18 (powers); appendix 5 (instructions).

6 Dates of all three marriage embassies in *DC*, no. 223n.

7 C 76/80, m. 18 (powers to conclude 5 and 28 year truce dated 7 October and 30 December respectively); *Foedera*, vii, 812 (French request), 820–32 (text of truce).

8 AN, J 644/16.

9 AN, J 644/18; J 644/17.

10 But the king did receive 25,000 and 120,000 francs respectively for their return – just over £24,000.

11 *Anglo-French Negotiations at Bruges*, 26–43.

12 *Foedera*, vii, 811–13 (instructions), 813–20 (marriage contract).

13 Ramsay, *Genesis of Lancaster*, ii, 305–6; Tout, *Chapters*, iv, 1–3; Steel, *Richard II*, 212–13.

14 Both fully described by Mirot, 'Isabelle de France', *RHD*, xix, 60–95.

15 AN, J 644/23 (Froissart, *Oeuvres*, xvi, 302–5, from copy), instructions to French ambassadors, August 1398. For what follows see E 364/30, mm. 6v–7 (accounts of English envoys); E 403/555, m. 16 (payments to same);

Foedera, vii, 832–3 (safe-conducts to French envoys); AN, J 644/20 (cf. n. 21); Perroy, *L'Angleterre et le grand Schisme*, appendix 13 (cf. n. 19).

16 AN, J 644/21 (= Mirot, 'Isabelle de France', *RHD*, xix, 64–5), undated draft from Charles to Richard *c*. July 1396, for Henry and Michelle; AN, J 644/20 (cf. n. 21); *St Denys*, ii, 442–3; *Mémoires . . . Bretagne*, i, 77; Lehoux, *Jean de Berri*, ii, 358, n. 5; and Viriville, 'Notes sur l'état civil des princes et princesses nés de Charles VI', *BEC*, xix, 477 for Rutland and Joan.

17 Mirot, *RHD*, xviii, 551–4, 560–1 for John of Alençon; *Mémoires . . . Bretagne*, ii, 644–5, 657 for Mary and Henry.

18 AN, J 644/19 (= Froissart, *Oeuvres*, xviii, 582–3).

19 Ehrle, 'Neue Materialien zur Geschichte Peters von Luna', *Archiv für Literatur- und Kirchengeschichte*, vi, 243; Perroy, *L'Angleterre et le grand Schisme*, appendix 13; *St Denys*, i, 470–3. There are interesting differences of detail between these three copies.

20 Perroy, appendix 15.

21 *Foedera*, vii, 850–1 (instructions to English ambassadors, 27 February 1397); AN, J 644/20 (French reply, 14 April); for what follows, Palmer, 'England and the Great Western Schism, 1388–99', *EHR*, lxxxiii, 520–2, and below, 221.

Chapter Eleven

Christendom and the Turk

On 15 May 1395, in a long and ecstatic letter to his rival, Charles VI outlined a programme for their future co-operation:

> Beloved brother, we devoutly pray to God that through His
> Grace He will cause us to meet together in person as soon as this
> can well be arranged. We greatly desire this meeting, for which
> you will always find us ready and willing; and we hope that
> through Him who said to His apostles, 'Peace be with you, I give
> you my peace', we shall meet not in royal pomp but in all
> humility in the love of God, trusting that He will show us grace
> and restrain His chastizing rod, which has long belaboured
> Christianity through the faults of our predecessors.
>
> Then by your holy labours, fair brother, and by our own, the
> enemies of Christianity in all countries will be converted to a true
> peace; and by virtue of this peace between us, descended from
> Heaven and confirmed in our two persons by the Holy Spirit,
> our mother, Holy Church, crushed and divided this long time by
> the accursed Schism, shall be revived in all her glory through the
> prayers of the most gentle Virgin Mary.
>
> Then, fair brother, it will be a fit moment, and one pleasing to
> God, that you and I, for the propitiation of the sins of our
> ancestors, should undertake a crusade to succour our fellow
> Christians and to liberate the Holy Land, first won for us by the
> precious blood of the Lamb who was slain for His flock. And so
> through the power of the Cross we shall spread the Holy
> Catholic Faith throughout all parts of the East, demonstrating the
> gallantry of the chivalry of England and France and of our other
> Christian brothers.

Historians have judged this programme to be so utopian that they have been unable to believe that the letter was written by, or even on behalf of Charles VI, and they have rejected it as a forgery.[1] Not only is the letter certainly authentic, however, but its proposals were neither as visionary nor as improbable as has been thought. In fact, the three-point plan for peace, unity and a crusade had been elaborated over a decade previously, and had already been implemented in part when this letter was penned.

The earliest evidence of this plan appears in the year 1384, on the morrow of the first truce of the period. At this date hopes of peace were high. Not only had a truce been concluded for the first time in seven years, but a draft treaty had been negotiated at the beginning of the year which seemed to offer the prospect of a final settlement. It was in these circumstances that Philip de Mézières produced his first work advocating an Anglo-French peace as the essential precondition for restoring the unity of the Catholic Church and organizing a crusade against the Turk. One-time chancellor of Cyprus, counsellor to Charles V, tutor to Charles VI, and promoter of a new crusading order, de Mézières was not a prophet crying in the wilderness. Throughout his life he had been a man of action first, a writer second; and his written works had always been closely related to immediate political events and designed to influence them. If he thought it worth advocating peace, unity and a crusade in 1384, then the programme was not as visionary as the unfortunate scantiness of our evidence might make it appear. His first essay on the theme of Anglo-French co-operation – the central theme of all his subsequent work – may be taken to mark the birth of an idea which was to haunt the minds of the leaders of England and France until it was all but destroyed on the field of Nicopolis some twelve years later.

It was also in 1384 that the ex-patriate King Leo of Armenia first appeared at the French court. Leo was to play an active role in Anglo-French relations in the following years, a role he used to forward the cause of a crusade in Asia Minor. It may have been pure coincidence that he arrived in France at this juncture – he had spent the two previous years in Aragon – but it is equally, if not more probable that he was drawn there by the prospect of Western aid to recover his recently lost kingdom in the Taurus. The changed atmosphere in Anglo-French relations which had inspired de Mézières had also kindled hope in King Leo.[2]

Finally, it was in 1384 that a significant change occurred in the diplomatic formulae employed by the chanceries of England and France, a change which reflected their mutual interest in the wider possibilities of an Anglo-French peace. Up to this date both sides had announced their desire for peace in meaningless platitudes common to all ages, in phrases which described peace as no more than the cessation of war, an end in itself. Peace, they announced, was sought 'for the honour of God', 'for the reverence of the Church', or 'out of respect for the pope'; and conferences were held 'from compassion for the people'. But in 1384 the idea was introduced that the negotiations were designed not only to regulate relations between the two countries but also to remedy the sorry plight of Christendom. Peace, it was declared, was desired in order to avoid the spilling of Christian blood and to ameliorate the 'very great evils and injuries which have befallen the whole of Christianity' because of the war between the two countries. This remained the official reason for all the negotiations which took place during the following decade. When the formula was varied, it was altered only to make it more specific. By 1395 peace was said to be desirable not only for the good of England and France but for that of 'all Christianity, to the benefit and union of the universal Church and to the confusion of infidels and enemies of the Catholic faith'. In the following year even greater precision was given to this programme when it was announced that an Anglo-French peace would be concluded

> In order that Christendom might be saved from the malice and evil onslaught of the infidels, who are attempting to destroy and annihilate it in various areas; and so that the king (of France), his adversary of England, and the princes of either side would be able to concern themselves with achieving good peace and true union in our Holy Mother Church, which has so long been divided and in Schism.

By this date a crusade and the restoration of Catholic unity had long since been accepted as the ultimate objectives of the Anglo-French peace negotiations, not only in England and France but elsewhere in Europe. The popes sent representatives to the peace conferences of the early 1390s and crusading plans were discussed there. In 1394 the king of Navarre could describe peace between England and France as 'what every man of goodwill should want and desire, as something on which the service of God, the glorification of the Faith, and the well-being, honour and recovery of all Christendom' depended. He was not announcing a new or revolutionary programme, nor indulging in idle moralizing, but simply summarizing the professed aims of the two countries.

To a certain extent these aims were forced upon Richard and Charles by the political situation in Europe. At the end of the fourteenth century Christendom appeared to be in a state of moral and physical collapse. The Schism which rent it in two had already lasted for more than a decade when the truce of Leulingham was sealed in 1389, and it still showed no sign of being healed. With the example of the previous 'great' Schism between the Eastern and Western Churches before them, contemporaries were becoming acutely worried that their division into two camps would prove to be equally permanent. The Schism, moreover, could not have occurred at a worse possible time, for while Europe was rent internally pressure from without was rapidly increasing. The ominous expansion of the Turks in the Balkans shook even the most complacent and parochial rulers in the West. In 1387 Thessalonika had fallen; in 1388 the Bulgarian kingdom had been crushed; and in 1389, on the field of Kossovo, the Christian empire of Serbia was destroyed. The Turk now confronted the Holy Roman Empire, and at his present rate of progress he would soon be in its midst. After Kossovo the Sultan, Bayezid I (1389–1402), boasted that he would soon bring his armies to France, *en route* feeding his horse on the altar of St Peter's, Rome. Confronted by threats backed up by such alarming progress in the Balkans, the Christian rulers of the West were forced to take notice. Henceforth they could no longer contemplate their internal dissensions with equanimity, nor continue to regard a crusade as a visionary concern for the Holy Places which could be indefinitely put to one side. It had become vital for the safety of Christian Europe to end the Schism and organize resistance to the Turk.

At first the challenge produced no response. The two popes devoted their energies to organizing crusades against each other; the king of the Romans was a drunken nonentity who could not even defend his own rights, let alone impose a common programme of action on others; and the Spanish and Italian kingdoms continued to be fully absorbed by their own internal affairs. Only Sigismund of Hungary, impelled by the proximity of the Turkish menace, showed any inclination to do anything about it; but by himself he was not nearly strong enough, and his comparative weakness frightened off potential allies. Venice, whose naval co-operation was indispensable, refused to commit herself until assured of substantial military support from the Western powers;[3] and although the alliance of the Eastern empire was available, it had no more than a moral value. In these circumstances it was inevitable that the eyes of Europe should turn towards England and France as soon as they showed signs of abandoning their fratricidal struggle, and understandable – if not also inevitable – that the two kings should feel morally constrained to attempt to heal the Schism and lead a united Christendom towards the Balkans and the East.

But the policies of Charles VI and Richard II were also affected by more immediate political considerations, for they could expect a number of very practical advantages from their role as defenders of Christendom. Any sort of success would bring immense prestige, no insignificant attraction in itself. On top of this, however, the end of the Schism would ease domestic problems, particularly in France and Flanders, and help cement the peace between England and France, which would otherwise be subject to continual stresses and strains over factional religious differences. A crusade could be expected to have a similar effect, while at the same time providing an ideal opportunity to rid the West of unemployed soldiers and so reconcile the more militant of the kings' subjects to an unaccustomed peace.

The last of these factors would have had a particular appeal to France, torn and ravaged as she was by the companies of 'English'. No sooner was the war at an end than Philip de Mézières was advising his sovereign to rid France of their presence by organizing a crusade.[4] The crusade took too long to materialize, however, and before it had got under way most of the country had been cleared of the 'English' by luring them into Italy or Aragon or by simply buying them off with a fat indemnity. Paradoxically enough, it seems that England benefited more than did France. Although England was never at the mercy of roaming bands of unemployed mercenaries like her neighbour, the north-west of the country was periodically disturbed by the depredations of small bands of desperadoes who were probably composed mainly of discharged soldiers. On one occasion these bands became a serious political menace. In 1393 a rebellion in Cheshire and the neighbouring counties was provoked by rumours of a permanent and dishonourable peace with France and led by a veteran of the wars. According to Walsingham, who appears unusually well-informed on the whole episode, after he had suppressed the rising the duke of Lancaster took the bulk of the rebels into his pay for service in Aquitaine in the following year. This army was not raised simply to overawe the Gascons, however, but to accompany John of Gaunt on the Nicopolis crusade. Although Gaunt himself eventually withdrew from this venture, there is good reason to believe that most of his Cheshire troops marched towards the Balkans under the leadership of his illegitimate son John

Beaufort, and fought and died on the banks of the Danube. In addition to this, it is very likely that Gaunt originally intended to enrol large numbers of his new Gascon subjects in his crusading force as a means of palliating their objections both to his rule in the duchy and the peace with France. In the event the success of their revolt defeated these plans; but the very fact that they were made shows how important – and in a sense how practical – a role the idea of a crusade played in the Anglo-French *rapprochement*.

The enrolment of unruly elements for a crusade not only helped the king by relieving him of his more uncontrollable subjects but also made those who remained at home less ill-disposed towards peace, as Walsingham acutely observed. This was no trifling consideration. Towards the end of the century a visiting foreign ambassador jokingly observed to the king that his subjects hated the French so intensely that they would risk eternal damnation to spite them.[5] The ambassador might be amused, but given his foreign policy this was not a state of affairs the king could contemplate with equanimity, and he did all that he could to moderate the francophobia of his subjects. One obvious method was to encourage fraternization and he employed this extensively. No sooner was the war over than he held a great 'peace tournament' at Smithfield to which foreigners, and especially the French and Scots, were invited,[6] and the Smithfield tournament itself was preceded by a similar event at St Ingelvert, organized by the French, where the English were the main guests, as the location of the tournament (near the Calais march) clearly anticipated they would be. More than a hundred English knights and squires took part with the king's encouragement and approval, and as a result of the encounter a very substantial English contingent joined the duke of Bourbon's crusade against Barbary in North Africa later that summer. In 1391 and subsequent years large numbers of English and French knights crusaded together in Prussia,[7] and in the mid-1390s a joint Anglo-French force was sent to aid Sigismund of Hungary keep the Turks at bay until a larger Western army could be raised. Finally, apart from the great Nicopolis crusade itself, which was planned from the beginning as a joint enterprise, Charles VI and Richard II also projected an Anglo-French expedition to Lombardy in 1397 in order – as Richard informed his parliament – to foster good relations between the two countries.[8]

But if the end of the Schism and a crusade offered certain practical political advantages, these were not, of course, their main attraction or their main impetus. The element of idealism cannot be discounted. The feeling of unity and solidarity within Christendom was still too strong for the Schism to be accepted as a matter of course, and the compulsion of the call to defend eastern Europe against the infidel cannot be explained solely in rational political terms. This idealism expressed itself in a variety of ways. It is apparent for example in some of the correspondence between the two kings – Charles VI's letter quoted above is one such example, and Richard's reply another – but above all it is apparent in the choice of intermediaries between the two courts.

Foremost among these must be placed Philip de Mézières. De Mézières had played an important role in the Near East in the mid-century, his career there culminating in the position of chancellor of Cyprus under Peter of Lusignan (1359–69). After the assassination of his master in 1369 he had returned to the West, looking for assistance against the growing Turkish menace; but his efforts met with negligible success, and in 1373 he entered the service of Charles V of France, becoming one of his close counsellors and – what was more important – tutor to the future Charles VI. On Charles's accession in 1380 Philip retired to the convent of the Celestines in Paris, remaining there until he died in 1405. But he did not retire from political life when he donned the habit of the Celestines.[9]

During the middle years of his life, and in particular after the failure of the crusade of 1365 against Alexandria, he had taken up the pen in an effort to arouse more widespread support for a crusade. In 1366 he had written a life of Peter de Thomas, a Carmelite whose enthusiasm for the crusading ideal had done much to form his own outlook. A year later he produced the first redaction of his *Nova Religio Passionis Jhesu Christi*, a plan for a new crusading order which he was to cherish and continually re-edit later in life. Finally, at about the same time, he wrote a brief eulogy of Peter de Lusignan. After this burst of activity, however, he produced no further crusading propaganda for over fifteen years. He presumably laid down his pen because he found it ineffective: political circumstances in the West did not favour his plans after the renewal of the war between England and France in 1369.

This long silence was suddenly broken in the mid-1380s with the rapid succession of three new works: the *Pèlerinage du pauvre pèlerin*, the *Petit pèlerinage du pauvre pèlerin* (neither extant), and the second redaction of the *Nova Religio Passionis* (1384). After another interval the *Songe du vieil pèlerin* appeared towards the end of 1389, shortly followed by the *Oratio tragedica* (1389–90). After a further five years the *Epistre au roi Richart II* was completed in the spring of 1395 and was immediately followed by the third redaction of the *Nova Religio Passionis*. De Mézières' last work, the *Epistre lamentable*, was elicited by the disastrous outcome of the Nicopolis crusade and followed hard on its heels (1397). With it, he laid his pen finally to rest, worn out perhaps by his labours and almost certainly disillusioned by their lack of results.

This bulky corpus of works produced in retirement has two features which have an important bearing on Anglo-French relations during the same period. The first of these is the remarkable correspondence between the dates of de Mézières' tracts and the ups-and-downs – particularly the ups – of Anglo-French relations. His first burst of activity came immediately after the conclusion of the first truce of the period (1384) and was terminated by the resumption of war. The ensuing silence lasted exactly as long as the war itself, and the truce of Leulingham (1389) produced his two major works, the one following the other in rapid succession. The tangled period of negotiations between 1390 and 1394 was matched by another literary interlude, before the crisis year of 1395 stimulated him to take up his pen once again. Finally, the Nicopolis disaster, and the destruction of all the hopes he had built on an Anglo-French *rapprochement*, elicited one last pamphlet, which was followed by eight years of total silence.

When de Mézières' ideas are examined, this coincidence becomes less surprising. Throughout all these works there run one or two common threads, and the strongest of these is his insistence that peace and co-operation between England and France must be the essential condition of any attempt to heal the Schism and succour the East. De Mézières argued that no attempt could be made to ameliorate the distressing situation within Christendom while England and France were at war, and that the first priority must therefore be to bring about peace and understanding between the two foremost Christian nations. Until this was accomplished all efforts to reunite the Church and to expel the Turk were doomed to failure. Given these views, it is scarcely surprising that the production of his works was closely geared to the ups-and-downs of Anglo-French relations. Though he was an idealist, de Mézières had also been a man of affairs and was hard-headed in his idealism. He pressed his plans only when political developments made them feasible.

When he retired to the Celestines Philip did not retire from public life. He continued to advise his pupil, Charles VI, and to impress his ideas on the young king, who became an ardent advocate of his tutor's views.[10] According to Froissart, Charles declared at the beginning of the decade that he thought of nothing else, night or day, but a crusade; and his recorded actions prove beyond any doubt his intense concern for unity in the Church and peace with his neighbour. His outlook became so conditioned by that of his mentor that in a moment of crisis with England in 1395 he could commission de Mézières to write on his behalf the famous *Epistre au roi Richart II*, a plea for peace as a prelude to ending the Schism and organizing a crusade. Because of his influence on Charles, de Mézières can properly be described as one of the main intermediaries between England and France at this period. His ideas became the common property of both sides; his crusading order attracted the patronage or membership of the highest nobility of each country; and his disciples were extensively employed in relations between them. More than any other person, Philip de Mézières was responsible for the pervasive idealism behind the desire for peace.

The activities of his four evangelists – he chose the term with deliberation – illustrate the force of this idealism and the place it occupied in relations between the two courts. John de Blaisy, Robert le Mennot (better known as Robert the Hermit), Louis de Giac and Otto de Granson were enrolled by their master in 1385, during the first truce of our period and immediately after he had completed the second redaction of his *Nova Religio Passionis*. They did their recruiting for this order between 1390 and 1395, the years of peace. Louis de Giac, chamberlain to the king and the duke of Burgundy, has unfortunately left little trace of his work, though it is known that he accompanied Boucicaut to Jerusalem just before the end of the war; but his three fellow evangelists all played an important role in Anglo-French relations. Otto de Granson was both *chevalier d'honneur* to Richard II and John of Gaunt and *persona grata* at the Burgundian court. He accompanied the earl of Derby on his expedition to the Holy Land in 1393 and he fought before the duke of Burgundy under the patronage of Richard II. He was clearly an important, if informal intermediary between the two courts. John de Blaisy was employed more formally, on matters which required a very special tact and delicacy. He supervised the evacuation of the 'English' *routiers* from the southern provinces of France in the years following the truce of Leulingham, and he was given the thankless task of arranging Scotland's inclusion in the truce in a way which would soothe English feelings. But the most remarkable member of this group is undoubtedly Robert the Hermit, whose name reveals the unconventional nature of his qualifications as a diplomat. Robert appears to have returned from the East at the beginning of the 1390s to preach a crusade. Such was the atmosphere in Paris and London at this date that he immediately gravitated to the French court, where his ardour for the crusade was judged to qualify him as an envoy between the two kings. His services as an ambassador were called upon in the ensuing years when relations between the two courts had become badly strained, or when they had joint business of the highest importance to transact – at moments, in fact, when both sides needed to be reminded of the great issues that hung upon their peace and co-operation. He was first employed by Charles VI immediately after the Breton crisis of August 1392, when he was dispatched in great haste to England to avert the possibility of war and put the peace negotiations back on a firm footing. Three years later he was similarly employed when Richard II's marriage plans precipitated another crisis. On this occasion he was again sent to England in a hurry, this time to urge Richard to abandon his ambitions, to persuade him to accept a French wife, and to remind him that the crusade and the unity of the Catholic Church depended upon the continued co-operation of England and France. Finally, just over a year later both kings entrusted him with a joint mission to Rome and Avignon to prepare the two popes for the formal Anglo-French embassies which were to follow some six months later demanding their resignation. The Hermit's career in the 1390s in fact illustrates to perfection the close interdependence of the three great issues of peace, unity and a crusade, and the extent to which all three preoccupied Charles VI and his rival. When Philip de Mézières described the Hermit as 'the special messenger of God and St James to the kings of England and France to conclude peace, end the Schism, and arrange a crusade', he was stating no more than the bare truth.[11]

Apart from any beneficial influence they may have had on the general atmosphere of Anglo-French relations, Philip and his four evangelists did much to spread enthusiasm for his visionary programme among the politically prominent members of the nobility on either side of the Channel. Some idea of their success may be obtained from the list of those who pledged their support to his crusading order.[12] Between 1390 and 1395 over eighty knights, lords and peers either enrolled themselves in the order or promised to give it their patronage. A mere handful of these came from Scotland, Italy, Germany or Spain, by far the greater number being English and French, who enlisted in roughly equal proportions. They included the most powerful and influential figures from each country: the dukes of Berry, Bourbon and Orleans, the admiral, the constable and the renowned Boucicaut from France; and the dukes of Lancaster, Gloucester and York, and the earls of Huntingdon, Rutland, Nottingham and Northumberland from England. In effect, if not in intention, Philip's order was to have been an Anglo-French one. Its membership may be taken as an index of the crusading enthusiasm which existed on both sides of the Channel, and of the degree to which England and France had – jointly – taken upon themselves the task of unifying Christendom and defending it against the Turk.

Though he was not formally one of them, King Leo of Armenia deserves to be considered alongside Philip's four evangelists, since he played a similar role to their own in Anglo-French relations at this time. He arrived in Paris in 1384, perhaps attracted by the truce of that year and the hopes it inspired of a crusade. In the following decade these hopes never became sufficiently dim to drive him elsewhere in search of assistance to recover his kingdom, and during that period he took an important part in the peace negotiations between England and France, particularly in the critical years 1385 to 1387. He naturally used his position to forward the idea of a crusade, and he was presumably employed for this very reason. Though he took no further part in the formal negotiations after the truce of Leulingham, he maintained informal contacts with the English court until his death, and twice – at the peace conferences of 1392 and 1393 – appealed to the assembled ambassadors of the two countries to lead a crusade in the near future. In between these appeals he paid a last visit to the Balkans and the East, a visit which may well have been undertaken to prepare the way for the crusade he had solicited and been promised. Long before this finally matured, however, Leo himself was dead. He died in Paris on 29 November 1393. His obsequies symbolized exactly what he had lived and worked for over the past decade: his executor was Richard II, he was buried by Charles VI, and he was laid to rest in de Mézières' convent of the Celestines.[13]

The career of King Leo, the influence of Philip, and the employment of Robert the Hermit and his fellow evangelists as diplomats in preference to more conventionally trained chancery clerks, all illustrate the element of idealism which affected the policies of the two governments in the decade or so after 1384. Though its precise effects cannot be measured, it is clear that the vision of reunited Christendom led by England and France against the encroaching Turk was one which excited the imagination of both sides, contributing to their desire to end the war and to put peace on a more stable basis. Sustained by this vision, Charles VI and Richard II more than once came within grasp of peace, and each time they did so they attempted to translate their ideals into a programme of practical action.

Initially there were several false starts, failures intimately related to the ups-and-downs of the peace negotiations. The truce of 1384 was too shortlived, and its unresolved problems too serious to permit immediate action in the mid-1380s. There was, however, one hopeful pointer to the future in a clause in the truce forbidding either side to harm the other on the pretext of the Schism in the Church. In subsequent truces this prohibition was extended to cover the allies of each side, thus guaranteeing them against 'crusades' such as those led by Bishop Despenser and John of Gaunt.[14] But for the moment this was the sole achievement. With the resumption of war in 1385 the question of the Schism and a crusade were pushed into the background. After a short burst of activity, Philip de Mézières lapsed again into silence for several years; and although King Leo tried to stir up enthusiasm for a crusade during his embassy to England in the winter of 1385–6, nothing practical came of his efforts.

The truce of 1389 was more productive. Not only was it longer-lived, but it promised to be so from the very beginning. Even before it was concluded, in fact, John of Gaunt had taken the first tentative steps towards realizing part of the programme mapped out by Philip de Mézières. At the end of 1388, when he had reached his agreement with Castile and arranged a truce in southern France, Gaunt was anxious to do all that he could to limit or terminate the war between England and France in order to safeguard his gains from the treaty of Bayonne. With this in view, he secured the support of Castile and Navarre for the convocation of a general council in Bayonne in the spring of 1389 to discuss the related questions of a general peace and the means of ending the Schism. Invitations were issued to Clement VII and to England, Navarre and Aragon, and the first three of these notified their acceptance. It is not known whether France was invited; but in any case, the allegiance of those who did receive invitations shows that even at this early date Gaunt envisaged some sort of compromise solution to the Schism. He would scarcely have invited Clement VII, King John of Castile and Charles III of Navarre if he intended to propose universal acceptance of Urban VI as the best means of reunifying the Church.[15]

In the event the conference of Bayonne did not meet. The setback was not particularly serious, however, as the conference had been made redundant by the initiation of direct negotiations between England and France at Leulingham at the very end of 1388. When these had been successfully consummated in the truce of 1389, the stage appeared to be set for a concerted attempt to heal the Schism; but before any action could be taken, events were precipitated by the death of Urban VI in October.

On receiving this news, the English council showed that it was favourable to a compromise solution to the Schism by agreeing not to recognize the new Roman pope until parliament had had the opportunity to review the entire situation. Before parliament could meet, however, further news from Italy and Flanders effectively killed any chance that it would advocate a moderate course of action; for in both areas the French had initiated aggressive moves on behalf of Clement VII.

Unlike England, France had a direct political stake in the continuance of the Schism, and was therefore slower to modify her policies to suit the new conditions of peace. In return for French support, Clement VII had arranged for the succession of Louis I of Anjou to the kingdom of Naples; and in return for their continued support the French were shortly to demand the bulk of the States of the Church for the king's brother, Louis of Touraine. Charles VI's advisers may even have aspired to the Imperial Crown for their master as the price of leading Clement VII to Rome. These were tempting political prizes, and the end of the war with England released resources which appeared to put them within reach. Within a few months of the conclusion of the truce of Leulingham, and at the very moment of Urban VI's death, Charles VI was at Avignon, concerting plans with Clement for an Angevin invasion of Naples, and possibly also for a Franco-Milanese invasion of north and central Italy on behalf of the pope and Louis of Touraine.

News of the interview at Avignon would have reached Westminster at about the same time that equally disturbing information arrived from Flanders. Seizing the opportunity afforded by Urban's death, Philip of Burgundy tried to seduce his subjects into the Clementist camp. He summoned the three Estates to Oudenaarde in January 1390 to reconsider their allegiance; and although his chancellor promised the assembly that no constraint would be used to coerce men's consciences, the episode was none the less disquieting from an English and Urbanist viewpoint, particularly in view of Philip's confident assertion that the Flemish nobility was prepared to abandon Urban at his behest.

With both Italy and Flanders under increased French and Clementist pressure, the English council was forced to abandon its conciliatory attitude. Any other course might have precipitated mass desertions from the Roman camp, leaving Clement VII the victor by default and Italy open to French aggression. Before the end of March 1390, therefore, England had recognized Boniface IX, and in the middle of the following month Richard II assured the city of Ghent of his support in the event of Charles VI or Philip of Burgundy trying to impose Clement VII on Flanders.[16]

England's recognition of Boniface IX did not immediately deter the French from their designs on Italy. On the contrary, disappointment at the decision seems to have acted as a spur, and throughout 1390 they pursued their plans for an invasion in force. In July Louis II of Anjou sailed for Naples, and by the end of the year diplomatic preparations for an attack on north and central Italy were virtually complete. Alliances with the Empire, Scotland and Castile were renewed, and in January 1391 Philip of Burgundy and Louis of Touraine set out for Milan to conclude an offensive alliance with the duke. In the following month the French army was ordered to concentrate at Lyons in the middle of March, and Clement VII himself began preparations to accompany Charles VI to Rome, the declared objective of the expedition.

At this point the English government intervened. Charles was informed that an invasion of Italy would constitute a *casus belli*, and that if he invaded Italy he would be invaded by England. This was no idle threat. Throughout the second half of 1390 the government had been busy building up a string of alliances to neutralize those of France, and in the new year parliament voted a subsidy to renew the war if it proved necessary. Convinced that Richard meant business, Charles climbed down. On 24 February 1391 he agreed to a personal interview with his rival in June. By choosing peace with England, he implicitly renounced armed support for Clement VII. Never again did he endorse the *voie de fait* – the termination of the Schism by military means. Though his brother Louis continued to hope for a kingdom in Italy carved from the States of the Church, Charles expressly dissociated himself from the execution of the project. Even Louis did not seem too sanguine about his prospects after 1391, and at the beginning of 1394 he asked Clement to allow him to defer his intervention in Italy for a further four years – a lifetime in the time-scale of international politics.[17]

Having abandoned the *voie de fait* Charles adopted the more conciliatory English attitude. By the time of the Amiens conference in the spring of 1392, Boniface IX could think it worth his while to invite French intervention to heal the Schism, hinting that he would be prepared to accept a conciliar solution himself. His emissaries, two saintly Carthusian monks (one of each obedience), were warmly received at the French court, and a rumour that they had been ill-treated on their way there by Clement VII provoked considerable antagonism towards the 'French' pope. This was by no means an isolated incident. At the very beginning of the next year, Charles VI himself headed a public procession to intercede for unity in the Church, and in the ensuing months similar processions were held in different parts of France. Clement VII became so alarmed for his position that he engaged public disputants to argue his case, and that of the *voie de fait*, before the university of Paris, but to no avail. This volte-face in French policy was arguably the most important single development in international relations in the 1390s. It was the essential condition for all the subsequent attempts to heal the Schism by the concerted action of England and France and other powers.

Precisely when and how the two kings first agreed on a common policy it is unfortunately impossible to determine; but the broad outlines of an agreement would seem to have been reached by the beginning of 1392. According to an eyewitness, the duke of Lancaster told a Clementist legate at the Amiens conference in the spring of that year that[18]

> When there is peace between England and France, then we shall have one pope, not before. The Roman pope was not the true pope, but then neither was Clement properly elected. Both would have to resign in favour of a third candidate. The king of England would never agree that Clement remain pope and Boniface be condemned . . . Because of the alignment of kings and kingdoms it was necessary that both elections be annulled.

It is difficult to believe that he could have made such a pronouncement without some sort of prior understanding with France. Even if the details had yet to be discussed, the two sides had evidently formulated a common policy to the extent of agreeing that peace must take precedence over the solution of the Schism, and that that solution must take the form of a compromise based on the resignation of both existing popes.

Given that precedence was accorded to the conclusion of peace, it is not surprising that little more is heard of the Schism during the two years which followed the Amiens conference. Nevertheless, the silence is not absolute, and it is clear that the Schism was discussed during the peace negotiations of 1393 and 1394. Clementist legates attended the all-important summit conference which produced the provisional treaty of June 1393; and the French historiographer-royal tells us that he too was present 'for the affairs of the Church', which suggests that there were formal discussions of some sort. The same writer also ascribed to the duke of Lancaster a tirade against the Clementist legates substantially similar to that attributed to him by Honoré Bonet in the previous year. He is reported to have told the Cardinal de Luna – the future Benedict XIII – that 'once peace is concluded you will be forced to put an end to the Schism or be exterminated.' In 1394 Gaunt reiterated these views once again, and he was to continue to do so in later years.

Up to this point the peace negotiations had made insufficient progress to allow any positive action to be taken to terminate the Schism. As we have seen, however, the negotiations came within reach of success during the summer of 1393, when only the sudden illness of Charles VI prevented a settlement. With his recovery at the end of the year the last obstacle to peace appeared to have been removed, and it became possible to make more definite plans for the future. (As will be seen, it was at precisely this time that the first practical preparations for a crusade were put in hand.) In January 1394 Charles VI made a pilgrimage to Mont St Michel to give thanks for his recovery, and while there he commissioned the doctors of the university of Paris to explore all possible ways and means of ending the Schism and to report back to him as soon as they had completed their investigations. This commission caused widespread astonishment, both at the university and at the French court. For years – indeed, since the very beginning of the Schism – the university had been importuning the king and his entourage to do something to bring about the reunification of the Church, without any success whatsoever. Unaware of the imminence of peace with England, and of all that this would entail, observers could not understand the sudden and apparently inexplicable volte-face of the French king.

Even less could they understand his second about-turn, which followed hard on the heels of the first. Throughout the first half of 1394 the doctors of the university pursued their work, though complaining of obstruction, rebuffs and positive hostility on the part of the royal council. When they had completed their investigations early in June,

they had considerable trouble in securing the right to present their conclusions to the king; and even when audience was eventually granted,
it was a secret session from which all but the king's uncles were excluded. To complete their discomfiture and crown their indignation,
the doctors were then ordered to keep both the proceedings and their
conclusions to themselves. All this was in such painful contrast to the
public encouragement they had received at the beginning of the year
that the doctors were as bemused as they were distressed, and their
chronicler was compelled to cast around for scape-goats. The number
he found testifies to his own bewilderment.[19]

Charles's second volte-face was almost certainly causally related to
his first. When he had set up the commission in January the success of
the negotiations with England had appeared assured; by July, when he
received the commission's report, they had been postponed indefinitely because of the Gascon revolt. It thereupon became imperative
to call a halt to the preparations to end the Schism. For the moment, and
possibly for some years to come, the work of the commission of inquiry
could not be followed up, and public discussion of ways and means of
procuring the abdication of Clement VII would antagonize him without
serving any useful purpose. Hence the silence imposed on the university.

The situation was transformed for a third and final time by the death
of Clement VII in September. The opportunity appeared to be too good
to be allowed to pass, and the French court hastily intervened, first in
an attempt to prevent the election of a new pope, then to secure the
promise of Benedict XIII to resign when he was called upon to do so.
Neither of these actions is comprehensible except on the hypothesis
that Charles VI had already reached some sort of informal agreement
with England. He would never have weakened his diplomatic position
in this way without some assurance that his rival would make similar
demands upon Boniface IX when it was opportune to do so. Even with
English support, Charles subsequently got himself into an extremely
unenviable position in his relations with Avignon, and his precipitate
action in the autumn of 1394, though undertaken from the highest
possible motives, was to have a baneful influence on all the later
efforts to reunify the Church. Virtually at war with Benedict XIII from
the beginning of his pontificate, Charles became over-anxious for a
settlement within the Church; and since England remained committed
to her original programme of peace first, unity later, the two sides
were often at cross-purposes during the later 1390s, a situation which

did nothing to help solve an already complex and intractable problem.

At first these difficulties were not apparent. When the new pope refused to bow to his demands, rejecting an ultimatum presented to him in the spring of 1395 by the dukes of Burgundy and Orleans in person, Charles could turn to his neighbour with some confidence. Formal discussions for the precise formulation of a joint policy towards the two popes proceeded *pari passu* with the truce and marriage negotiations throughout 1395 and 1396, culminating in the agreement of 5 November 1396 to demand the simultaneous resignation of both popes and the election of a third – the solution outlined by the duke of Lancaster in 1392 at the Amiens peace conference. The two kings sent Robert the Hermit to Rome and Avignon to inform the popes of their decision and to announce the arrival of a formal joint embassy in the following spring or summer; and both sought to enlist the support of the king of the Romans. They agreed that if Boniface or Benedict refused to comply with their demands, they would compel them to do so, possibly by withdrawing their obedience;[20] and they also agreed to lead a joint Anglo-French expedition to Italy in the following summer to prepare the way for the unanimous election of a new pope. As we have seen, the first part of this policy was carried out without a hitch; and until at least the summer of 1398 Anglo-French policy towards the Church was a triumph of moderation and co-operation, promising an early end to the Schism which had bedevilled the religious and political life of Europe in the previous two decades.

Plans for a crusade evolved *pari passu* with those to deal with the Schism, and like them were intimately related to the progress of the peace negotiations. Though there was plenty of crusading activity after 1389, it was not until 1392, and more especially from 1393 that there is any clear evidence that an expedition was to be sponsored by the two governments. From that date, however, signs that a joint crusade were under consideration become more and more numerous, culminating in the definite formulation in 1394 of plans for an Anglo-French attack on the Turkish empire in the Balkans in 1395 – the blueprint for the Nicopolis crusade.

So far as is known, the considerable crusading activity of the early 1390s was privately inspired and unrelated – except in the most general way – to the policies of the two governments. The duke of Bourbon's Barbary crusade of 1390 was the largest, if not the most successful of this period; the earl of Derby's Prussian expeditions of 1390 and 1392 the best documented.[21] English contingents participated in the Barbary expedition, and Derby, who had originally intended to accompany Bourbon, was joined by French knights in Prussia. Further substantial English and Burgundian contingents arrived in Prussia in 1391, and only atrocious weather prevented the English effort from being capped by an imposing expedition under the duke of Gloucester. Traffic to Jerusalem was equally heavy at this time, though unfortunately it is not equally well documented. Froissart records casually the passage of a group of French knights just before the end of the war; the chronicler of St Denys mentions incidentally the return of another group at the end of 1391; a lucky manuscript survival has preserved a vivid account of the pilgrimage of Sir Thomas Swinburne in 1392; and the unfortunate or heroic deaths of John, Lord Roos, Sir John Clanvow and Thomas, Lord Clifford moved contemporaries to record for posterity journeys to Palestine which would otherwise have been too common-place to merit their attention. The invaluable Lancastrian accounts add the names of the earl of Derby and his retinue – among whom was Otto de Granson, one of Philip de Mézières' four evangelists – and of one or two others they met on their way to and from Jerusalem in 1393; and an odd reference in the Burgundian accounts supplies the names of two more pilgrims who made the journey to Mount Sinai and the Holy Land. Finally, Charles VI himself sent costly furnishings to the Holy Sepulchre in Jerusalem in the spring of 1393.

Research may yet establish a relationship between some of these pilgrimages and expeditions – which may well have been exploratory missions for the rulers who financed many of them – and the policies of the two governments; but at present the earliest direct evidence of their plans for a joint crusade appears to date from the period of the Amiens conference, the first of the summit meetings of the1390s. According to the French historiographer-royal, this conference was in fact arranged in order to facilitate a crusade. He relates that Charles VI was so moved by the plight of the Holy Land as described to him by a group of knights returning from the East at the end of 1391 that he immediately dispatched an embassy to Richard II to seek peace. Richard was amenable, and the Amiens meeting was duly convened. This is, of course, a gross over-simplification which omits many of the factors which contributed to the decision to hold this conference. But it may nevertheless contain an essential grain of truth. Froissart recounts that at Amiens Charles VI urged on the duke of Lancaster the necessity of peace so that their two countries could co-operate in a crusade against the Turks, and according to the same writer John of Gaunt responded favourably. Official sources tend to corroborate both chroniclers. On 23 December 1391, immediately after the Amiens conference had been arranged, Philip the Bold sent one of his advisers, Guy de la Trémouille, to Venice and Hungary on business which he held 'very close to our heart', business which can surely only have concerned a crusade. In the following February, on the eve of the conference, Charles VI negotiated a draft treaty with Genoa, one of the clauses of which stipulated that the Republic should provide naval aid in the event of a French army being sent against the infidel. Three months later, immediately after the conference, Richard II confided to Antonio Adorno, Doge of Genoa, that he too was contemplating a crusade when the moment was ripe. All three rulers may of course have been independently inspired; but it seems more likely that their plans had been laid jointly and were contingent upon the successful outcome of the peace negotiations.[22]

The Breton crisis and the madness of the French king during the summer of 1392 produced a momentary break in the negotiations and a temporary setback to the prospects of a crusade; but by the new year amicable relations had been restored and preparations and discussions resumed. Early in the year King Leo returned from his visit to the Balkans, and the earl of Derby capped his tour of the eastern marches of Europe with a visit to Jerusalem. At some time during the year – the precise date cannot be pinpointed – a small Anglo-French force was sent to aid Sigismund of Hungary against the Turks. It was against this background that the conference of 1393 met. At the conference Leo made another appeal for a crusade, and according to Froissart, who was in the vicinity, his appeal was well received and graciously answered by the dukes of Lancaster and Gloucester, who had been instructed by Richard II to conclude the negotiations as swiftly as possible so that something could be done about the growing Turkish menace. On 27 May, just before he was stricken down by a recurrence of his insanity, Charles VI authorized the dispatch of chapel furnishings to the Holy Sepulchre in Jerusalem, symbolizing his intention of leading a crusade there. Finally, a few weeks later Derby reached France on his return from the Holy Land and hastened towards Leulingham, where the negotiations were taking place. He arrived just too late for the conference itself, but spent four days at the French court at Amiens, where he no doubt passed on the information he had acquired about conditions in the East. By this stage rumours of a major Anglo-French expedition appeared to be so well founded that the Turkish sultan, Bayezid, retired to the heart of his empire to collect an army large enough to repel the Christian forces. His preparations proved unnecessary, however. The illness of the French king threw everything into disarray.

During the six months of Charles's incapacity nothing further was done; but as soon as he had recovered preparations were resumed. It may be remarked that from this point – which was also the point at which the first definite steps were taken to end the Schism – the plans and projects of the previous two years were translated into practical action. Charles recovered his sanity at the very end of 1393. In January 1394 John Holand, earl of Huntingdon – the king's half-brother and John of Gaunt's son-in-law – was accredited to the Hungarian court. He may possibly have been instructed to negotiate with Venice on his way to Hungary, since he travelled there via Savoy, rather a roundabout route. Early in the following month Sir John Golofre, one of the king's most trusted chamber knights, was similarly accredited to the Polish court. Both ambassadors were expected to remain abroad for some considerable time, and both were in fact absent for the better part of a year. At roughly the same time Sir John Beaufort, Gaunt's illegitimate son, was in Prussia; and although it is not known for certain whether he was there in a private or official capacity, the fact that he was subsequently to command the English crusading force suggests that he was exploring the ground on behalf of his father, who was at this time designated leader of the English army.

The English embassies were accompanied by the joint ambassadors of Philip the Bold and Louis, duke of Orleans.[23] On 10 January 1394 Rénier Pot was sent 'hastily' to Hungary, either accompanied or shortly followed by his half-brother, William de la Trémoille, marshal of Burgundy. At about the same time another of William's brothers, Pierre, was sent to Prussia. All three ambassadors were away until the end of the year, and when they returned, they returned together in the company of the English envoys. It is clear from all this that the English, Burgundian and Orleanist embassies worked together for a common objective, an objective precisely defined by Philip the Bold himself in a letter written to his cousin, William of Namur, some five months later.[24] In this, Philip asked his cousin for an *aide* to finance a crusade which was to be lead jointly by himself, John of Gaunt and Louis of Orleans to Prussia or Hungary early in 1395. The triple embassy had evidently been entrusted with the preliminary planning of this crusade.

Practical preparations were put in hand long before the English and French ambassadors had returned. On 30 May 1394, the day after the dissolution of the final summit conference, Philip made his way to St Omer where he convoked the Estates of Flanders to grant him an *aide* to finance a crusade to Hungary. During the remainder of the summer he, his wife and their eldest son John de Nevers, were to devote a considerable amount of time and energy to financial negotiations with the Burgundian territories, negotiations which eventually produced extraordinary taxes totalling 220,000 francs (*c.* £37,000). By the early autumn the negotiations were complete and the task of collecting the taxes had begun.[25]

It is unfortunately not known how Louis of Orleans and John of Gaunt proposed to finance their share of the crusade. It is probably no coincidence, however, that on 15 May 1394 – a fortnight before Philip summoned the Estates of Flanders to grant him an *aide* for Hungary – the duke of Orleans was granted by his brother, Charles VI, the royal *aides* from his lands for the period of one year from the previous 1 February. As soon as this grant expired, the *taille* and *gabelle* of his lands were conferred on Orleans for a further year, to run from 1 February 1395. It looks as if Charles intended to defray much of the cost of his brother's crusade, and it is probable that John of Gaunt expected somewhat similar assistance from Richard II. He enjoyed £4,000 a year for the 'defence' of Aquitaine, and in August 1394 he was given a bonus of £6,000 towards the cost of the army he took to Gascony that autumn. On top of this he received substantial sums for his part in the peace negotiations. Altogether, the exchequer disbursed almost £10,000 to him in the year from 26 February 1394 to 1 March 1395. In the financial year beginning on 2 February 1394, his receiver-general recorded an income of approximately £17,000, no less than £7,300 of which came from the royal exchequer. Of the balance almost exactly two-thirds – £6,550 – came from the annuity paid to the duke under the treaty of Bayonne, a reminder of the immense personal fortune he had amassed in 1388. He can scarcely have spent much of the £100,000 he had received on that occasion. In short, there is no reason to suppose that Gaunt had any serious difficulty in financing his share of the crusade. He was the first of the three leaders to collect an army. Before the end of 1394 he had recruited some 1,500 men-at-arms in England, and in the autumn he set sail for Aquitaine, where he intended to raise the remainder of his troops once his quarrel with the Gascons had been appeased.[26]

From the beginning of these preparations more emphasis was laid on the possibility of a crusade in the Balkans than in Prussia, and any remaining doubts as to its destination were resolved by the discouraging tenor of the Prussian reply to the embassy of Pierre de la Trémoille. The Grand Master of the Teutonic Knights informed Philip that the difficulties of the terrain, combined with the effects of recent heavy floods, made it impossible for him to give a firm assurance to co-operate in a crusade in the coming year. In existing conditions only God himself could plan that far ahead.[27]

By contrast the embassies to Hungary were completely successful. King Sigismund had no hesitation whatsoever in accepting the Anglo-French proposals and enthusiastically agreed to co-operate with the dukes of Burgundy, Orleans and Lancaster. By September he had informed the Venetian senate that he intended to put a powerful army into the field by the following May, the date already selected by the three dukes for the launching of their crusade. This agreed, the allies then sought the co-operation of Venice, who promised on 6 September to commit herself to the project once the Western powers had given firm pledges of their participation. Meanwhile Boniface IX had thrown his weight behind the Western powers – despite the prominent part played by the French – and in two bulls issued on 3 June and 15 October 1394 ordered the proclamation of a crusade in the territories stretching roughly from Austria in the west to Dalmatia in the south. Sigismund himself sought the alliance of the remaining independent princes of the Balkans – and notably the ruler of Wallachia – while the Western rulers appear to have sought aid from those who had something to gain from the Turks in the east. Unfortunately the evidence on this point is somewhat scanty; but Charles VI was certainly negotiating an alliance with the king of Cyprus by 1395, and Venetian correspondence with Constantinople at this date reveals that the allies hoped for assistance – if unintentional – from the Tartar khan, Tamerlane. A number of German princes also took the Cross. Finally, the Eastern emperor, Manuel II Palaeologus, would give what assistance he could; though since Constantinople was under siege from the Turks and contingency plans had had to be made for the rescue of Manuel, this was not likely to amount to very much.[28]

Having secured a firm assurance from Sigismund and a conditional promise from Venice, the Anglo-Burgundian embassies returned home at the end of 1394, having agreed to meet the Hungarians again at Venice on 6 January 1395 to complete their own plans and to conclude the promised alliance with Venice. The three dukes entrusted their final arrangements to William de la Trémoille, Philip's marshal. Early in the new year he arrived in Venice, where he was forced to fret and fume in the absence of the Hungarian ambassadors, without whom nothing could be done. By 21 January the senate found it necessary to write to Philip of Burgundy, John of Gaunt and Louis of Orleans excusing the delay and stating that they had persuaded de la Trémoille to stay in Venice a little longer to await the Hungarians, despite his urgency to report back to them. Two weeks later the Hungarians had still not arrived and de la Trémoille, his patience exhausted, decided to return to France, though this necessarily meant returning empty-handed. In the absence of Sigismund's ambassadors the Venetians would make no hard and fast promises.

Another month passed before the Hungarians finally arrived in Venice. They were given their first formal audience on 5 March, and by 12 March the senate had decided to commit itself to naval support for the crusade. It agreed to supply 25 per cent of the total shipping provided by the allied powers on condition that this did not exceed twenty-five ships – not perhaps an over-generous contribution, but certainly a very useful one.

Even after this, however, there was a further inexplicable delay before the Hungarian ambassadors met the dukes of Burgundy and Orleans at Lyons early in May. After lengthy discussions Philip sent his chamberlain, Rénier Pot, and Louis of Orleans his secretary, Louis de Buno, to Paris to inform the king of the latest developments, while the Hungarians proceeded to Bordeaux to confer with the duke of Lancaster. After seeing the king, Pot and Buno were instructed to make their way to Bordeaux to complete arrangements with John of Gaunt and the Hungarian ambassadors. The four-power conference at Bordeaux occupied the months of June and July.[29]

By this date it was of course too late for a crusade in 1395. For this the Hungarians were undoubtedly to blame, as Philip himself remarked in a letter to his wife written from Lyons on 14 May, immediately after his interview with Sigismund's envoys.[30] Why they were so dilatory is a mystery, for of all those involved in the project Sigismund had the most to gain from it. As it was the delay proved fatal to the whole enterprise. Had it set out in 1395 the crusade would almost certainly have conformed to its original conception. There is no sign that the original leaders had, as yet, decided to withdraw, and in the very letter in which he blamed the Hungarians for the delay, Philip made it clear that he still intended to lead the Burgundian contingent. But the delay combined with the political upheavals at Westminster, Bordeaux and

Avignon to necessitate a complete change of plan. With Anglo-French relations in disarray as a result of the Gascon revolt and Richard II's marriage plans, and with France virtually at war with her pope as a result of her intemperate reaction to the election of Benedict XIII, the political leaders of England and France could not be spared. Orleans withdrew completely; Philip made way for his son, John;[31] and John of Gaunt handed over the command of his contingent to his illegitimate son, John Beaufort.[32] These changes affected not only the leadership but the entire composition of the army. No one appears to have deputized for Orleans, and the Gascon revolt meant that the English contingent was almost certainly much smaller than originally intended. What had been conceived as an equal partnership of England, France and Burgundy was thus transformed into a predominantly Burgundian enterprise.

The change in the leadership and composition of the crusade had disastrous effects. When the allied Christian armies eventually confronted the Ottomans outside Nicopolis, just south of the Danube, on 25 September 1396, the outcome of the battle was decided by the incredible foolhardiness of the French and Burgundian knights, who tried to defeat Bayezid single-handed and win all the glory for themselves with a series of cavalry charges reminiscent of the French tactics at Crécy. The outcome was inevitable. Bayezid was able to ambush and destroy most of the cavalry, then defeat the remainder of the Christian army piecemeal. It is inconceivable that this would have occurred had either John of Gaunt or Philip the Bold been present. Philip's leadership in the field had always been characterized by an excess of caution, and the most remarkable trait of Gaunt's long and varied military career had been his ability to keep a tight rein on his troops under the most sustained and intense enemy pressure. Neither man would have succumbed to the temptation to vainglory which proved the undoing of John de Nevers; and since most observers believed that the battle would have been won but for the indiscipline of the Franco-Burgundian forces, the presence of Burgundy and Lancaster would in all probability have ensured a Christian victory.[33]

The Christian defeat at Nicopolis has some claim to rank as one of the most decisive battles of the later Middle Ages. It shattered the hard-won Christian unity which had produced the crusade – the first major Western effort for over a century; it paved the way for grave internal dissensions in England, France and the Empire, to the further confusion of Catholic Europe; and it consequently set the seal on Turkish power in Europe, with effects which are still visible today.

Its most immediate result was to put an end to plans for a second, and even greater expedition envisaged by Charles VI and Richard II. Though this fact appears to have escaped observation, the Nicopolis force was intended to be only the first of two great Christian armies whose ultimate destination was to have been Jerusalem itself. In accordance with contemporary crusading theory, the Nicopolis army was to have cleared the ground and established a forward base from which the second and greater of the two armies could set out for the Holy Land under the leadership of Charles VI and Richard II themselves. This was the strategy advocated by Philip de Mézières. In all his later writings he assumed that the two kings would eventually lead a crusade in the wake of a lesser expedition (preferably one spearheaded by his own crusading Order of the Passion), and he had good grounds for this assumption. Other contemporaries testified to Charles VI's determination to lead a crusade in person; and Richard II gave vivid and enduring expression to his own readiness to participate in a joint royal expedition to the East when he commissioned the Wilton Diptych.[34] Whatever the degree of their personal zeal, however, their correspondence in May 1395 reveals that they had accepted joint responsibility to lead a crusade to the Holy Land. 'You and I', Charles had said, 'should undertake a crusade to succour our fellow Christians and to liberate the Holy Land', and Richard had applauded his proposal. In the following March, on the eve of the departure of the first crusade, both kings reiterated their determination to preserve Christendom 'from the malice and the evil onslaught of the infidels'. Finally, the most detailed surviving account of the Nicopolis campaign states that the two kings had definitely agreed in November 1396 during the course of their personal interview at Calais that 'they would set out in the following summer with a great force of men-at-arms and archers to conquer the Holy Land'. The tale is repeated by Froissart. As evidence of the kings' intentions, it is the more convincing for predicting something which did not happen.[35]

The Nicopolis disaster ruined the possibility of a royal expedition and appeared likely to put an end to all crusading activity for some time to come. Politically and financially the effects of the Turkish victory were felt well into the fifteenth century. The ransom of John de Nevers and his companions, for instance, may have cost Philip of Burgundy anything up to £100,000. But the political consequences were more important. In the years following Nicopolis there were serious political upheavals, followed by political revolutions in England, in France and in Germany. In none of these cases can the Christian defeat be said to have caused the troubles, but in each of them it facilitated conflicts which might well have been averted had the crusade been a success. In France, for instance, conflict stemmed from the rivalry of the dukes of Burgundy and Orleans, both of whom had been prepared to lead the first crusade and so would presumably have joined the second had not disaster intervened. In England Nicopolis was a blow to the prestige of the king, since the crusade was very much a part of his whole policy of friendship and co-operation with France. While the success of the crusade might well have stifled criticism, its failure allowed the duke of Gloucester to question the fundamental basis of royal policy. According to Froissart his reaction to Nicopolis was to demand that the king take advantage of the French losses by reopening the war! Yet on the eve of Nicopolis Gloucester himself had been preparing to go on a crusade.[36] Finally, in Germany Sigismund's association with the Nicopolis disaster not only lowered the prestige of the whole imperial family but also encouraged Sigismund himself to turn his back on the Balkans and embroil himself in internal German affairs, to their further confusion.

In these circumstances the continued interest shown in the West for a crusade is a remarkable tribute to its resilience and to the strength of the crusading ideal. In France a tax was levied to succour the Eastern empire and a quite respectable force some 800 strong sent to Constantinople under Boucicaut in 1399. There was talk of Louis of Orleans or Henry of Derby joining this or a subsequent expedition. England meanwhile sent money if not men to Manuel; and there was a busy passage of ambassadors between Westminster, Paris and Constantinople. Richard maintained an ambassador in Constantinople from July 1397 until February 1399, then again from June 1399 onwards. Several Byzantine ecclesiatics visited the West, and London honoured both the 'brother' and the 'cousin' of the Emperor Manuel, the latter being knighted by Richard II himself. The culmination of this activity was the decision of Manuel II to visit the West in person. His visit might possibly have provided the stimulus for the two kings to resurrect their earlier plans, but unfortunately for Manuel he left his visit too late. He set out from Constantinople for Venice towards the end of 1399 and by the time he reached France Richard II had been deposed and Anglo-French relations were in disarray. The Lancastrian revolution killed the last lingering hopes of a second major crusade. Though he remained in the West for the better part of two years and was fêted in both London and Paris, Manuel eventually returned home empty-handed. But for assistance from an unexpected quarter, Constantinople would probably have fallen in the next few years.[37]

The Turkish victory also set the seal on their power in Europe and hence on the political configuration of that part of the world for centuries to come. A Christian victory could easily have transformed this situation out of all recognition. In the greater part of the Balkans Turkish rule was still very recent and as yet unconsolidated. Serbia had been eliminated only seven years previously, Bulgaria and Thessaly only three years, and southern Greece a mere year or so before Nicopolis was fought. Only in Thrace had the Turks been entrenched for very long, and this was an area in which Greek traditions and self-awareness were almost certainly at their strongest. In these circumstances a single resounding military defeat might very easily have led to the complete expulsion of the Ottomans from Europe; and since their base in Asia Minor was neither very extensive nor very wealthy, they would have found it far from easy to make a comeback even after the withdrawal of the crusading forces.

Finally, the Nicopolis disaster had an adverse effect on the peace negotiations between England and France, though not in a way which can be precisely measured. Until the end of 1396 these negotiations had been carried out in an atmosphere which was conducive to success. The unity and safety of Christendom were held to lie in the hands of the two kings; and although this did not blind either of them to his own best interests, it did produce the sort of conditions in which even complex problems could seem less intractable. As Philip de Mézières remarked – with pardonable exaggeration – the contemptible mundane interests of the two kings would seem less important when they contemplated the kingdoms they should conquer for the love of God; and the sacrifice of a few castles would be a small price for a peace which would allow them to devote their energies to such a great design. Something of this attitude is discernible on both sides during the 1390s, which have left more traces of genuine good feeling and of active and even enthusiastic co-operation than has any other period of the Middle Ages. Nicopolis blighted this. Thereafter, though England and France remained on friendly, even warm terms until Richard's deposition, their co-operation was brought down to earth. Perhaps for this reason no new solution to the problem of Aquitaine was propounded, nor any old one put into effect.[38]

NOTES

1 *Anglo-Norman Letters*, no. 172 (very slightly abbreviated); for proof of its authenticity, see Palmer, 'The Background to Richard II's Marriage to Isabel of France', *BIHR*, xliv, 8–10.

2 For de Mézières and Leo see below; and for what follows, *Foedera*, vii, 429, 466, 491, 610, 715, 753, 814, 823; *Anglo-Norman Letters*, no. 106.

3 *Régestes des délibérations du sénat de Venise*, i, 189–90; *Calendar of State Papers: Venetian*, i, no. 117.

4 *Songe du vieil pèlerin*, ii, 409. For what follows see *RP*, iii, *passim* (almost every parliament produced complaints of the turbulence of Cheshire); Walsingham, *Annales*, 159–61; and below, appendix 1 (o).

5 Valois, *La France et le grand Schisme*, iii, 622.

6 For *Joustes de pees* see: E 28/6/89; cf. *Higden*, ix, 235. For St Ingelvert see *Foedera*, vii, 665–6; *Joustes de St Ingelbert*; for Barbary, Atiya, *Crusade in the Later Middle Ages*, 408; E 403/533, m. 14; E 404/14/96, no. 30; C 81, nos 6266, 6268–9, 6283, 6289, 6281.

7 For English crusading activity see E 403/530, m. 7; C 81, nos 6212, 7233, 7241, 7258, and file 529 *passim*; E 30/1515; *Hansisches Urkundenbuch*, v, 32–3, 86–7; *Foedera*, vii, 705–6; *Higden*, ix, 258–9; *Expeditions to Prussia and the Holy Land made by Henry, Earl of Derby*. For French activity see Jarry, *Louis, duc d'Orleans*, 55–6; Vaughan, *Philip the Bold*, 61; and ACO B 1479, fos 55, 68v, 72, 83, 142–3, 147v, 149, 152v–3v; B 1487, fos. 76v, 78v–9v, 85, 81; B 1492, fos 42v–5; B 1500, fos 65v–6v, etc.

8 *RP*, iii, 338. For next paragraph see *Anglo-Norman Letters*, no. 173.

9 Iorga, *Philippe de Mézières*; Atiya, *Crusade in the Later Middle Ages*, chapter 7; *Songe du vieil pèlerin*; Molinier, 'Description de deux manuscrits contenants la règle de la "Militia Passionis Jhesu Christi" de Philippe de Mézières', *Archives de l'Orient Latin*, i, 335–64, 719; Hamdy, 'Philippe de Mézières and the New Order of the Passion', *Bulletin of the Faculty of Arts*, xviii, 1–105; Philippe de Mézières, *De la Chevallerie de la Passion de Jesu Christ*–both latter works kindly lent to me by Professor G W. Copland.

10 *Songe du vieil pèlerin*, ii, 431. For what follows see Froissart, *Oeuvres*, xiv, 280; BM, Royal MS. 20 B VI (the *Epistre*).

11 Froissart, *Oeuvres*, xii, 39 (de Giac); *Expeditions to Prussia . . . by Derby*, 309; E 403/546, m. 4; E 403/551, m. 19; E 403/554, m. 18; E 403/556, m. 17 (de Granson); *DC*, no. 219n; Durrie, *Gasons en Italie*, 21ff.; AN, KK 322, fos1–44 (de Blaisy); *DC*, no. 151; Palmer, 'The Background to Richard II's Marriage to Isabel of France', *BIHR*, x/iv, 9–13; Froissart, *Oeuvres*, xvi, 311–18; Molinier, 'Description de deux manuscrits', *Archives de l'Orient Latin*, i, 362 (the Hermit).

12 Molinier, i, 363–4.

13 Above, chapter 4 and *Higden*, ix, 77 for negotiations with England; for

subsequent contacts, C 76/75, m. 11; C 76/76, mm. 12, 9; *Foedera*, vii, 706; C 76/79, m. 9; and, in general, Froissart, *Oeuvres*, xiv, 387, xv, 116–18, xx, 111.

14 *Foedera*, vii, 443, 627, 714–22, 748, 770, 824.

15 Palmer, 'England and the Great Western Schism, 1388–99', *EHR*, lxxxiii, 516–22 for this and next two paragraphs.

16 Palmer, 'English Foreign Policy, 1389–99', *The Reign of Richard II*, 75–107, for the Italian crisis; Cartellieri, *Phillipp der Kühne*, 53ff., appendices 5–7; ADN, B 1337/14601*bis* = Kervyn de Lettenhove, 'Des alliances de la commune de Gand avec Richard II', *BARB*, II, xx, 314–5, for Flanders.

17 Durrieu, 'Le royaume d'Adria', *RQH*, xxviii, 43–78. For next paragraph see, *St Denys*, ii, 46–61; Valois, *La France et le grand Schisme*, ii, 398–404; *Annales avignonnaises*, xii, 129–38.

18 *L'apparicion de maistre Jehan de Meun*, 92. For this and next paragraph, Palmer, *EHR*, lxxxiii, 519–20.

19 *St Denys*, ii, 94–101, 130–85.

20 For events of 1395–97 see Valois, iii, chapters 1–2, and especially Perroy, *L'Angleterre et le grand Schisme*, chapter 9; and for the projected expedition to Italy, Palmer, in *The Reign of Richard II* (cf. n. 16).

21 Atiya, *Crusade in the Later Middle Ages*, chapter 17; *Expeditions to Prussia . . . by Derby*. For what follows, above nn. 6–7; Froissart, *Oeuvres*, xii, 39; *St Denys*, i, 708; *Archives de l'Orient Latin*, ii, 380–6 (Swinburne); *DC*, no. 183; Walsingham, *Annales Ricardi Secundi*, 164–5 (Roos); *Higden*, ix, 261–2 (Clanvow and Clifford); ACO B 1500, fo. 67v; Moranvillé, 'Extraits des journaux du trésor (1345–1419)', *BEC*, xlix, 389.

22 *St Denys*, i, 708–10; Froissart, *Oeuvres*, xv, 116–19; Pot, *Histoire de R. Pot*, 33; Jarry, *Origines de la domination française à Gênes*, 35; *DC*, no. 145. For what follows see also, *Expeditions to Prussia*; *Chronique des quatre premiers Valois*, 326, 335; *St Denys*, ii, 122–5, 386–91; Moranvillé, *BEC*, xlix, 389.

23 For all these embassies see appendix 1 (p).

24 Cartellieri, *Philipp der Kühne*, appendix 10.

25 ACO, B 1276/12987 for preliminary negotiations; Vaughan, *Philip the Bold*, 63–4 for the grants and their collection.

26 *Quelques pièces relatives à . . . Orléans*, 100–2; Nordberg, *Les ducs et la royauté*, 20; E 403/546, mm. 22, 23; E 403/548, mm. 1, 4, 20; E 403/549, mm. 6, 14; Armitage-Smith, *John of Gaunt*, appendix 6 (for finances); and for Gaunt's army, Froissart, *Oeuvres*, xv, 135; Walsingham, *Annales*, 161; C 61/104, mm. 9–1.

27 *Codex diplomaticus prussicus*, v, 70–1.

28 For the negotiations with Cyprus see MS. Français 14371, fos 267v–8v; and for those involving Venice, *Mon. spect. hist. Slavorum*, iv, 335–43; *Mon. Hungariae historia*, iii, 755–6; *Régestes de Venise*, i, 189–205; *Cal. State Papers: Venetian*, i, 35–6.

29 ACO, B 1503, fo. 46v; BM Add. Ch. 3371–4, 3376–7, payments by Burgundy
   and Orleans to their ambassadors, who left Lyons on 8 May and returned
   to Paris on 6 August.
30 Cartellieri, *Philipp der Kühne*, appendix 13.
31 Philip had intended to take his son from the very beginning: ADN, B
   18822/23270, undated letter (?22 June 1394) in which John de Nevers refers
   to the crusade as 'mon premier voiage et pour mon chivalerie'; cf. B
   18822/23258 (undated, ? 30 June 1394).
32 For this see appendix 1 (o).
33 The main secondary authorities are Delaville le Roulx, *La France en
   Orient*; Atiya, *Crusade of Nicopolis*, and Vaughan, *Philip the Bold*, chapter 4.
34 See appendix 1 (q).
35 Above, pp. 180, 182; and Froissart, *Oeuvres*, xv, 450, 242–3.
36 C 66/356, m. 8 (relevant section not in *Calendar*).
37 Delaville le Roulx, *La France en Orient*, 355–79; Jarry, *Louis, duc d'Orléans*,
   216–18 for France; and for England *Anglo-Norman Letters*, no. 103;
   Correspondence of T. Bekyngton, i, 285–7; *Foedera*, viii, 65–6, 82–3; *DC*, no.
   241; E 101/320/17 (cf. E 403/555, m. 17 for correct date); E 403/561, mm.
   12, 14; E 403/562, m. 7; E 404/16/373; and for Manuel's visit, Ostrogorsky,
   History of the Byzantine State, 554–6, and Schlumberger, 'Un empereur de
   Byzance à Paris et à Londres', *Byzance et les croisades*, 87–148. Add now
   two major works which became available after the completion of my book:
   Barker, *Manuel II Palaeologus*, chapter 3; Nicol, 'A Byzantine Emperor in
   England', *Univ. Birmingham Hist. Journal*, xii, 204–25.
38 According to the official French chronicler (*St Denys*, ii, 520–2), the news
   of Nicopolis threw everyone into such a state of despair that it ruined the
   prospects of final peace between England and France.

Chapter Twelve

The End of the Reign
1397–9

The three years which followed the Nicopolis crusade, the interview between the two kings, and Richard's marriage to Isabel form a depressing anti-climax to an exciting and constructive period in Anglo-French relations. The two courts appeared to resign themselves to the impossibility of concluding a final peace, and negotiations hung fire; their joint efforts to end the Schism ran into difficulties which strained their relations without greatly advancing their cause; and the project for a crusade led by the two kings themselves disappeared without trace, to be replaced by only minor and spasmodic efforts to prop up the tottering Eastern empire. No other achievements served to compensate for these three failures; and the earlier hopes for securing peace, reuniting Christendom and expelling the Turk were obscured, and at times almost obliterated by a confusion of short-lived, self-interested, parochial and often conflicting schemes whose objectives were often as obscure as their results were negligible. Nevertheless, in this chaos of futile diplomatic manoeuvrings, historians have discerned one development which – they argue – both imposes a certain coherence on the period and at the same times explains its apparent incoherence. This factor was the foreign policy of Richard II.

Despite agreement on this point, however, there are widely divergent – indeed, diametrically opposed – views as to what Richard's foreign policy was in these years. It has been argued on the one hand that it consisted quite simply in following the lead given by the French court, and on the other that it was deliberately designed to oppose French interests throughout Europe. According to the first view, Richard's one unwavering aim was to shore up his domestic tyranny. Driven by a desire for internal security which he was convinced he could achieve only with French support, he resigned himself to becoming virtually a French puppet in international politics, recklessly subordinating English interests to those of France. In so doing, however, he merely increased the discontent of his own subjects, whose unanimous opposition forced him from time to time to go back on his more extravagant promises to his father-in-law, thereby introducing the element of instability which was to frustrate many of the plans of the period. Ultimately, his craven attitude towards France precipitated his downfall; and since no one else in England endorsed his policies, his removal entailed an immediate revolution in English relations with France.

The alternative view indicts the king for precisely the opposite failings. Far from being a puppet of the king of France – it is argued – he deliberately jettisoned the advantages of the French alliance in a reckless bid for the imperial throne. To realize this megalomaniac ambition, he was forced to reverse all his earlier policies. In order to induce Boniface IX to use his electoral influence in Germany on his behalf, Richard went back on his promise to Charles VI to withdraw obedience from the pope if he refused – as he did – to agree to the *voie de cession*. To the same end, he denounced a projected Anglo-French expedition to Milan (the pope's ally), to which he had agreed in 1396; withdrew his support for the enterprise; and then allied with the duke of Milan himself. Finally, he lavished money fiefs on the German electors. All this, of course, had a disastrous effect on his relations with France. Both the end he had in view, and the means by which he sought to achieve it clashed violently with her best interests, opening once again an abyss between the two countries. Only his eventual failure averted conflict. But though the peace was not in fact broken, it had become a hollow one from which he could derive none of the advantages he had originally sought. When his hour of crisis came the French not only failed to assist him but actually gave their support to his supplanter.[1]

Such abnormally divergent interpretations presuppose an unusual degree of ambiguity in the evidence, much of which consists of plans or projects undertaken and then abandoned for reasons which were rarely stated and can only be surmised. In order to understand their true significance, it is imperative to grasp at the outset the background against which they were formulated. During these three years matter-of-fact relations between the two courts are peculiarly crucial to an understanding of their foreign policies.

The most conspicuous feature of this relationship is undoubtedly the continuing absence of signs of serious strains or stresses. The instalments of Isabel's dowry were paid promptly and in full by Charles VI, and Richard lavished every care and attention on his young queen, as

French observers were quick to remark.[2] At no time before Richard's deposition did either government show any inclination to break or condone breaches of the truce. Charles VI did indeed complain in the summer of 1398 that Richard had not yet published the twenty-eight-year truce concluded two years previously, despite several requests that he do so; but he also made it clear that he suspected his son-in-law of nothing more sinister than lethargy or mild opportunism, a suspicion which was duly confirmed when the truce was published on 30 August, just as it was due to take effect.[3] Thereafter there was never any question as to its observance, and in this respect the last years of Richard's reign provide a stark contrast with the uneasy and unstable conditions which prevailed under his successor.

More positive evidence of amicable relations between the two courts is by no means lacking. At Richard's request, Charles VI agreed to put diplomatic pressure on Scotland to observe the truce more rigorously, and his ambassadors were fêted in 1397 and 1398 when they passed through London on their way north.[4] Similarly, at the end of 1397 Richard pardoned certain Gascon lords of English allegiance for breaches of the truce after being requested to do so by Charles himself.[5] In December 1397 one of Richard's *chevaliers d'honneur* fought a duel before the French court in Paris, and in the following autumn every member of the French royal family was represented at the duel which was to have been fought between Mowbray and Bolingbroke. Throughout the entire period informal embassies bearing news, gifts or family correspondence were exchanged with uncharacteristic frequency, the envoys invariably returning home richly laden.[6]

Apart from the absence of conflict and the more direct evidence of friendly contacts between the two courts, the best insight into the nature of their relationship is provided by the accounts of a number of Frenchmen who visited England during the last three years of Richard's reign. Two of these accounts – the 'metrical history' of Jean Creton and the anonymous *Chronicque de la traison et mort de Richart II* – are well enough known, but it is perhaps worth emphasizing one or two of their features which have a bearing on the matter in hand. Both were written immediately after the Lancastrian revolution to condemn its architect and to justify its victim; and the alacrity with which two Frenchmen leapt to the defence of the deposed king may perhaps be taken as symptomatic of the French attitude to him in general. It has, it is true, been suggested that their anti-Lancastrian bias is to be attributed to the deterioration in Anglo-French relations which occurred some time after Richard's death. But this is highly improbable. The two works were completed before the deterioration had set in; and both their form and their contents reveal them to have been inspired by the revolution itself, and by the events which produced it rather than by its repercussions. They were written out of sympathy for Richard rather than hatred of Henry, as even the most cursory reading will reveal.

The propaganda purpose of both writers sufficiently indicates their attitude towards the king and his government, but one or two details in their narratives deserve emphasis. The anonymous author of the *Chronicque* was particularly impressed by the care and affection lavished upon the young French queen and her household; and although he may have heightened his picture for dramatic purposes, there is no reason to believe that it is in any way inaccurate. It is, in fact, substantially corroborated by the account of another French visitor, Pierre Salmon, whose evident dislike of the king himself increases his authority on this point. Futher evidence of Richard's continuing goodwill towards the French court is supplied by Creton, who goes so far as to say that he lost his throne because of his love for his father-in-law.

The circumstances which placed both writers in a position to collect their material is yet further evidence of the amicable relations which continued to exist between the two countries down to the moment of the Lancastrian revolution. The author of the *Chronicque* was an eyewitness to many of the events he relates, and was evidently employed as a herald in the household of the king's half-brother, John Holand, from at least 1397 until the beginning of 1400, when he presumably returned to France. Some of the details he provides of the king's travels in the Midlands in 1398, and of his departure for Ireland from Windsor in 1399, show that he was accustomed to move around with the royal court; and his familiarity with the names and titles of the nobility, as well as with some of their domestic affairs reveals that he had constant access to the court and was present at many of its functions. In an age when foreigners were apt to be regarded with suspicion and were normally kept under surveillance, such latitude was unusual.

The freedom accorded to the poet Creton was even more remarkable. He arrived in England in the spring of 1399 to accompany the king on his last Irish expedition and remained at court throughout the summer, leaving the king's immediate entourage only for the return trip to England, when for 'the sake of song and merriment' he accompanied the earl of Salisbury, a fellow poet. In the hectic days which followed, Salisbury and Creton were rejoined by the king, with whom they remained until the bitter end, being among the last dozen or so of his companions who refused to abandon him. Of this small band of stalwarts only Creton subsequently committed his experiences to writing; and so by a singular paradox, the only eyewitness account of the most important domestic event of the later Middle Ages comes from the pen of a Frenchman. It is entirely appropriate that it should do so.

Had Pierre Salmon been in Creton's position we might have had a very different picture of Richard's last days of freedom, for Salmon was at no pains to disguise his dislike of the king, whom he considered to have wronged him. For this reason his memoirs are among the most valuable sources of the period. Salmon had come to England in the train of Queen Isabel in 1396 and was subsequently employed by Richard as an intermediary with the French court on business concerned with the health of his father-in-law. During the course of the somewhat incredible adventures in which these missions involved him, Salmon fell foul of a number of influential people – including the king himself – with the result that he eventually found himself in disgrace both in England and France, where it was rumoured – not without some foundation in fact – that he had stolen Isabel's crown and some of her jewels. His reaction to this unenviable position reveals – quite unintentionally – just how close were the relations between the two courts at this date. Convinced that if he returned to England with news of the good health of the French king all his faults would be forgiven him, Salmon spent an uncomfortable period in enforced exile in the Low Countries awaiting arrival of the news which was to prove his salvation. In the event, he was unable to put his expectations to the test; and for reasons which had nothing to do with his assessment of Richard's character, he was forced to return to France while still under a cloud. Though he took the precaution of writing in advance to Charles VI and a number of his more influential counsellors, he was immediately seized and thrown into prison, the fate he had nervously anticipated since he had first had the misfortune to give offence to the king of England.

At about the time that Salmon was undergoing the most uncomfortable of his various experiences the English court was honoured by the visit of yet another French notable, one Aymard Broutin, a knight from the Dauphiné, who arrived during the summer of 1398. His business was unfortunately of a semi-official nature, to which his account[7] is almost exclusively devoted. Even so, it is revealing in one or two limited respects. Broutin was apparently given free access to anyone of importance and allowed to perambulate the royal court at will. He had lengthy conversations with the king, the duke of Lancaster, the abbot of Westminster, and important officials of the royal household. If we can accept his word for it he was allowed astonishing freedom of speech, telling the king himself that his ecclesiastical policy was misguided, his subjects perverse, and his pope a schismatic. Despite this, he was allowed to finish his discourse and was then dismissed without rancour and allowed to continue his efforts to convince the court of the superior claims of the pope of Avignon. His audacity, and the king's tolerance both presuppose a background of amicable, if not positively cordial relations between England and France.

The last and most eminent Frenchman to have left his impressions of the English court is Raymond, *vicomte* of Perelhos and Roda. Though now established in Aragon, Perelhos was born and brought up in France and had since maintained close relations with the French court. His *Voyage au Purgatoire de Saint Patrice* is, as its title implies, predominantly a narrative of a pilgrimage to Ireland; but this narrative is prefaced and concluded by an account of the author's journeys through England which is in effect a eulogy on the hospitality of the English court. Like Creton and Salmon, Perelhos arrived in England armed with letters of introduction from Charles VI and his uncles which guaranteed him a fulsome reception. When he reached the court near Oxford towards the middle of November 1397 he was honoured by the king himself, then lavishly entertained for ten days before being allowed to proceed with his pilgrimage. When he finally left for Ireland he was provided with guides and letters of introduction to the earl of March, the king's lieutenant there. His reception in Ireland was consequently no less hospitable than it had been in England. He was entertained in Dublin by the earl of March himself who, after trying to dissuade him from a journey which would take him through the heart of rebel Irish territory, paid all his expenses and provided him with guides to escort him to the archbishop of Armagh, who then gave him a veritable army of a hundred men-at-arms to see him safely to his destination. Returning without mishap, he was once again fêted in Dublin and in England before parting regretfully for France early in 1398.

With only the partial exception of Salmon, the impression left by the writings of these five Frenchmen is one of unreserved approbation of the king and his court, an impression which can scarcely be reconciled with the existence of serious tension between England and France. As foreigners in a country which was by long tradition their natural enemy, they would certainly have detected any such tension, and indeed would probably have embroidered it. Their silence is therefore eloquent. Other writers – Froissart, the monk of St Denys, and the English chroniclers – had less cause to be affected by the nuances of Anglo-French relations, and they were in any case less well-placed to observe events; but for what it is worth, none of them give any reason to suspect that the picture painted by Creton and his fellow writers was in any way distorted. On the whole they have very little to say about Anglo-French relations – in itself an indication of tranquility – and what they do say tends to corroborate the accounts of the French travellers. Walsingham's story of Richard's plans to sell Calais to Charles VI in 1398 may be taken as representative. Although the story is incredible in itself and improbable in all its details, it could nevertheless only have been conceived against a background of the closest and most amicable of relationships between the two courts. Without this background not even the most gullible and hostile of Richard's subjects could have given a moment's credence to so malicious a rumour.

The conclusions suggested by these literary sources are borne out by some of the more important domestic events of the period, and notably by the treatment accorded to Henry Bolingbroke in 1398 and 1399. When Charles VI heard of the quarrel between Bolingbroke and Mowbray he immediately sought to patch matters up as best he could. In August 1398 he sent an imposing embassy headed by the count of St Pol to try to persuade Richard to cancel the duel they were to have fought and to do what he could to 'save the honour' of both parties. This is precisely what Richard then did. Moreover, after sentencing Henry to ten years' exile, he then allowed him to retire to the French court and to remain there for the remainder of his reign – no great hardship – during which time he received very substantial remittances from the king: 1,000 marks in October and again in December 1398, £500 in the following February, and shortly afterwards a pension of £2,000. Richard evidently felt that this arrangement was to his advantage, a feeling he could scarcely have enjoyed had his relations with the French court been at all uneasy. Until the moment of Henry's invasion he was never given cause to regret his decision. In the spring of 1399 he received a momentary jolt when he heard that Bolingbroke was negotiating for the hand of a daughter of the duke of Berry; but as soon as he expressed his disquiet the French court withdrew its blessing and nothing further was heard of the projected marriage. In such circumstances it is not really surprising that Richard felt secure enough to turn his back on England in order to undertake an Irish expedition in 1399.[8]

In view of all this evidence, it is impossible to endorse the view that Richard reversed his policies towards France in the last years of his reign. On the other hand it is equally clear that good relations with France were not purchased at the expense of English interests abroad. Though there is no proof that Richard made any very serious or sustained effort to secure his election as emperor, he certainly allowed the scheme to be canvassed among some of the German princes and at the papal court, thereby securing considerable diplomatic advantages both in Rome and in the Low Countries. Since 1393 he had been trying to build up a network of alliances in the Low Countries to act as a bulwark against Burgundian expansion in that areas. It was his success in this direction which prompted some of the German princes of the lower Rhine to propose his candidature for the Imperial throne. By ostensibly accepting their proposal he encouraged them in their opposition to Burgundy, while at the same time obtaining the temporary backing of Boniface IX during the domestic crisis of 1397–8. Boniface, who had been alienated by Richard's adhesion to the *voie de cession*, was encouraged by his candidature for the Imperial Crown to believe that the king might yet be won back to his side. With this hope in mind, he did everything that was asked of him during the critical months which followed the king's attack upon his domestic enemies, transferring Thomas Arundel to the schismatic see of St Andrew's, replacing him at Canterbury by the royal nominee Roger Walden, and then underwriting the oaths and anathemas promulgated by the parliaments of 1397 and 1398.[9] Once he had secured this all-important support, Richard then lost interest in his imperial pretensions, which suggests that his interest had been feigned for the purpose of securing the temporary political support of the papacy.

Whatever the true explanation of this episode, it certainly revealed that English foreign policy was not solely designed to gratify the French court. A number of other events point to a similar conclusion. During the last years of his reign Richard persisted in his earlier efforts to create a pro-English bloc in the Low Countries, adding Rupert III of the Palatinate – the future emperor – the duke of Berg and count of Ravensberg, and the heir to the duchies of Guelders and Juliers to the allies he had acquired in the earlier part of the decade. During the same period an alliance was concluded with the duke of Brittany, and marriage alliances sought with the king of Aragon and the duke of Milan, both of whom were at odds with France at this time.[10] Finally, in the years 1397 and 1398 Richard sent substantial quantities of weapons, and several retinues of men-at-arms and archers to assist the king of Portugal in a war against his rebellious half-brother and the king of Castile, an ally of France.[11]

If these events are considered in the light of the amicable relationship which Richard continued to enjoy with the French court, then it would appear that his foreign policy in the last years of his reign was neither avowedly hostile nor cravenly subordinate to that of France, but rather designed to uphold essential English interests with the minimum of necessary provocation. There is much to support this conclusion. In the first place, the view that Richard pursued a *new* foreign policy after 1397 rests upon a fundamental misconception as to the nature of his policy before that date. Despite a generally accepted belief to the contrary, he had pursued a consistently hard-headed policy in the earlier part of the decade, opposing French activity wherever English interests demanded that he do so, and doing so with a very marked degree of success.[12] In this respect his relations with Italy, Aragon, Brittany and Milan after 1397 merely continued the policies he had pursued before that date and cannot be taken as evidence that he had developed a more hostile attitude towards France. Furthermore, a closer examination of his activities after 1397 will reveal that although he did not hesitate to uphold English interests where this was necessary, he did so with as little provocation as circumstances permitted. This is most immediately obvious in his relations with Portugal. Though men and supplies were sent to King John as soon as he asked for them, Richard stipulated that they were only to be used for defensive purposes, to quell the rebellion of the king's half-brother Don Denis; in no circumstances were they to be employed in an aggressive war against Castile, even though the rebellion of Don Denis was backed by Castile: for this would have constituted a breach of the truce of Leulingham.

A similar combination of firmness and restraint can be observed in Richard's handling of an Italian crisis which arose in the winter of 1397–8. Indirectly, this crisis grew out of the Anglo-French plans to end the Schism. To facilitate the resignation of the two existing popes and the unanimous election of a third, the two kings had agreed in 1396 to lead a joint Anglo-French expedition to north Italy in 1397, a project which had to be postponed after the Nicopolis disaster and the subsequent illness of Charles VI. In the autumn of 1397, however, the project was given a new twist and a new lease of life by certain elements at the

French court who hoped to turn it to the dynastic advantage of the count of Armagnac at the expense of the duke of Milan. When informed of this development by the duke of Milan himself, Richard immediately forbade his own subjects to participate in the expedition, and then intervened at the French court to secure its cancellation. He took the opportunity to remind Charles that their original purpose had been to put an end to the Schism; and he asked him, politely but firmly, to forbid the Armagnacs to pursue their aggressive designs against Milan. Thereupon the entire project was shelved.

The firm yet discreet and friendly way in which this minor crisis was handled can be paralleled by other episodes of a similar nature, and notably by the manner in which negotiations with the German princes of the Low Countries were conducted. As we have already seen these negotiations were carried on more or less continuously throughout the 1390s, resulting in a series of alliances by which the princes rendered homage and pledged their military support in return for an annual pension from the English exchequer. One feature of these alliances which has escaped comment deserves emphasis. Like most such agreements at this period they avowedly excluded certain rulers from their scope; and although the particular individuals thus excluded varied from agreement to agreement, there were two omissions common to all of them: the duke of Burgundy and the king of France. Taken in conjunction with the geographical situation of the countries involved, this leaves no room to doubt that the alliances were designed to inhibit the further expansion of Burgundian power and influence in the Low Countries. But though they were aimed at France and Burgundy, their purpose was essentially defensive, as the terms of one particular agreement with the archbishop of Cologne clearly reveal. In this,[13] it was stipulated that although the king of France was not expressly excluded from the scope of the alliance, he was nevertheless 'to be understood to be excepted, and to be held to be excepted' provided the archbishop promised to renounce his homage to Charles VI within three months of being requested to do so. In other words, if the alliance was to be used against anyone, it would probably be used against France and Burgundy; but the English government had no immediate intention of using it in this way, nor any desire to make an issue of the archbishop's continued allegiance to the French Crown. Provided the government had a prior claim on his support, it was content to let sleeping dogs lie.

It is against this background that Richard's attitude towards the Schism during the last years of his reign must be viewed. On this vital question he is universally believed to have reversed his policy, either because he was unable to secure the support of his own subjects for the *voie de cession* or because he wanted to ingratiate himself with Boniface IX in order to secure papal support for his candidature for the Imperial throne.[14] In fact, however, it is very far from certain that he modified his policy in any important respect. When he agreed to work with Charles VI to secure the joint resignation of the two popes, his agreement had been conditional upon the promise of Charles VI to continue the peace negotiations, a promise which Charles had failed to honour.[15] Without reneging upon his own pledges in any way, Richard had, therefore, every reason to withhold his co-operation after the spring of 1397. But although he naturally became more hesitant in his support, he certainly did not categorically refuse to continue his efforts to secure the resignation of the two popes. According to Charles VI himself, Richard was still committed to the *voie de cession* in the spring of 1398;[16] and at this date at least Charles believed that his commitment was a genuine one, backed up by positive co-operation. This emerges very clearly from a letter written by Charles to his son-in-law in the spring of 1398 to thank him for the recent assistance he had given to a French embassy sent to Germany. The embassy in question had been sent to secure the support of the king of the Romans and the German princes for the Anglo-French proposals to end the Schism, a task in which it had been greatly assisted by an English envoy sent to Germany on a similar mission. According to the French king, the English ambassador had remained in Germany for some considerable time after completing his own mission, for the sole purpose of assisting his French colleague, upon whom he had lavished every attention and honour. He had been instructed to do this by Richard himself, for which his father-in-law was effusively grateful.[17] When all due allowance has been made for the customary superlatives of contemporary diplomatic usage, it would seem reasonable to conclude from this that Charles was without serious doubts as to the English attitude at this date.

There is no sign that he found cause to change his mind in the next few months. In summer of 1398 the French finally decided to go ahead with their plans to withdraw obedience from their pope, and requested that the English government follow suit. In response to this request, Richard referred the matter to an assembly of the higher clergy and to the universities of Oxford and Cambridge, demanding their replies by February 1399.[18] Shortly after this date, and before taking a final decision, he set sail for Ireland, where he was to remain until the invasion of

Henry Bolingbroke brought him hurrying back to England and his death. We cannot know for certain, therefore, what he would eventually have done. He had clearly become hesitant about following the course taken by France, but his hesitancy may well have been a tactical, diplomatic one. He had maintained all along that an Anglo-French peace must precede, or at least accompany a solution to the Schism, and he may therefore have been holding back in the hopes of extracting concessions on this point. But whatever the reasons for this hesitancy, Charles VI still appears to have had no qualms about his ultimate intentions. Had he suspected that the English government would refuse point-blank to implement the *voie de cession*, he would scarcely have withdrawn obedience from Benedict XIII. No other major Urbanist power was openly committed to this policy, and a unilateral withdrawal of obedience from Benedict would only embroil France with her pope to no useful purpose. Despite delays on the English side towards the end, therefore, it does not seem likely that they were due to a radical change in policy. The factor which effectively destroyed the Anglo-French plans to end the Schism was the Lancastrian usurpation.

Although the enthusiastic co-operation which had characterized the mid-1390s had somewhat diminished by the latter part of the decade, therefore, Anglo-French relations remained basically amicable, the two countries continuing to co-operate in many spheres. To this prevailing atmosphere of harmony and goodwill, however, one partial exception must be made, an exception which goes a long way to account for the ambiguities and apparent paradoxes of the period. Although Charles VI and his government continued to be well-disposed towards England the king's brother, the duke of Orleans, certainly was not, and it was his activities – rather than the alleged instability of the king of England – which were to introduce an occasional moment of unease into Anglo-French relations and which were responsible for the disaster with which the century closed.

Throughout the earlier part of the decade the ambitions of Louis of Orleans had been continually frustrated by the steady determination of the English government to oppose French aggression in Italy, where Louis had hoped to carve out a kingdom for himself at the expense of the States of the Church.[19] He was therefore far from happy with the prevailing state of peace. At the same time he grew increasingly out of sympathy with the ecclesiastical policy of his brother's government, since he himself required the support of the Avignon papacy, and hence the continuation of the Schism for the realization of his Italian ambitions.

In the earlier part of the decade he was still too young and inexperienced to make much headway against the resolution of the English government, backed up as it was by the refusal of the duke of Burgundy to countenance policies which entailed the risk of conflict with England. But as the decade wore on, he began to find his feet and to react with increasing political acumen and a steadier sense of purpose against his political tutelage, attracting to himself all those elements within France whose ambitions had been circumscribed by peace with England. Those with a vested interest in intervention in Italy (the house of Anjou) and in Brittany (the house of Blois); those who favoured the *voie de fait* or were otherwise hostile to the decision to abandon the pope of Avignon in favour of a compromise solution to the Schism; and those who stood to lose directly by peace with England (the duke of Berry and the Armagnacs): all these were available allies, ready to make common cause with Louis if opportunity presented itself. Had the crusading projects of the 1390s been successful, Louis might conceivably have found an outlet for his energies in eastern Europe. But the disaster at Nicopolis ruled out this possibility, and it was in the years that followed that Louis began to emerge as a major disruptive force within France. Short of publicly denouncing his government's policy, he did everything he could to hinder the execution of the *voie de cession* and to prevent the withdrawal of obedience from Benedict XIII in 1398.[20] At the same time, he endeavoured to frustrate the projected Anglo-French expedition to Italy;[21] and in pursuit of this aim he steadfastly supported the duke of Milan, and then initiated negotiations for an alliance with Wenzel of Bohemia. By March 1398 the alignment of Wenzel, Milan and Orleans – a veritable 'Urbanist' league – had been cemented by the conclusion of a marriage contract between Orleans' son (Giangaleazzo's grandson) and the niece and heiress of Wenzel. This agreement was supplemented by a political alliance between Wenzel and Orleans against all men except Charles VI himself and the marquis of Moravia. The failure to exclude either Richard II or the duke of Burgundy was equally significant, for in pursuing policies which might bring him into conflict with England, Louis could not avoid, and apparently no longer tried to avoid collision with his uncle. During the course of the interview between Charles VI and Wenzel at Rheims in the spring of 1398 – an interview from which Philip was significantly absent – Louis initiated a policy of acquiring vassals and allies in the Low Countries and the Rhineland, evidently with the purpose of opposing Burgundian interests in that area. The seneschal of Luxembourg and the count of

Cleves received pensions in March and April 1398 in return for their homage, and in the following June the duke of Lorraine joined their number. At this point, the existence of the English and Burgundian blocs inhibited Louis' further progress; but when Henry IV failed to hold together the network of alliances which his predecessor had so laboriously constructed, Orleans added most of the ex-allies of England, including the all-important duke of Guelders and Juliers to his growing clientage.

By 1398 there could therefore be no doubt as to the opposition of Louis of Orleans to the policies of his government, nor of his determination to make his opposition as effective as possible. For as long as Philip of Burgundy maintained his control over the French government, however, its policy towards England remained essentially unchanged. At the very end of this period, this was effectively demonstrated by an incident which occurred during Henry Bolingbroke's exile in France. As we have seen, Richard had been quite happy to allow his cousin to remain in France under the surveillance of Charles VI and his uncle, even paying him a substantial pension while he was there. Henry, however, was by no means content to sit out his exile in Paris in passive resignation and immediately entered into negotiations for a marriage alliance with the 'opposition' princes in France. Through the mediation of the duke of Orleans he sought the hand of the widowed countess of Eu, a daughter of the duke of Berry. As soon as Richard heard of the project he asked Charles VI to quash it, a request which was immediately complied with.

Thus, although the attitude of the duke of Orleans introduced an element of uncertainty and occasional unease into Anglo-French relations, Richard appeared to have no cause for serious concern while Philip of Burgundy was alive, and he could turn his attentions to Irish affairs with a relatively easy mind. While he was absent in Ireland, however, a series of unforeseen contingencies combined with the reckless opportunism of Louis of Orleans to give Bolingbroke the opening which he was to exploit so effectively.[22] From May until November 1399 Paris and the central provinces of France were ravaged by an outbreak of the plague which caused most members of the government to disperse to their estates. Philip of Burgundy spent the entire period in the Low Countries. But Orleans remained in Paris, gained temporary control of the government, and pushed through a series of measures designed to strengthen his position. His possessions were erected into a *pairie* on 28 June; his enemy, de Craon, was found guilty of *lèse-majesté* and banished on 7 June; on 19 July, another enemy, the count of Périgord, was similarly condemned and banished; and on 17 June Orleans concluded an alliance with Henry Bolingbroke, who thereupon left Paris to make his bid to seize the English throne.

Each of these last three measures was an affront to both England and Burgundy, and taken together they afford presumptive evidence that Orleans did – as Henry himself subsequently claimed – lend his support to the Lancastrian usurpation. The disinheritance of the count of Périgord (whose possessions Orleans was shortly to acquire for himself) brought the French frontier into direct contact with English Guyenne, a matter of considerable concern to the English government, especially when Périgord was in the hands of Orleans himself. The banishment of de Craon was an even more unfriendly act; for as well as being a friend and ally of Philip of Burgundy, de Craon was a vassal of Richard II. At the very moment he was banished from France, he was in fact serving Richard in Ireland. Finally, although the alliance of Orleans and Bolingbroke specifically excluded the king of England from its scope, it is morally certain that Henry received secret assistance from Orleans as a consequence of this alliance. Apart from Henry's own subsequent claim to this effect, the timing of the alliance, the marriage negotiations which had preceded it, its coincidence with other unfriendly acts, and the fact that Louis was in control of the French government at the moment when Henry set out for England – many officials must have averted their eyes at this juncture – all tend to validate this conclusion. Although Henry was not offered *French* assistance as Walsingham claimed, he was almost certainly given Orleanist aid and encouragement.

The damage done by Orleans' opportunism was never to be repaired. At one stroke it destroyed the prospects of a stable peace and all that depended upon it. For France good relations with the supplanter and murderer of Charles VI's son-in-law were evidently out of the question. Hostility towards England therefore became a respectable policy after 1399, and with it the resumption of ambitious policies in Italy and of support for the Avignonese papacy. The rivalry between Burgundy and Orleans thereby became more intense, to the further detriment of any sort of stable relationship between England and France. In these conditions all possibility of mutual co-operation 'for the good of Christendom' vanished: in the last half-dozen years of his life Philip de Mézières withdrew into a disillusioned silence. From whatever angle it is viewed, the Lancastrian revolution marks a decisive break with the past, and one almost uniformly unfavourable in its political consequences.

NOTES

1 Perroy, *L'Angleterre et le grand Schisme*, 376–90, and *The Hundred Years' War*, 196–200; and Bueno de Mesquita, 'The Foreign Policy of Richard II in 1397', *EHR*, lvi, 628–37, for the most able statements of these views.

2 *Foedera*, viii, 25; AN J 644/22 for dowry; *Chronicque de la traison et mort de Richart II, passim.*

3 AN J 644/23; *Foedera*, viii, 43.

4 *Foedera*, vii, 850; AN J 644/20; E 364/31, m. lv.

5 C 61/105, m. 12; for next sentence, E 403/556, m. 14; E 403/561, m. 4; *Chronicque de la traison*, 153, 158; ACO B 1514, fo. 86.

6 The list would be a long one: materials in C 76/82; E 403/556, 559, 561, 562; E 364/31, 32; ACO B 1513, 1514, 1517, 1518; and in the chronicles discussed below.

7 Published by Valois, *La France et le grand Schisme*, iii, 620–3.

8 AN J 644/23 (Charles's intervention); E 403/561, mm. 4, 6, 14; E 403/562, m. 12 (payments to Henry); Collas, *Valentine de Milan*, 253.

9 Perroy, *Schisme*, 344–6.

10 *Foedera*, viii, 21–4, 36–8, 66, 80–2 (Low Countries); *PPC*, i, 79–80 (Brittany); *DC* no. 236n. (Aragon); Bueno de Mesquita, *EHR*, lvi, 634–5.

11 *Foedera*, viii, 29, 40–1; C 76–/82, mm. 13, 5–4.

12 Palmer, 'English Foreign Policy, 1388–1399', *The Reign of Richard II*, 75–107, for this and next two paragraphs.

13 C 76/82, m. 13.

14 See works cited in n. 1.

15 Above, 282–4.

16 Ehrle, 'Neue Materialen zur Geschichte Peters von Luna', *Archiv für Literatur- und Kirchengeschichte*, vi, 274–5.

17 *Anglo-Norman Letters*, no. 175; undated, and assigned to the years 1396–9 by the editor, this letter can be dated March–April 1398 by reference to *Deutsche Reichstagakten*, iii, 1–18 and E 364/32, m. 6v.

18 Perroy, *Schisme*, 284–7.

19 Palmer (as n. 12); Durrieu, 'Le royaume d'Adria', *RQH*, xxviii, 43–78.

20 Valois, *La France et le grand Schisme*, iii, 164–83.

21 Pitti, *Cronica*, 102–9; for what follows, Schoos, *Der Machtkampf zwischen Burgund und Orleans*, 119–37; Nordberg, *Les ducs et la royauté*, 156–69.

22 I hope to deal with the circumstances of Bolingbroke's usurpation in more detail elsewhere.

Appendix 1

(a)

(See pp. 21–3 and nn. 32–4, and appendix 2 for the text of the letter.)

In the absence of other direct evidence, this letter is by far and away the most important source on the origins of Anglo-French intervention in Flanders; but it has only been utilized by Kervyn de Lettenhove (see appendix 2), who missed its true significance by assigning it to the year 1383. The objections to this dating are formidable. By April 1383 Richard II had long since been recognized as 'king of France' by Ghent. Moreover, in April 1383 the Despenser crusade to Flanders was in an advanced state of preparation. Openly discussed in the parliament of October 1382, the invasion of Flanders was finally sanctioned by the parliament of February 1383. By March troops and shipping had begun to concentrate on the south coast, and by April all the world knew of the size, leadership and destination of the crusading force – all the world, that is, except those Flemish spies whose job it was to unearth such information. So great a degree of incompetence is incredible: clearly, they were not writing about the events of 1383.

The only alternative to this date is April 1382. The letter cannot be later than 1383, for it would then have been addressed to the duke of Burgundy. On the other hand it cannot be earlier than 1382, since relations between Richard II and Louis de Mâle had certainly not deteriorated to the extent described at the end of this letter before the winter of 1381 at the very earliest (Quicke, *Les Pays-Bas*, 328–35). Furthermore, the activities of the English government described in the letter tally more or less exactly with those of April 1382. Though no parliament was summoned to meet at Windsor for 26 April in 1382 – or indeed in any other year – parliament did meet at Westminster on 7 May. Its business was to discuss a projected *royal* expedition to France, as predicted by Louis' spies. Moreover, this parliament was preceded by a series of meetings between the royal council and the merchants (*RP*, iii, 122), again as described by Louis's spies. Finally, the letter refers to the writers' efforts to secure restitution for recent losses suffered by three burgesses of Sluys at the hands of certain Englishmen. The episode to which this alludes had occurred in September 1381 (*CCR, 1381–5*, 10, 14), so the letter must be subsequent to that date; and since nothing further is heard of these claims, they were in all probability settled in the following year. Taken together, these points leave no room to doubt that the letter was written on 22 April 1382. It is consequently the earliest surviving evidence of the negotiations for an alliance between England and Ghent, and the only evidence prior to October 1382 to hint at the content of those negotiations.

One final point connected with these negotiations deserves mention. The accounts of an English herald, one Richard Hereford, appear to reveal that he and William Gunthrop, a baron of the exchequer, undertook two missions to Flanders in 1381, the first (6 July–2 August) 'to obtain a safe-conduct for Philip van Artevelde and others', and the second (December) for some unspecified purpose (E 101/318/11, 18; E 364/19, m. 2). Both embassies have been the subject of a certain amount of learned exegesis, and the mention of van Artevelde has given rise to the belief that these embassies were concerned with the subject of an alliance between England and Ghent. In fact, however, neither took place in 1381. A comparison of Hereford's accounts with the relevant entries on the Issue Rolls (E 403/480, m. 9) shows that his July mission occured in 1382, not 1381. As for the December mission, this occured in 1379, the entry under 1381 merely recording – somewhat belatedly – sums paid to him for his expenses on that occasion by the treasurer of Calais.

(b)

(See p. 25 and n. 37, p. 33 and n. 7.)

This poem – often cited by historians – has usually been taken to refer to the peace negotiations of 1394. However, the details given in the poem do not tally with this date and will only fit the year 1384. According to Deschamps, the negotiations he is describing took place at *Boulogne*, in *August*, when the king was under age, and when the poet himself was present. All four of these facts rule out the year 1394, and no two of them can be squared with any date other than 1384. In 1384, however, the negotiations were held at Boulogne, they did take place in August, the poet was then present (*Oeuvres*, 11, 42); and if Charles VI was not technically under age, he was nevertheless a mere youth.

(c)

(See p. 33 and n. 8, p. 153 and n. 4.)

This letter – Archives Tarn-et-Garronne, A 33/2; published in *Histoire de Languedoc*, x, 1691–2 – from the Lord Albret to an unnamed count of Armagnac is dated Paris, 17 July, without year. It can only have been written in 1384. The writer commiserates with Armagnac over the recent death of his father, evidently alluding to the death of Count John II on 25 May 1384. Furthermore, he refers to an Anglo-French peace conference due to meet at Boulogne at the end of July, at which the dukes of Burgundy and Berry will be present. The only conference which will fit this description is that held in the summer of 1384.

(d)

(See p. 45 and n. 2.)

All three of these letters – ADN B 277/14452, published by Kervyn de Lettenhove (Froissart, *Oeuvres*, xviii, 543–5) without archival reference – are addressed to the count of Flanders. The first, dated Melun 22 May (without year), is from a king of France, inviting the count to attend an Anglo-French peace conference in Picardy on 8 June when the king's uncle, the duke of Burgundy, would be present. The second and third letters, both dated Paris, 1 June (also without year), are from the king and his uncle thanking the count for his prompt acceptance of the invitation of 22 May. All three have been assigned to the year 1376; but as Perroy has pointed out ('Louis de Mâle et les negotiations de paix franco-anglaises', *RBPH*, xxvii, 146), only Charles VI could have described Philip of Burgundy as his uncle. The letters were therefore written after Charles' accession and before Philip himself became count of Flanders, i.e. in 1381, 1382 or 1383. Of these, Perroy suggested 1383; but this is clearly wrong. The only one of these three years in which an Anglo-French *summit* conference was scheduled to meet in Picardy in June was in 1382 (*Foedera*, vii, 347–8). In that year too Charles VI was at Melun on 22 May (*Séjours de Charles VI*, 415).

Several interesting deductions can be drawn from this correspondence. In the first place, it is clear that Louis de Mâle was invited to attend only at the very last moment, in circumstances of considerable haste. The most probable explanation of this is that the French had been prompted by recent events in Flanders to try to get the 'Flemish question' put on the agenda of the peace conference before Flanders was dragged into the Anglo-French war. This would have been the first time that a count of Flanders had attended an Anglo-French peace conference, and he had evidently not been invited for merely social reasons. Secondly, it seems fair to deduce from subsequent events that the English government refused to include the Flemish question on the agenda of the conference. Within a very few days of this exchange of correspondence, the projected summit meeting had been cancelled. The only new factor in the situation was Flanders; and since the French were willing, if not eager to include this among the subjects for discussion, the English presumably were not.

(e)

(See p. 91 and n. 9, pp. 123–4 and n. 4.)

Despite their importance, these negotiations between the baronial council and Ghent in 1386 and 1387 have hitherto escaped detection. There are two major sources from which they can be reconstructed:

(1) The reports of the Burgundian authorities of their interrogations of two spies, captured at the end of 1386 and the end of 1387 respectively. The first report, on the activities of one Willekin Erembout, has been published by Coussemaker, 'Annalectes historiques', 46–8; the second and more important report, on Clay Delit, by Cartellieri, *Philipp der Kühne*, appendix 4. There are also one or two important unpublished documents relating to Delit's case in ADN B 18822/23461, 23464.

(2) The Issue Rolls of the English exchequer, which record payments made to many of the agents named in these two reports, and which enable the negotiations to be dated with some precision (E 403/515, mm. 8, 11, 13, 14, 18, 22, 25; E 403/517, mm. 2, 16, 19).

Willekin Erembout was captured at the beginning of December 1386. He had been entrusted with a mission to Francis Ackermann in Ghent by the treasurer of Calais and Peter van Bos, Ackermann's one-time colleague who had fled from Flanders at the end of 1385 and was at this time serving in the garrison at Calais (E 101/40/29). The precise nature of his mission is not revealed in the report; but in view of the attitude of the Burgundian authorities, and of the standing of the three principals involved, there can be little doubt that his charge was in some way subversive.

This was certainly the case with Clay Delit, who acted as an inter-

230

mediary between Ackermann and the English government. According to the Burgundian authorities, these negotiations were designed to procure an alliance between England and Ghent against the count of Flanders and the king of France. The negotiations were evidently spread over many months and involved a considerable number of agents: Rovelkin le Lit, Henry Baylew, William van Oreigne, Lievin Leleu, brother Adam Bamford, and Peter Wenk. Most of these agents can be traced in the records of the English exchequer, which corroborate the allegations of the Burgundian authorities and also allow the negotiations to be dated with reasonable precision. William van Oreigne, the first to figure in these records, was awarded the handsome sum of £10 on 31 October 1386 for an embassy from Ghent to the king on behalf of the city authorities. On 17 December 1386, and on 5 and 28 February 1387, he was again rewarded for similar missions between England and Ghent. At approximately the same period, brother Adam Bamford and Peter Wenk received similar commissions, for which they were paid substantial sums on 26 November and 11 December 1386 and 19 March 1387. At a slightly later date Henry Baylew continued the negotiations. On 28 February 1387 he was paid £5 for 'coming from the town of Ghent to declare to the king and his council certain facts concerning the inclinations [status] of the town'. On the advice of the council he was then sent back to Ghent 'on the king's secret business' escorted – significantly enough – 'by a certain armiger of the earl of Arundel'. He received a final payment for his services on 19 August 1387. Finally, one important agent apparently escaped the notice of the Burgundian authorities. Master Nicolas Barbitonser, clerk of the city of Ghent, was rewarded at the exchequer on 2 May and 27 July 1387 for embassies to England from the city authorities. But by this date the negotiations had tailed off and the possibility of an alliance with Ghent had all but disappeared: it was recorded that master Nicolas dare not return to Ghent for fear of his life.

(f)

(See p. 95 and n. 18.)

The date of Ackermann's death is variously given as 22 July 1386 or 22 July 1387. If the former were correct, Ackermann could not have played the important role assigned to him in this narrative, and it is therefore important to decide which (if either) of the two dates is the correct one. According to one redaction of the Flemish chronicles (*Istore*, 383) he was assassinated on 29 June 1386; but according to the *Memorieboek* of Ghent (i, 120) the assassin struck on 22 July 1387. Of the two, the *Memorieboek* is the better authority. Moreover, so far as the year of Ackermann's death is concerned its statement is supported by a number of other pieces of evidence. The accounts of Ghent (*Rekeningen*, 386) record certain sums paid to Ackermann during the course of the year 1387; documents relating to negotiations between Flanders and the Hanse (*Hanserecesse*, ii, 414) imply that he was alive on 1 May 1387; and Clay Delit's testimony makes no sense whatsoever if Ackermann had in fact died before the spring of 1387 (appendix 1(e)). This last source makes it certain that Ackermann was dead before the end of 1387, but the precise date of his death must remain open to question. According to the Issue Rolls of the exchequer (E 403/515, m. 27), he was dead by 1 April; but it can be inferred from the records of the Hanse that he died between 1 May and 17 June; and as we have already seen, the Flemish sources give two conflicting dates, 29 June and 22 July. All that can be said with certainty, therefore, is that his assassination took place in 1387, probably between the late spring and early summer of that year.

(g)

(See p. 96 and n. 21.)

When he made his peace with Charles VI in October 1388, the duke of Guelders claimed that he was not responsible for the letter of defiance, which had been drawn up in England. Had he drafted the document himself he would, he added, have phrased it in very different terms (AN J 522/20). In view of the offensive wording of the defiance, the duke's disclaimer rings true, and there seems no good reason to reject it. It is moreover supported by one slight piece of circumstantial evidence. A copy of the letter of defiance found its way into an ecclesiastical formulary bound up with the register of Archbishop Alexander Neville of York (Borthwick Institute, York; fo. 8 of formulary). In 1388 Neville was succeeded as archbishop by Thomas Arundel, the chancellor who would have been responsible for the drafting of the defiance had it in fact been produced by the English chancery. In these circumstances it would seem quite likely that Arundel was responsible for the original document, from which one of his clerks had taken a copy for his own purposes.

(h)

(see p. 108 and n. 13.)

This letter – published in *DC*, no. 126n. – is dated Gisors, 5 October, without year. Its editor assigned it to the year 1390 on the grounds that Charles VI's itinerary ruled out any subsequent year of the reign. But Charles could not have been at Gisors on 5 October 1390 since he was in Paris on the 6th; there is no other evidence that he issued such an invitation at this date; and the general political circumstances make it improbable that he would have done so. On the evidence of Charles's itinerary, the letter can only be assigned to the year 1387. In that year Charles spent most of October at or near Gisors. It is not known where he was on the 5th, but on 4 October he was at Beauvais, a gentle day's ride from Gisors, where he spent the remainder of the month. More-over, we know that one of the two kings issued an invitation of this kind in the autumn of 1387 from other sources. Finally, one other detail tends to support the year 1387. The letter is countersigned 'Yvo', that is, Yves Derien. There survive other letters countersigned by Derien at this date (AN J 915; BN, MS. Française 20590, fo. 39), but none apparently for the year 1390.

(i)

(See p. 117 and n. 33.)

This memorandum survives in three manuscripts in the Bibliothèque Nationale: BN, NAF 6215; MS. Française 15490, and MS. Dupuy 306, the first of which preserves the earliest and most accurate text. Its contents are indicated by the rubric:

> Memore abrege grossement de la matiere de la guerre d'entre le roy de France et le roy d'Angleterre, extrait des lettres et instruc-tions sur ce faites ou temps passe, lesquellez fauldroit veoir qui vouldroit veoir et bien clerement entendre tout le fait, qui ne pourroit pas estra comprins en si pou d'escripture comme est ceste present, [qui fut faite l'an de grace Mil CCC IIII^{xx} et X].

After analysing the main features of the negotiations since 1369, the author continues:

> Item, pour une aultre instruction qui fut faite l'an CCC IIII^{xx} et VIII *ou environ*, presens nosseigneurs de Berry et de Bourgongne,

> les offres dessusdictes *furent restrainctes* par ce que le roy voult
> que le pais de Rouergue, qui ne fust oncques de la duche de
> Guienne, luy demourast. Et oultre que en toutes les aultres for-
> teresses que son adversaire tient en la marche [de Picardie] fussent
> delivrez au roy pour le restituer a ceulx a qui il appartendroit de
> leur heritage. Etau fort, se le roy d'Angleterre requeroit, que la
> forteresse de Calaiz fut abatue . . . Et oultre en celle instruction
> est contenu que le roy voulloit que les villes et chasteaulx de
> Chierbourc et de Brest luy fussent renduz.

It is apparent both from the wording of the rubric and from the contents of the memoir that the writer had access to the royal archives. In
all probability his account was compiled for one of the French diplomats at the peace conference of 1390; for not only was the memoir
originally completed in that year, but it was subsequently supplemented by the addition of an important collection of documents relating to the peace conferences of 1390 to 1393 (published by Moranvillé,
BEC, l, 355–80), documents which would have been readily available
only to the small circle of those involved in the peace negotiations.

Since he had access to the royal archives, the writer's uncertain
reference to '1388 or thereabouts' would seem to imply that he was
analysing an undated and incomplete documentation, in which case it
can most plausibly be assigned to the abortive conference arranged for
the end of 1387. Some support is given to this conclusion by the statement that these instructions were drawn up in the presence of the
dukes of Burgundy and Berry. For if they were not drafted for the projected conference of 1387, they can only have been drawn up for that
which met in December 1388. In this last case, the two royal uncles are
unlikely to have supervised the diplomatic arrangements, since they
had been dismissed from the government of the kingdom by Charles VI
at the beginning of November.

(j)

(See pp. 128–9 and n. 21.)

The story of these marriage negotiations has been told in some detail
by Froissart (*Chroniques*, xiii, 114–16, 127–35, 276). His account, however, has been dismissed as entirely fictitious by Perroy (*L'Angleterre
et le grand Schisme*, 234–5) and Russell (*English Intervention in Spain*,
495–6) on the grounds that it is unsupported by other evidence, in-

herently improbable, and chronologically impossible. The first point must be conceded, and the second is certainly true as far as Froissart's interpretation of the *motives* of Gaunt and Berry are concerned; but this does not necessarily invalidate his *facts*, of course. As for his chronology, this does present certain minor difficulties, but it is not in fact impossible. On the internal evidence of Froissart's narrative, Perroy dated the main phase of the marriage negotiations from mid-June to early August; and since Gaunt had finally agreed to marry his daughter to Henry of Castile in July, he concluded that this was impossible and that the marriage negotiations with Berry never took place at all. However, he misunderstood Froissart's chronology, which in fact assigns the main phase of the negotiations to the period early May to late June or early July, before the conclusion of the agreement with Castile. In this case, the marriage negotiations with Berry can be fitted into the events of the first half of 1388 without any difficulty. But this chronological problem is really a red herring. Froissart's chronology is vague, probably concealing his own ignorance of the precise dates of the events he describes. It is more important to note that he claimed first-hand knowledge of these negotiations. At the time he was staying on the borders of Blois and Poitou, and he relates that he was there able to collect his information from those involved. To refute his story, therefore, it would be necessary to demonstrate that he had some reason to invent it and some expectation that it would not be challenged. Neither possibility seems very likely.

(k)

(See p. 135 and n. 25.)

The date of this council and the chronology of Franco-Breton relations at this crucial juncture can be pinpointed fairly exactly. Berry, Burgundy and de Montfort eventually met at Blois between 31 May and 2 June (*Itinéraires de Philippe le Hardi*, 193–4). Since Philip himself set out from Paris for Blois on 26 May, he had evidently received an assurance that de Montfort would put in an appearance by that date. Between the meeting of the royal council and the departure of Philip for Blois there had occurred an interval sufficient to allow a French embassy to travel to Brittany, secure de Montfort's promise to appear at Blois, and then report back to Paris. Whatever its haste, this embassy could not have completed its work in less than ten days. The meeting of the royal council must therefore have taken place before 16 May. The *terminus a quo* can be fixed with greater precision. Charles VI remained in Orleans for most of the month of April, waiting for de Montfort to keep the appointment made in the previous December. He did not return to Paris until the beginning of the following month (*Séjours de Charles VI*, 439). At this date both Berry and Burgundy were absent from Paris; Philip did not return to the capital until 11 May, and his brother could not have preceded him by many hours (*Itinéraires*, 193–4; Lehoux, *Jean de Berri*, iii, 472). Since both the king and his uncles attended this council, it met between 11 and 16 May, and probably nearer the earlier date. Le Fèvre (*Journal*, i, 523–4) mentions a number of important sessions of the royal council beginning on 12 May.

It is apparent from this chronology that the French council assembled and acted with unusual speed and decision after de Montfort's non-appearance at Orleans in April, a measure of its assessment of the dangers of the situation.

(I)

(See p. 100 and n. 33, p. 127 and n. 15, p. 134 and n. 31.)

This project for an Anglo-Breton alliance and for the immediate dispatch of an English expeditionary force to Brittany is outlined in 'Les articles du volunte monseigneur le duc de Bretagne', preserved in BM, Cotton MS. Julius B VI, no. 55. The document – subscribed 'passe par moy duc de ma main' – is undated but endorsed in a later hand 'A.D. 1380'. This date is patently incorrect. In clause four, de Montfort required certain obligations under the seals of four royal counsellors: the duke of Gloucester and the counts of Arundel, Derby and Warwick. Quite clearly, therefore, the document belongs to the period of Appellant rule, between December 1387 and May 1389. Furthermore, it must be later than the summer and earlier than the winter of 1388, since it alludes to Arundel's 1388 expedition on the one hand and to the *possibility* of peace or truce negotiations on the other: Arundel was at sea from mid-June to the beginning of September and truce negotiations actually began in December. A slightly earlier *terminus ad quem* than December is very strongly suggested by the fact that de Montfort was (once again) restored to his earldom of Richmond on 20 November. In view of his conduct during the summer, this is incomprehensible unless we assume that he had meanwhile made amends; and the offers contained in this document constituted his apology.

The 'articles' can therefore be dated between August and early November 1388 with some confidence. It may also be suggested – though rather more tentatively – that the most probable date is late August, when Arundel was still at sea but just about to return to England. Once he was back in his duchy, de Montfort had every incentive to renew contact with the English government and every reason to do so without delay. The French were about to invade Guelders, providing an ideal opportunity for an English army to land in Brittany unopposed. De Montfort's insistence on the *immediate* despatch of an expeditionary force, even a small one, may well have been prompted by this consideration. Finally, his failure to mention the truce published at Blaye on 18 August when referring to truce negotiations with France may possibly indicate that he did yet know of its existence.

(m)

(See p. 136 and n. 36.)

Rather astonishingly, this petition appears to have escaped attention. Its importance is underlined by the fact that Knighton incorporated it verbatim in his chronicle, thereby assigning it equal significance with the impeachment of 1386 and the political trials of 1388.

At first sight the petition appears to be misplaced in the chronicle, whose chronology is very muddled at this point. The references to recent peasant risings and to the inordinately heavy taxation of the previous *five* years immediately suggest that it was the product of the parliament of November 1381, which met in the *fifth* year of the reign and in the immediate aftermath of the Peasants' Revolt. But closer examination reveals that the petition was lodged during the second session of the Merciless parliament. This is indicated by a number of minor points, but the decisive argument is provided by the following clause: 'Most dreaded lords: many other reasons might be declared before you to explain why the said commons have revolted, and notably because of the long time consumed by you, our lord [the king], and by the other lords in *this present parliament*.' Clearly the revolt referred to here cannot be the Peasants' Revolt of 1381 since parliament was not in session at any time during its course; but if the clause is compared with a passage in Favent (*Historia*, 21), it will be seen that it alludes to risings which occurred in April and May 1388. According to

237

Favent, these risings were provoked by the enormous amount of time devoted to the trial of Sir Simon Burley, which lasted from 12 to 20 March and then from 13 April to 5 May. This, and the reference to the length of the parliamentary session dates the petition to the second session of the Merciless parliament (13 April–2 June), and in all probability to a date fairly late in the session.

In conclusion, it may be remarked that the evidence here provided of fairly extensive peasant risings in southern England in the spring of 1388 is of considerable interest and some importance, for the rising appears to have escaped attention (e.g. most recently Dobson, *The Peasants' Revolt of 1381*, 29, 333–5).

(n)

(See p. 153 and n. 3.)

This document – entitled 'Raisons pour lesquelles le conte d'Armagnac fit assembler les gens des trois estats des pays d'Agenois, Quercy, Rouergue et Bigorre pour avoir leur conseil sur la manière dont ils se devroint gouverner pour l'onneur et profit du roy et des pays et conservation de leurs bonnes coutumes et privileges' – survives in an authenticated seventeenth-century copy, in BN, Doat MS. 194, fos 294–7 (Gascon) and 298–301 (authorized French translation). It is undated and has been attributed to the year 1361. On internal evidence, however, it is at least a quarter of a century later than this. There is an unmistakable allusion to the Gascon appeals of 1368, and the count of Armagnac names one of the Appellants – a previous count of Armagnac – as his grandfather. The document must therefore have been drawn up in the name of either Count John III (1384–91) or of his brother, Count Bernard VII (1391–1418). Of the two, Bernard VII is the more probable author. Clause 1 of the document states that 'on tient communement et publiquement que le roy donne la paix au roy d'Angleterre'. This immediately rules out the period after 1399 and effectively limits the choice before that date to the years 1384 or 1393–4, the only two occasions when a final settlement was seriously in prospect. But although a draft treaty was negotiated in 1384, the hope of a settlement proved to be short-lived. Moreover, at the time it arose Count John was busy taking stock of his inheritance (his father died on 26 May 1384), and by the time he had done so the peace negotiations had broken down (August). Although the year 1384 cannot be excluded, therefore, 1393–4 is a more probable date. But in any case, the document certainly belongs to the period when the creation of a Lancastrian duchy of Aquitaine was under consideration.

(o)

(See p. 184 and n. 4, and p. 204 and n. 32.)

The size, composition and leadership of the English contribution to the crusading army of 1396 have long been subjects of controversy, and a recent attempt has even been made to prove that no Englishmen whatsoever participated in the crusade (Tipton, 'The English at Nicopolis', *Speculum*, xxvii, 528–40). Tipton points out that there is no concrete evidence that an English army crossed the Channel in the spring of 1396, and argues that the 'English' alluded to by a dozen or so European chroniclers were in fact soldiers of the English province of the Knights Hospitallers at Rhodes. This last argument is too far-fetched to merit much attention. Just conceivably, some central European chroniclers might have adopted this weird terminology without explanation; but that Froissart should do so, or that *all* the chroniclers should simultaneously conspire to deceive historians in this manner, is inconceivable. As for the 'unrecorded' departure of the English army, this – as we have seen – took place at the end of 1394, not in the spring of 1396. By leaving early and travelling via Aquitaine, John of Gaunt's army had hitherto escaped detection. According to Froissart, this army was about 1,500 strong, a figure which approximates reasonably well with that given by the Italian chronicler Fiorentino (1,000 men-at-arms), the only writer to have specified the size of the English contingent at Nicopolis.

Fiorentino is also the only writer to identify the leader of the English force, whom he named as 'a son of the duke of Lancaster'. Tipton has shown conclusively that neither the earl of Derby, Gaunt's one legitimate son, nor the earl of Huntingdon, his son-in-law, could have been at Nicopolis. But Gaunt had three illegitimate sons and the eldest of these, Sir John Beaufort, was almost certainly the English commander. Gaunt, like Philip of Burgundy, would surely have wished one of his sons to deputize for him. Beaufort fits Fiorentino's description; he had accompanied his father to Aquitaine at the end of 1394 (C 61/104, m. 7); there is no trace of his presence in England during the next two and a half years; and when he did return, he was immediately created earl of Somerset for (unspecified) crusading exploits which had redounded to the honour of his country (*RP*, iii, 343). The evidence may be circumstantial but it could scarcely be stronger.

One other Englishman from among the ranks of the aristocracy can be positively identified as having fought at Nicopolis: Sir Ralph Percy. A younger son of the earl of Northumberland, Percy had an enviable reputation in his own day, and was considered by some to be the superior of his far more famous brother, Hotspur. According to the Evesham chronicler, he was captured and slain by the Turks in 1396 (*Historia*, 130). Though not the most reliable of writers, the monk of Evesham is on this occasion corroborated by documentary evidence which, if circumstantial, is nevertheless convincing. Percy left England in the early summer of 1396 (C 76/80, m. 4), and there is no sign that he ever returned. According to the royal inquisition taken in January 1400, he died abroad on 15 September 1397 (C 137/1, no. 6).

(p)

(See pp. 200–1 and n. 23.)

Letters of protection and attorney for Huntingdon and Golofre are dated 18 and 20 January and 12 and 2 February 1394 respectively (*Foedera*, vii, 764; C 76/78, m. 9). Both men were sent *in ambassiatam regis . . . ibidem moraturus*, a formula employed only when an embassy was expected to be absent for a long period. Before his departure Huntingdon was granted 700 marks towards his expenses (E 403/546, m. 21), another indication that he was expected to be abroad for some considerable time. Nothing is known about Golofre's travels; but Huntingdon went to Hungary via Savoy, where he arrived early in March 1394 (Gabotto, *Gli ultimi principi d'Acaia*, 218), a detour which suggests that he may have been instructed to negotiate with Venice. During the course of his embassy he also visited Austria (*CPR 1391–6*, 594). Before leaving England he had been licensed by the pope to choose a confessor to accompany him on his journey 'against the Turks and other enemies of Christ', so there can be no doubt as to the purpose of his embassy (*Cal. Papal Letters*, iv, 489).

The date of the return of the English ambassadors can only be fixed approximately, by circumstantial evidence. Neither accompanied Richard II on his Irish expedition, though both joined him in Ireland at a later date. On 1 February 1395 Golofre was given letters of protection for a journey to Ireland, and on 10 February shipping was ordered to convey Huntingdon there; Golofre witnessed his first Irish charter on 16 February 1395, and Huntingdon received wages of war in the royal army from 8 March onwards (*CPR, 1391–6*, 536, 587; Curtis, *Richard II in Ireland*, 84, 109; E 101/402/20, m. 32v). All this strongly suggests that both men returned to England together at the beginning of 1395. On his return Huntingdon at least came through Paris, where Philip de Mézières enrolled him in the Order of the Passion and presented him with a shortened version of its rules and regulations (Clarke, *Fourteenth Century Studies*, 288–9).

The French embassies to Hungary and Prussia were also absent for almost the whole of the year 1394, though this has been obscured by the unusual manner in which they were paid. It appears that they were jointly financed by Burgundy and Orleans, Orleans paying for the first few months, Burgundy for the last. Consequently, the Burgundian accounts – our main source of information — give the misleading impression that the two embassies only lasted for about half a year, from roughly May to December 1394. In fact, however, when the accounts state that an ambassador was 'absent' for some six months, what they mean is that this was the period for which the Burgundian authorities were financially liable. This can be shown most clearly in the case of the two leaders of the Hungarian embassy, Rénier Pot and his half-brother, William de la Trémoille, marshal of Burgundy. On 5 December 1394 Pot was paid 1,125 francs for an embassy to Hungary which is stated to have lasted about half a year. But at the beginning of the year, on 10 January, he was paid an almost identical sum (1,200 francs) by the duke of Orleans 'to go hastily on a certain long voyage' to Hungary (Pot, *Histoire de Rénier Pot*, 38). His embassy lasted, therefore, ten or eleven months, not five or six, from about late January to early December 1394. Similarly with de la Trémoille. He too received 1,125 francs from the receiver-general of Burgundy in December 1394, from which it might be deduced that his embassy lasted only six months. But fortunately de la Trémoille was given a bonus on top of his wages, and here it was stated that the *total* period of his embassy was 'about ten months', i.e. from January to December 1394. This same entry also states that the remaining thirteen members of this mission were absent for precisely the same period, though elsewhere, in the entries recording the wages they received, their embassies are said to have lasted for only half a year. In view of this it seems reasonable to assume that the embassy sent to Prussia, said to have lasted from May to December, also set out in January 1394 (ACO B 1502, fo. 19v; B 1503, fos 78–78v, 82v–95 *passim*).

It appears from all this that the English and French embassies set out at about the same time, returned at about the same time, and had the same destinations. It seems reasonable to infer that they travelled together and worked for a common purpose. As soon as his ambassadors had returned to France, Philip sent one of them on to Bordeaux to inform John of Gaunt of the results of their mission (ACO B 1503, fo. 94v).

(q)

(See Plates and p. 205, n. 34.)

Despite almost a century of scholarly investigation the Wilton Diptych (see Plates 2 and 3) remains an enigma. What, precisely, does it portray? What is its inner meaning? Theories abound, but none command general acceptance. Three features of the painting – its Christian symbolism, its heraldic peculiarities, and its date of composition – demand explanation, and all three must somehow be reconciled with each other. The hypothesis advanced in the text – that the Diptych portrays Richard II vowing to lead a crusade with Charles VI – satisfies all these requirements.

In the first place it explains the most puzzling of all the features of the painting, the lavish use made of the personal emblems of the two kings, Richard II's badge of the White Hart and Charles VI's Broom Cod collar. Richard himself is decked out in both from neck to toe on one panel, while on the other the entire band of angels wears his badge on their right shoulders and Charles's collar around their necks. Why? Richard's badge does not seem to call for special explanation, but the presence of the personal emblem of the French king has caused so much bewilderment that the author of the most recent attempt to analyse the meaning of the Diptych (Harvey, *Archaeologia*, xcviii, 1–28) was driven to conclude that the Broom Cod collar must have been adopted by Richard II as another of his own personal emblems. But this conclusion is flatly contradicted by all the available evidence. In the first place, there can be no doubt at all that the collar was Charles VI's (e.g. *BEC*, ciii, 119); secondly, in all the abundant literary and record evidence concerning Richard's use of liveries there is no reference to his ever having given this collar to any of his retainers; and finally these same sources – all of them English – several times describe the Broom Cod collar as 'of the livery of the king of France'. There can therefore be no doubt that the persistent pairing of the two emblems in the Diptych is a deliberate allusion to Anglo-French affairs, and more specifically to some form of Anglo-French co-operation. This established, however, there remains the even greater puzzle of why the angels are made to wear the emblems of the two kings, for this smacks of sacrilege. What could have induced the patron (Richard II) to cause the angels to be represented as personal retainers of himself and the French king? Surely, only the mutual association of all three parties in a project so holy as to justify this liberty could have provided the motive. And what could that enterprise be other than the liberation of the Holy Land?

This conclusion is supported by the Christian symbolism of the Diptych. The Christ child wears the emblems of his Passion, the Crown of Thorns and the nails of his Crucifixion. He gestures towards the banner of his Redemption – the banner frequently adopted by crusaders – which Richard himself is about to receive. What could this signify other than the king's readiness to undertake the liberation of the Holy Land with the aid of the French king? The Holy Land was Christ's bequest to the Christian world, won for it with his Blood: hence the symbols of His Passion. The allusion would have been apparent to contemporaries. The symbolism is in fact restated in two contemporary works commissioned by Charles VI himself. The first of these we have already examined (above, p. 180) in connection with the Anglo-French crusading projects of the 1390s. This is Charles's letter of 15 May 1395, in which he outlined the project for a crusade led by himself and Richard II to liberate the Holy Land which, he remarked, '*was acquired for us* by the precious Blood of the Lamb'. At the same period Charles also commissioned Philip de Mézières to compose a treatise destined for Richard II – the famous *Epistre à Richart II* – which was prefaced by an illumination showing the Crown of Thorns linking the Crowns of England and France (see Plate 1). The symbolism here was exactly that expressed in the letter of 15 May and in the Diptych: the Passion of our Lord required the recovery of the Holy Land, and the task of recovering it had devolved upon, and had been accepted by, the kings of England and France.

Finally, the date of the Diptych fits this hypothesis to perfection. The ingenious detective work of a number of scholars, most notably

Clarke (*Fourteenth Century Studies*, 272–92) and Harvey, has now established beyond any reasonable doubt that the painting was executed between 1395 and 1397, and very probably between May and December 1395. This is precisely the period when the possibility of a royal crusade was under discussion, as we have already seen.

Appendix 2

Letter from Flemish spies in London to two counsellors of the count of Flanders detailing recent secret negotiations between the English government and envoys of the city of Ghent, 22 April [1382]. (Lille, ADN B 1337/14596, contemporary copy; published, without archival reference, by Kervyn de Lettenhove, 'Des alliances de la commune de Gand avec Richard II', *BARB*, II, xx. 307–9.)

(See above, pp. 21–3 and 32–4, and p. 45 and n. 3; for a discussion of the date, see appendix 1 (a); for a translation see p. 247 below.)

Copie. Harde, edel, moghende, gheducht here, onse naturlike, gheduchte here ende prinche, onse here van Vlaendren. Ghelieve u, edel here, te wetene hoe dat ane ons commen es in de name van u, edel here, Gheerkin Toluin, uwes baillius clerc van uwer stede van der Nieupoort, onslieden ghegheven heift te kenne in secrete dat hi van uwen weghe commen es te Lonnen om enighe sticken die hi ons ghegheven heift te kenne, die u, edel here, atouchieren. So dat wii dertoe ghedaen hebben, edel here, onse vermeughen, also wii sculdich ziin te doene ende ooc, waerde here, gherne doen ende blide ziin dat ghi ons dies betrauwet. Waerbi, edel here, dat wii verstaen hebben dat iii persone van Ghend te Lonnen waren, die wii zelve zaghen, met brieven van der stede van Ghend, versoukende an den coninc, zinen raed ende an de stede van Lonnen met i brieve, metten andren ende metten derden, principael wesende i Lieven de Crane, Gheraerde zone. Maer d'ander twee niet en moghen wii weten hoe se heten. De welke, edel here, wii gherne ghevolght hadden, dermede dat was Gheerkin deis briefs bringher, om u, edel here, de vorseide personen te bringhene. Dwelke wii, edel here, niet volbringhen mochten mids dat zii gheconvoiiert waren van den Inghelsche tot Colchestre hii de havene ende voeren van denen over in Holland. Dwelke onslieden zonderlinghe leet es dat wii't niet consten ghebetren. So, edel here, dat wii wel verstaen hebben dversouken van hemlieden. Ende hebben ghepresenteerd in de name van der stede van Ghend manscepe hulde te doene den coninc van Ingheland ende zinen lieden, mids dat zii zegghen dat de coninc van Ingheland recht coninc van Vrankerike es ende dat so wie coninc van Vrankerike es dat hi es sculdich te zine hare gherechte here. Also wii hebben ghehoren zegghen, ende zii den coninc ende zinen lieden ghegheven hebbe te kenne, dies de Inghelsche wel blide ziin, ende ooc de meesters van scepen die de coninc omboden heift voor hem ende zinen raed, zegghen dat hem de coninc van Ingheland cortelike zal doen scriven grave van Vlaendren. Ende voord, edel here, zo hebben die van Ghend an den coninc ende der stede van Lonnen begheert soccours ende hulpe van sinen lieden van wapenen tot vichtich duust volx, ende dese zouden, edel here, commen in contrarien van u. Ende zii hebben den coninc ghegheven te kenne ende der stede van Lonnen dat se binnen harer stede van Ghend hebben tot C^m ende XX^m. Ende den coninc ende ziin volc hebben wille over te commene met IIII^{xx} hooftscepen zonder d'andre, ende die meenen toe te commene d'And-werpen. Ende, edel gheducht here, dat wii hebben wel verstaen dat die dese brieven brochte ute Ghend ziin grotelike gheghift van den coninc ende van der stede van Lonnen. Ende zii hebben brieven van den coninc ende van der stede weghe van Lonnen. Also ons gheseid van den zelven lieden die si in hande hadde, daerof dat die van Ghend certaine andworde te bringhene belooft hebben tusschen nu ende Assencioens daghe nu eerst commende. Ende, edel here, zo ne can niemene commen ute Vlaendren, men vraecht hem wat manne het es. Zeicht hi dat hi come ute Ghend, zo es hi wellecomme, ende anders niemen, edel here, van uwen lieden. Ende als enighe brieve commen van uwen weghe, die ziin qualic commen. Ende, edel here, die van Ghend hadden hare andworde ende brieven na Paesschedaghe avonde laest verleden, ende voeren over Smaendaghs daer naer. So waerde here, noch een commen es met brieven van der stede van Ghend an den coninc ende an de stede van Lonnen, up dwelke dat gheordenert es een parlement den derden dach naer Sinte Joris dach eerst com-mende, ende dat zal me houden te Wiinshoren in de herberghe daer ziin zal de coninc ende 't ghemene land. Ende, edel here, om dat wii willen dat ghii 't haestelike weit, so zenden wii over Gheerkine, uwen bode, de welke vaerd ende keerd over copman ende anders niet om u, edel here die te kenne te ghevene. Ende voord, edel here, ten parle-mente vorseide zullen wii ziin omme te wetene hoe ende waerup 't parlement sceeden sal. Ende zeker here, wii waren zelve overcommen het en ware dat wii ligghen ende volghen omme 't goed dat de Inghelsche ghenomen hebben poorters van der Sluus. Van welken goede wii ghesend ziin van Jan Buke, Janne van Cleyhem, filius Heinrix, ende

Aernoud vander Mare. Ende voord, edel here, of ghi te Lonnen weder-
zend, dat ghi niement daer en zend danne den vorseide Gheerkin, mids
dat hi over coopman bekent es. Harde, moghende here, ghebied over
ons als over uwe aerme knechten die u altoos gherne dienen zouden
also wii sculdich ziin te doene. Harde, edel here, God moet u bewaren
ende verleenen goed lyf ende lang. Ghescreven te Lonnen den XXII
dach van Aprille.
[Names of the writers have been obliterated.]
[Dorse: A Messires Josse de Halwin et Henry de Donzy.]

TRANSLATION

Copy. Most noble, powerful and feared lord, our natural feared lord
and prince, our lord of Flanders. May it please you to know, noble lord,
that Gheerkin Toluin, clerk to the bailiff of your town of Nieuport, has
come to us in your name, noble lord, and has told us in secret that he
has come to London on your behalf about some matters of which he has
informed us which concern you, noble lord. In these matters we have
done our best, noble lord, as we are bound and as we are pleased to do,
worthy lord; and we are glad that you have entrusted us with them.
Know then, noble lord, that three persons – whom we ourselves saw –
came from Ghent to London, with letters from the town of Ghent
appealing to the king, his council and the town of London, each of
whom received a separate letter. The head of this embassy was Lievin
de Crane, Gerard's son; but we were unable to discover the identity
of the other two. We would have liked to have followed them, noble
lord, with Gheerkin, who brings this letter to you, in order to bring
them to you, noble lord; but we were unable to do this, noble lord, as
they were conveyed to Colchester harbour by the English, and from
thence went over to Holland. We are very sorry that we could not do
better. However, we did learn their business, noble lord. They have
offered in the name of the town of Ghent to do homage to the king of
England and his people, as they say that the king of England is rightful
king of France, and that as king of France he is their rightful lord. We
have also learnt that they have let the king and his people know [that
they would recognize the king as count of Flanders], with which the
English are well pleased. Also, the masters of ships, whom the king
called before him and his council, say that the king will shortly assume
the title count of Flanders. In addition, noble lord, the envoys from
Ghent have asked the king and the town of London that the English

247

should aid and succour them with weapons and with 50,000 men to be used against you, noble lord. And they have informed the king and the town of London that there are 120,000 in the town of Ghent. And they want the king and his men to come over with 80 large ships, not counting the [small ones]; and they will come to Antwerp. And, noble and feared lord, we have learnt that those who brought these letters from Ghent have been richly rewarded by the king and the town of London, who have entrusted them with letters to Ghent to which they have promised to bring a definite reply between now and next Ascension day [15 May]. And, noble lord, no one can come from Flanders without being asked who he is. If he says that he is from Ghent, he is welcome; but none of your men, noble lord, are welcome; and if any letters come from you, they are badly received. And, noble lord, the envoys from Ghent received their answer and were given letters to take back on the evening of Easter day [6 April], and returned to Ghent on the following Monday. Since then, noble lord, another person has come with letters from the town of Ghent to the king and the town of London, as a result of which parliament has been summoned for the third day after St. George's day [26 April] at Windsor, where the king and the Commons will be present. Because we wish you to know all this as soon as possible, noble lord, we send Gheerkin your messenger, who travels as a merchant (and not otherwise) to inform you of this, noble lord. Further, noble lord, we shall be at the aforementioned parliament to discover how and what parliament shall decide. We would certainly have returned to you ourselves, lord, were it not for the fact that we are seeking restitution of the property which the English have taken from the citizens of Sluys, for which purpose we were sent here by Jan Buck, Janne von Cleyhem, the son of Henry, and Arnold van der Mare. If you sent again to London, noble lord, send no one other than the aforesaid Gheerkin, as he is known as a merchant. Most powerful lord, command us as your poor servants, who shall always gladly serve you as we are bound to do. Most noble lord, God preserve you and give you a good and long life. Written at London, 22 April [1382].

Appendix 3

Letter of Philip of Burgundy of 6 May 1387 concerning the aide granted by the duchy of Burgundy to finance the invasion of England in 1386, incorporated in a mandate addressed to one of his receivers. (Dijon, ACO B 2299, fo. 1.)

(See above, pp. 72–3 and n. 11, p. 74 and n. 15, p. 79 and n. 30.)

Copie du povoir du dit Guillaume [Bataille].

Les esleuz ou duchie de Bourgogne sur le fait de XL^m frans octroyez a monseigneur de Bourgogne en Mars Mil CCC IIII^{xx} et Cinq [sc 1386], et sur ung don de XX^m frans qui nagaires fu octroyez a nostre dit seigneur a la presence de monseigneur le conte de Nevers et baron de Donzi, filz de nostre dit seigneur, par les gens d'eglise, nobles et bourgeois du dit duchie, *pour sostenir les fraiz que mon dit seigneur a faiz pour le passaige d'Engleterre que le roy et nostre dit seigneur entendoient a faire ou dit pais d'Engleterre*, a Guillaume Bataille, receveur des diz foaiges es baillages d'Ostun et de Moncenis, salut. Nous avons receu les lettres de nostre dit seigneur contenantes la forme qui s'ensuit:

Philippe, filz de roy de France, duc de Bourgogne, conte de Flandres, d'Artois et de Bourgogne, palatin sire de Salins, conte de Rethel et seigneur de Malignes, aus esleuz et receveur qui ont este ordonnez sur le fait des quarente mille frans a nous octroyes par les gens d'eglise, nobles, bourgeois et habitans de nostre pais de Bourgogne deca la Saoune en l'annee novellement passe, salut. *Comme environ a ung an monseigneur le roy, ayent en propoux de passer en personne a toute sa puissance ou pais d'Engleterre pour grever et domaigier ses ennemis at mectre fin en sa guerre*, eust mis sus en tout son royaume, tant en Languedoc comme doyl, pour convertir ou dit fait certains aides et empruns, les quelx touz les princes, barons, prelaz, et autres de son dit royaume consentirent et acorderent estre levez en leurs terres; et pour ce que lors les gens de nostre dit pais nous avoyent freschement octroyez les diz XL^m frans, dont encores n'estoit escheu fors le premier paiement; et qu'il eussent este moult grevez se, avec la dite somme, eussent paie le dit aide; Nous, pour les relever de ce, eussions fait baillier en lieu de l'aide que mon dit seigneur eust peu liever en nostre dit pais a maistre Nicolas de Plancy (ordene de recevoir le dit aide) deux paimens de la dit somme de quarente mille frans, montans a la somme de vint mille frans, parmi ce que les gens de nostre dit pais (qui pour ce furent assemblez par nostre ordenance en nostre ville de Diion) consentirent en la presence de Jehan nostre filz, conte de Nevers et baron de Donzi, et des gens de nostre grant conseil illenc estans et envoyez pour ce depart nous, nous recompenser de la dite somme apres le paiement des diz XL^m frans. Et ia soit ce que mon dit seigneur n'ait acompli le veaige et passaige dessuz dit, *niantmoins il ait fait – et aussi nous qui avions entencion de passer en nostre personne avec tout nostre povoir en sa compaignie – touz les fraiz qui povyent cheoir ou dit fait, tant en paiemens de gens d'armes, salaires de navioes, provisions de vivres, comme d'autres choses quelxcumques; et n'ait tenu fors que a l'indisposicion du temps et vent, qui furent du tout contraires si comme ces choses sont noctoires.* Nous vous mandons et enioignons estroitement et commectons se mestier est que les diz vint mille frans faites imposer, cuillir et liever sur les gens de nostre dit pais selon les instructions que vous eustes des diz XL^m frans, a deux termes et en telle maniere que a ceste prochaine feste de Saint Jehan Baptiste puissons avoir touz levez et preste les dix mille frans, et a la feste de Saint Remy ensuyent les autres dix mille en lieu des ii paiemens dont dessuz est faite mencion, montans a la somme par nous baillie au dit maistre Nicolas de Plancy, a la descharge de nostre dit pais comme dit est. Et de ce faites telle deligence qu'il n'y ait aucune faute, car nous nous en prendrons a vous de ce faire, vous donnons povoir et mandement especial, mandons et commandons a touz noz iusticiers et subgez que a vous et a voz commis et deputez en faisent les choses dessuz dites ou c[ir] constances et despendences d'icelles obeissent et entendent diligentement et vous prestent et donnent confort et aide se mestier est et requis en sont. Donne a Compiegne le VIe jour de May l'an de grace Mil CCC IIII^xx et Sept. Ainssi signe: Par monseigneur le duc, vous present: J. Hue.

Appendix 4

Indenture between the captain of Calais and four bourgeois of Flanders on the subject of a commercial agreement between England and Flanders, dated Calais 22 October 1387. (Lille, ADN B 517/11679.)

(See pp. 113–15 and n. 28.)

Copie. Ceste endenture – faite entre honnore et poissant seignour monsieur Guillame de Beauchamp, frere du conte de Warrewyk et capitaine de Calois et gouvernour de la marche pour le roy de France et d'Engleterre nostre tressouverain et liege seignour d'une partie, et Lubrecht Scuttellaer, bourgois de la ville de Bruges en Flandre, ensamble avoec autres trois bourgois souffisans et gens d'estat du dit pays de Flandre d'autre partie – tesmoigne que comme nadgaire de temps le dit Lubrecht Scuttelaer fust venu au dit lieu de Calois pour certaines choses que il avoit illoeques a negocier et besongnier; sur quoy fut avenu que paroles doulces, plaisantes et traictables eussent este parlees par le dit Lubrecht a William Elarton, escuier, mareschal de Calays, et a Jehan Ultyng, escuier et merchant de la dite ville de Caloys; contenantes en effect et soubstance une maniere de traitie que il desiroit estre fait entre le roy nostre dit seignour, son royaume d'Engleterre et tous les autres pays, terres et seignouries d'une partie, et le dit pays et la seignourie de Flandres d'autre, a fin que cours de marchandise peust estre use par mer et par terre en dit pays de Flandres en temps advenir en la maniere et estat que il fut et estoit use audevant de la guerre et division darreinement meue et usoie en dit pays de Flanders: c'est assavoir, que tous les liges, subges, allies et bienvuillans du roy nostre dit seignour peussent estre et feussent benignment receuz et franchement, liberalment et sans aucun danger ne desaese peussent venir es parties du dit pays de Flandres et illoeques converser, demourer, habiter, marchander, et residence faire sans aucun molestacion, empeschement, destourbier, arrest ne violence leur estre fait ne a l'un de eulx a cause de la discencion qui a este entre le roy nostre dit seignour, son dit royaume et ses autres terres, pays et seignouries, et le dit pays de Flandres, ne autrement par nulle maniere indeue ne desraisonnable; et que aussi et par telle maniere tous les gens du dit pays de Flandres peussent estre et feussent benignement receus et franchement, liberalment et sans aucun danger ne desaese peussent venir par mer et par terre es diz royaume d'Engleterre et autres seignouries, terres et pays du roy nostre dit seignour, et illoeques converser, demourer, habiter, marchander et faire residence sans aucun molestacion, empeschement, destourbier, arrest ne violence leur estre faite ne a l'un d'eulz a cause de la dite discencion ne autrement par nulle maniere indeue.

Sur quoy les diz Elarton et Jehan Ultyng, voyans la volente du dit Lubrecht, lui eussent demande se il avoit aucun povoir de par le dit pays de Flandres ne de par la seignourie d'icellui par quoy il peust commencier, entamer ne entreprendre a parler de si haute matiere et royal fait comme de faire traittie en celle partie. A quoy il eust respondu que 'non'; mais – a fin que les diz Elarton et Ultyng peussent clierement sentir, veoir et appercevoir que sur efficaux matere son propos et desir estoit de veoir bon traittie de loyale et ferme paix en cas dessus dit – il leur dist que, se il povoit trouver en dit pays de Flandres et ovec la seignourie d'icellui que l'en voulsist entendre au dit traittie, il retourneroit pardevers les diz mareschal et Ultyng et les en certefieroit, a fin que part aucune mediacion avoec l'aide de Dieu le dit traittie se peust commenchier et cheoir en fourme comme le souverain desir d'icelluy Lubrecht estoit.

Et ce fait, le dit Lubrecht s'en fust retourne en dit pays de Flandres. Et par apres a certain jour fust venu au dit lieu de Calays sur le sauf-conduit du dit capitaine, qui adonques estoit retourne d'Engleterre ou il avoit este et estoit au temps que les dites paroles furent parlees parentre les diz Lubrecht, Elarton et Ultyng. Pardevvant le quel capitaine les paroles dessus dites eussent este recitees et de nouvel parlees et acordees par entre les diz Lubrecht, mareschal et Ultyng. Sur quoy le dit capitaine eust dit que, se il advenoit que traittie de paix se feist en cas dessus dit, il lui sembloit que la ville de Gravelinghes et le chastel de l'Escluse (qui a present sont gardees et tenues par les Francois, ennemiz du roy nostre dit seignour) convendroient premiere-ment et avant toutes choses estre mises a l'estat a quoy eulz estoient audevant de la dite descencion meue et commencie, ainsi que d'yceulx guerre, destourbier ne grevance ne fust fait par mer ne par terre au roy nostre dit seignour ne aux siens en aucune maniere. Sur quoy le dit Lubrecht eust respondu que se il advenoit que la dite traittie se prinst, il entendoit que tant serroit fait a l'aide de Dieu envers le roy de

France et le duc de Bourgongne que la dite ville de Gravelinghes ne le chastel de l'Escluse ne ferroient mal, guerre, destourbier, violence, molestacion ne damage au roy nostre dit seignour ne aux merchans et gens du dit royaume d'Engleterre ne des autres terres et pays et seignouries d'icellui nostre seignour le roy.

Et ainsi se fust parti le dit Lubrecht du dit lieu de Calois et ale vers les dites parties de Flandres, disant au capitaine que pour lui faire avoir cognoissance que son propos et sa venue au dit lieu de Calois ne la mocion de ses dites paroles ne estoient pas commencees ne fondees sur vanite ne par maniere frivoles, il feroit venir a certain jour certaines gens du dit pays de Flandres notables, soffisans et d'estat a l'abbaie des Dunes ou au dit lieu de Calois, en la presence des queux il recorderoit, recevroit et de nouvel parleroit les paroles et choses surdites, fust en la presence du dit capitaine ou des diz Elarton et Ultyng ou aultre quelconque personne qu'il plairot au dit capitaine a ce commettre. Et apres son dit departir de Calais, aussi comme sur la fin de son saufconduit, fust retourne a ycellui lieu de Caloys et eust requis le dit capitaine que pour ce que il ne povoit pas encore avoir amene les dites gens, il lui pleust lui aloigner le dit saufconduit iusques a certain jour, ainsi que a griegnour deliberacion il peust parler as dites gens et yceulx amener comme dit est pour oir la desclaracion de ses dites paroles, a l'entente que le dit capitaine peusse par lour response et contenance percevoir et avoir cognoissance comme eulx ont le dit fait aggreable. En quel cas soit avenu que yce Samady le XIXe jour d'Octobre darrainement passe le dit Lubrecht, ensamble avec trois bourgois soffisans, persones et gens d'estat . . . vindront au dit lieu de Calois sur le dit saufconduit; en la presence des queux le dit Lubrecht recita recorda et de nouvel parla toutes les choses dessus dites pardevant le dit capitaine, adonques estant a l'ostel des freres Carmes en la dite ville de Calais acompaignie de honnourable et puissant homme monsieur Esmon de la Pole, frere du conte de Suffolk et capitaine du chastel du dit lieu de Calois; monsieur Jehan de Say, baron de Wemme, et monsieur Robert de Whittenay, chivaliers; seignour Rogier Walden, tresorier de Calais; Richart Wodehale, mair du dit lieu; Jehan de Loucroft, le dit Jehan Ultyng, et Perrin Loharent, escuiers.

Et apres ce que les diz trois bourgois volentairement eurent dit plainement, sommierement et appertement que il leur sembloit la motion des dites paroles et tout ce qui avoit este fait, dit et commenchie en cas dessus dit par le dit Lubrecht este et estre deuement, loyaument, proufitablement et al honnour du dit pays de Flandres faictes, dites et parlees; et que l'endroit de la dite ville de Gravelinghes et du dit chastel de l'Escluse, eulz esporroient et esporrount que tant seroit fait envers les diz roy de France, duc de Bourgongne et siegnourie du dit pays de Flandres que les paroles du dit Lubrecht en celle partie seront entierement tenues et trouvees vraies.

Sur quoy fut demande de par le dit capitaine aux dessus diz se eulx avoient aucun povoir de proceder en fait du dit traittie, tout ainsi et en la maniere que il avoit audevant este demandie au dit Lubrecht. A quoy eulz responderent que 'non'. Et pour ce ne fust plus avant fait en la dite matiere, fors soulement que le dit Lubrecht et les autres diz troiz bourgoiz disrent tout a une vois que il leur sembloit que meritore chose et vraie oevre de charite seroit de labourer en fait du dit traittie se faire se povoit en aucune maniere, tant pour eschuer a l'effusion de l'umain sanc que pour destruire et anuller les pechies de orguil, d'envie et de rancune qui par la continuacion des guerres se nourrissent et enracinent es cuers des Cristiens, a la desplaisance de Dieu et confusion de leur aumes. Et aussi pour ouvrir le droit chemin du cours de marchandise qui par la dite discencion a longuement estre estouppe, encombre et tenu hors de usage entre le dit royaume d'Engleterre et les autres terres, pays et seignouries du roy nostre dit seignour et le dit pays de Flanderes, a grant damage, preiudice et grief[et] desavantage de chescune coste; ainsi que par ce le pueple cristien puisse en chescune des dites parties vivre en paix, amour, tranquillite et perseverance en bien, et de leur biens et de leur corps servir Dieu et vivre en charite et aumoigne l'amendement de leurs vies et de leur almes.

Et pour ce le dit Lubrecht pria le dit capitaine que puis que Dieu lui avoit donne grace d'avoir meu premierement les dites paroles, il pleust au dit capitaine – a la reverence de Dieu et pour contemplacion des choses surdites – escrivre du dit fait pardevers le roy nostre dit seignour et son royal conseil, a l'entente que par la grace de Dieu et sa bonne mediacion aucune jour de traittie se peust prendre a quoy les conseilx du roy nostre dit seignour et du dit pays et seignourie peussent estre pour appointer et mettre au fin le dit fait; la quele chose le dit capitaine lui acorda, et se charga d'en escripre comme dit est.

Et aussi le dit Lubrecht se charga d'aler devers le dit pays de Flandres et diligentement, curiousement et sans faintise faire par voie de supplicacion et de humilite tout son povoir envers son droit lige seignour le duc de Bourgongne de amener et mettre le pueple d'icelluy pays en volente, propos et entente de finalment, peremptoirement, effectuelement, sans fraude ne . . . le dit traittie, et en ycellui continuer iusques a la fin par la volente et licence du dit son seignour.

En tesmoingnance des quelles choses ces endentures [sont] entre changablement scellees du seel du dit capitaine pour sa partie et du seel du dit Lubrecht tant pour lui que pour les autres diz trois bourgois de Flandres demourante devers ycellui Lubrecht et les dizt rois bourgois.

Faite et donnee au dit lieu de Calois le XXIIᵉ jour de Octobre l'an de grace Mil CCC IIIIˣˣ et Sept.

Appendix 5

Instructions to the English ambassadors to France, dated Ledes castle 8 July 1395. (BM, Cotton MS. Vitellius C XI, nos 2–3; original on parchment; autograph signature; seals missing.)

(See pp. 169–71 and n. 5.)

L'instruccion donee a lui reverent pere en Dieu, l'ercevesque de Dyvelyn, as contes de Ruteland et Mareschal et as autres messages envoiez de par nostre tresredoute seignur le roy vers son cousin de France pur treter du mariage parentre nostre dit seignur le roy et Isabelle, eisnee fille de son dit cousin, en espoire de meillour et plus ferme et seure pees avoir entre les deux roiaumes; et pur ent accorder pleinement en manere desouz escrite; et aussint pur treter de la dite pees: c'est assavoir, de faire fin par la grace de Dieu de la mariage susdite et de reporter ce que serra faite touchante la dite tretee de pees.

Primerement, que touchante la dite pees les messages susditz entrent en tretee ovesque les Franceoys, fesantz protestacion en la plus honeste manere que faire se purra.

Item, que les ditz messages demandent pur la partie du roy nostre dit seignur toute la duchee de Guyene ovesque les feez, seignuries, avoesons et toutes autres choses si entierement et si avant come ils estoient grantez au roy Edward en le darrein pees et accord que se fist a Caleys entre lui et le roy Johan de France, a tenir a nostre dit seignur le roy et a ses heirs sanz faire aucune homage pur mesme la duchee.

Item, que le roy nostre dit seignur avera Caleys et la seignurie de Merk ovesque les marches de Caleys et le countee de Guynes et la seignurie de Pountif aussi entierement come ils estoient grantez au dit roy Edward en la dite pees et accord, sanz faire aucune homage pur ycelles ou pur aucune parcelle d'icelles.

Item, que les armes du roy nostre dit seignur queles il ad a present demoerent ovesque lui et ses heirs a touz iours.

Item, que les ditz messages demandent pur la partie nostre dit seignur le roy tout ce q'est a deriere de la raunceon du roy Johan de Fraunce, ensemblement ovesque les damages et coustages soeffertz et faitz par mesme nostre seignur le roy ou par aucun de ses progenitours puis la commencement de la guerre tanque encea.

Item, que nostre seint piere le pape Boniface soit compris en la dite tretee de pees.

Item, que s'il avyegne par la grace de Dieu touchante la dite mariage que nostre seignur le roy eit ovesque la dite Isabelle, fille de son dit cousin de France, un filz, adonques le dit filz soit duc de Normandie et conte d'Angoye et de Meyne, et eit mesmes les duchee et countees ovesque les fees, seignuries, avoesons et toutes autres choses si entierement et si avant come aucun roy d'Engleterre les ad euz avant ces heures.

Item, que si touchante mesme la mariage il avyegne que mesme nostre seignur le roy eit ovesque la dite Isabelle un autre filz ou fille, adonques l'eisne filz eit soulement le dite duchee de Normandie et l'autre filz ou fille les ditz countees d'Angoye et de Meyne.

Item, quant a mesme la mariage: si Dieu le veulle que nostre dit seignur le roy eit pluseurs filz ovesque la dite Isabelle; et si par cas il purra estre trovez que le roiaume d'Escoce soit en aucune manere confisquez, ou autrement qu'il deveroit devenir a la corone d'Engleterre; issint que le roy nostre dit seignur voudra doner as aucuns de ses ditz filz le dit roiaume d'Escoce, adonques son dit cousin de France serra tenuz de trover certein nombre de gentz d'armes et d'autres guerroiours tanque le dit roiaume soit conquis ou paisiblement enjoiez par le filz susdit, ou au meins durantz certeins ans.

En tesmoignance de quele chose les grand et prive sealx et aussi le signet de nostre dit seignur le roy de son commandement sont mys a ceste instruccion.

Don. au chastel de Ledes le VIII jour de Juyl l'an du regne de nostre dit seignur dys et noefisme.

Le Roy R S

Bibliography

MANUSCRIPT SOURCES

Public Record Office, London

The Record Office was the richest source of documentation for this study. The *Gascon Rolls* (C 61); *Treaty Rolls* (C 76); *Council and Privy Seal Files* (E 28); *Exchequer Diplomatic Documents* (E 30); *Exchequer Miscellaneous Books* (E 36); *Accounts Various* (E 101); *Memoranda Rolls* (E 159); *Enrolled Accounts* (E 364); and *Issue Rolls* (E 403) were consulted for the period covered by this book; and the *Chancery Miscellanea* (C 47); *Warrants for the Great Seal, Series 1* (C 81); *Inquisitions Post Mortem* (C 137); *Writs and Warrants for Issues* (E 404), and *Ancient Petitions* (SC 8) were sampled for particular purposes. The classifications of the PRO are described in the official *Guide*, and the contents of individual classes listed or analysed in the relevant volumes of *PRO Lists* or in the volumes distributed to subscribers by the *List and Index Society* (see bibliography for details).

British Museum, London

The *Cotton, Harley* and *Royal* collections, the *Additional Manuscripts,* and the *Charters and Rolls* all contain important materials; but in view of the arrangement—or rather, lack of arrangement – of these collections, they can only be profitably approached by reading through their catalogues, *viz: Catalogue* of Additions and of the Cotton, Harley and Old Royal collections, and *Index* to the Charters and Rolls. Other catalogues, both in manuscript and in print, are conveniently listed in *Catalogues of the MSS Collections.*

Archives Nationales, Paris

The *layettes* of the *Trésor des Chartes* concerning England (J 643–4) contained a number of important documents, but otherwise the Archives contributed only one or two minor items to this study. The *Etat sommaire* describes the main classifications of the archives, and series K is fully analysed in *Monuments historiques.*

Bibliography

Bibliothèque Nationale, Paris
The MSS. français proved the most rewarding source, though some of the
individual collections – Dupuy, Doat, Duchesne – yielded one or two items of
interest. As with the BM, the heterogeneous nature of the collections in the
BN makes it essential to approach them through the catalogues, the most
important of which are the *Catalogue générale des MSS français*; *Catalogue
des MSS . . . Clairambault*; *Catalogue de la collection Dupuy*; *Catalogue des
fonds Libri et Barrois*, and the manuscript catalogue of the *pièces originales*.
Other catalogues, both in print and in manuscript, are listed by Langlois and
Stein, *Archives de l'histoire de France*.

Archives Départementales du Nord, Lille
Apart from the PRO, the Lille archives proved the richest source for this
study. The *Trésor des Chartes*, particularly the subsections on treaties (B 277–
85), commerce (B 515–22), France (B 655), Flanders (B 1275–9), and Ghent
(B 1337), produced more than could be fully used, and the first register of
lettres missives was equally valuable.
The classifications of the Lille archives are fully described in the *Répertoire
numérique* and more extensively analysed in the *Inventaire sommaire*.

Archives Départementales de la Côte-d'Or, Dijon
The accounts of the receiver-general of all finances of the duke of Burgundy
(B 1467–1518) produced much useful, miscellaneous information of the kind
found in the *Issue Rolls* of the English exchequer.
The Dijon archives are fully described in the *Inventaire sommaire*.

Edinburgh University Library
Edinburgh University MS. 183 (formerly MS. Laing 351) produced one or
two important letters. The MS. is described in the introduction to *DC*, where
the bulk of the letters are published.

PUBLISHED WORKS

(Full titles of works cited in the notes)

Anglo-French Negotiations at Bruges, 1374–1377, ed. E. Perroy, RHS, Camden
Miscellany xix, London, 1952.
Anglo-Norman Letters and Petitions, ed. M. D. Legge, Anglo-Norman Text
Society, iii, Oxford, 1941.
Annales avignonnaises de 1382 à 1410 extraites des archives de Datini, ed.
R. Brun, *Mémoires de l'Institut historique de Provence*, xii (Marseilles, 1935),
17–142; xiii (1936), 58–105; xiv (1937), 21–52; xv (1938), 21–52, 154–92.
Antient Kalendars and Inventories of the Treasury of H.M. Exchequer, ed.
F. Palgrave, RC, 3 vols, London, 1836.

Apparicion de maistre Jehan de Meun et le Somnium super Materia Schismatis d'Honoré Bonet, ed. I. Arnold, Paris, 1926.

Archives de l'Orient Latin, ed. Count P. Riant, 2 vols, Paris, 1881–4.

ARMITAGE-SMITH, S., *John of Gaunt*, London, 1904; reprinted 1964.

ASTON, M., 'The Impeachment of Bishop Despenser', *BIHR*, xxxviii (1965), 127–48.

ATIYA, A. S., *The Crusade in the Later Middle Ages*, London, 1938.

—— *The Crusade of Nicopolis*, London, 1934.

BAILEY, C. C., 'The Campaign of 1375 and the Good Parliament', *EHR*, lv (1940), 370–83.

BALDWIN, J. F., *The King's Council in England during the Middle Ages*, Oxford, 1913.

BARKER, J. W., *Manuel II Palaeologus (1391–1425): A Study in Late Byzantine Statesmanship*, New Brunswick, 1969.

BOUTRUCHE, R., *La crise d'une société: seigneurs et paysans de Bordelais pendant la guerre de Cent Ans*, Paris, 1947.

BRANDON, J., *Cronique, 1360–1428*, ed. Kervyn de Lettenhove; *Chroniques relatives à l'histoire de Belgique sous la domination des ducs de Bourgogne*, i, 1ff., CRH, Brussels, 1870.

BUENO DE MESQUITA, D. M., 'The Foreign Policy of Richard II in 1397: Some Italian Letters', *EHR*, lvi (1941), 628–37.

——, *Giangaleazzo Visconti, Duke of Milan, 1351–1402*, Cambridge, 1941.

Calendar of Charter Rolls, 1341–1417, HMSO, London, 1916.

Calendar of Close Rolls, 1377–1399, HMSO, 6 vols, London, 1914–27.

Calendar of Fine Rolls, 1377–1399, HMSO, 3 vols, London, 1927–9.

Calendar of Letter-Books of the City of London, H, 1375–1399, ed. R. R. Sharpe, London, 1907.

Calendar of Papal Letters, 1362–1404, HMSO, 2 vols, London, 1902–4.

Calendar of Patent Rolls, 1377–1399, HMSO, 6 vols, London, 1895–1909.

Calendar of State Papers. Milan, i, 1385–1618, ed. A. B. Hinds, HMSO, London, 1913.

Calendar of State Papers: Venetian, i, 1202–1509, ed. R. Brown, HMSO, London, 1864.

CALMETTE, J. and E. DÉPREZ, *La France et l'Angleterre en conflit* (G. Glotz, *Histoire générale. Moyen Age*, VII, i), Paris, 1937.

CAMPBELL, J., 'England, Scotland and the Hundred Years' War in the Fourteenth Century', *Europe in the Late Middle Ages*, ed. J. Hale, R. Highfield and B. Smalley, London, 1965, 184–216.

CARTELLIERI, O., *Philipp der Kühne* (*Geschichte der Herzöge von Burgund, 1363–1477, i*), Leipzig, 1910.

Catalogue de la collection Dupuy, ed. L. Dorez, 2 vols, Paris, 1899.

Catalogue des manuscrits de la collection Clairambault, ed. P. Lauer, 3 vols, Paris, 1923–32.

Catalogue des manuscrits des fonds Libri et Barrois, ed. L. Delisle, Paris, 1888.

Catalogue générale des manuscrits français, ed. H. Omont *et al.* 17 vols, Paris,
1868–1918; *Index*, ed. A. Vidier and P. Perrier, 6 vols, Paris, 1931–48.
Catalogue of Additions to the Manuscripts in the British Museum, 1783–1935,
16 vols, London, 1843–1967.
Catalogue of Manuscripts in the Cottonian Library in the British Museum, ed.
J. Planta, RC, London, 1802.
Catalogue of the Harleian Collection of Manuscripts in the British Museum, new
edition ed. R. Nares *et al.* RC, 4 vols, London, 1808–12.
*Catalogue of Western Manuscripts in the Old Royal and King's Collections in the
British Museum*, ed. Sir G. F. Warner and J. P. Gilson, 4 vols, London, 1921.
Catalogues of the Manuscript Collections in the British Museum, Trustees of the
BM, London, 1962.
Choix de pièces inédites relatives au règne de Charles VI, ed. L. Douet d'Arcq,
2 vols, Paris, 1863–4.
Chronicque de la traison et mort de Richart II, ed. B. Williams, English Historical
Society, London, 1846.
Chronique des quatre premiers Valois, 1327–1393, ed. S. Luce, SHF, Paris, 1862.
Chronique du religieux de Saint-Denys, ed. L. Bellaguet, CDIHF, 6 vols, Paris,
1839–52.
*Chronique rimée des troubles de Flandres à la fin du XIVe siecle, suivie de documents
inédits*, ed. E. le Glay, Lille, 1842.
Chronographia regum francorum, ed. H. Moranvillé, SHF, 3 vols, Paris, 1891–7.
CIRCOURT, A. DE, 'Le duc Louis d'Orléans, frère du roi Charles VI. Les
débuts dans la politique. Origines de sa rivalité avec les ducs de Bourgogne,
1386–1391', *RQH*, xlii (1887), 5–67.
——, 'Le duc Louis d'Orléans. Ses entreprises en Italie, 1392–1396', *RQH*, xlv
(1889), 70–127.
——, 'Le duc Louis d'Orléans. Ses entreprises en Italie, 1394–1396. Savone et
Gênes', *RQH*, xlvi (1889), 91–168.
CLARKE, M. V., *Fourteenth Century Studies*, ed. L. S. Sunderland and
M. McKisack, Oxford, 1937.
COCHON, P., *Chronique normande, 1108–1430*, ed. C. de Robillard de
Beaupaire, Rouen, 1870.
Codex diplomaticus prussicus, 1217–1404, ed. J. Voigt, 6 vols, Königsberg,
1836–61.
COLLAS, E., *Valentine de Milan, duchesse d'Orléans*, 2nd edn., Paris, 1911.
CONTAMINE, P., 'Batailles, Bannières, Compagnies', *Cahiers vernonnais*, iv,
Caen, (1964), 19–32.
*Correspondence of Thomas Bekyngton, Secretary to Henry VI and Bishop of Bath
and Wells*, ed. G. Williams, RS, 2 vols, London, 1872.
COULBORN, R., 'The Economic and Political Preliminaries of the Crusade of
Henry Despenser, Bishop of Norwich, in 1383', University of London Ph.D.,
1931.
COUSSEMAKER, E. DE, 'Analectes historiques sur la Flandre maritime.

Chateau de Bourbourg; relations entre la France et l'Angleterre; un émissaire de Philippe d'Artevelde; Dunkerque, Gravelines et Bourbourg', *Bulletin de la comité flamande de France,* vi (1872–5), 36–48, 66–89.

CRETON, J., *French Metrical History on the Deposition of Richard II,* ed. and translated J. Webb, *Archaeologia,* xx (1824), 1–441.

Croniques de Franche, d'Engleterre, de Flandres, de Lile et especialement de Tournai, ed. A. Hocquet, Publications de la Société des bibliophiles belges, xxxviii, Mons, 1938.

DAUMET, G., *Etude sur l'alliance de la France et de la Castile au XIVe et au XVe siècles,* Bibliothèque de l'école des hautes études, cxviii, Paris, 1898.

DE LA BORDERIE, A. LE MOYNE and B. A. POCQUET DU HAUT-JUSSÉ, *Histoire de Bretagne,* 6 vols, Paris, Rennes, 1896–1914.

DE LA BORDERIE, A. LE MOYNE, 'Le siège de Brest en 1387', *Revue de Bretagne, de Vendée et d'Anjou,* ii (1889), 198–203.

DELACHENAL, R., *Histoire de Charles V,* 5 vols, Paris, 1909–31.

DELAVILLE LE ROULX, J., *La France en Orient au XIVe siècle. Expéditions du maréchal Boucicourt,* Bibliothèque des écoles françaises d'Athènes et de Rome, xliv, xlv, Paris, 1886.

DE MÉZIÈRES, P., *De la chevallerie de la Passion de Jesu Crist (1396),* ed. A. H. Hamdy, Typescript, Alexandria, 1964.

——, *Epistre au roi Richart II (1395),* ed. G. W. Coopland (forthcoming).

——, *Songe du vieil pèlerin,* ed. G. W. Coopland, 2 vols, Cambridge, 1969.

——, *La sustance de la chevalerie de la Passion de Jhesu Crist en francois,* ed. A. H. Hamdy, *Bulletin of the Faculty of Arts,* xviii (Alexandria, 1964), 43–105.

DESCHAMPS, E., *Oeuvres complètes,* ed. Q. de Saint Hilaire and G. Raynaud, Société des anciens textes français, 11 vols, Paris, 1878–1903.

Deutsche Reichstagakten, ed. J. Weizsäcker *et al.,* 16 vols, Munich and Gotha, 1867–1928.

Diplomatic Correspondence of Richard II, ed. E. Perroy, RHS, Camden 3rd series, xlviii, London, 1933.

DOBSON, R. B., *The Peasants' Revolt of 1381,* London, 1970.

Documents pour servir à l'histoire de la maison de Bourgogne en Brabant et en Limbourg, ed. H. Laurent and F. Quicke, *BCRH,* xcvii (1933), 39–188.

Dokumente zur Geschichte des grossen abendländischen Schismas, 1385–1395, ed. S. Steinherz, Prague, Reichenberg, 1932.

DUBOSC, N., *Voyage pour négocier la paix entre les couronnes de France et d'Angleterre,* ed. E. Martène and U. Durand. *Voyage littéraire de deux religieux bénédictins de la congrégation de Saint-Maur,* ii, 307–60, Paris, 1724.

DURRIEU, P., *Les Gascons en Italie. Etudes historiques,* Auch, 1885.

—— 'Le royaume d'Adria. Episode de la politique française en Italie sous le règne de Charles VI, 1393–1394', *RQH,* xxviii (1880), 43–78; reprinted separately, Paris, 1880.

EHRLE, F. 'Neue Materialen zur Geschichte Peters von Luna', *Archiv für Literatur- und Kirchengeschichte des Mittelalters,* vi (1892), 139–308; vii (1900), 1–310.

Bibliography

England's Export Trade, 1275–1547, ed. E. M. Carus-Wilson and O. Coleman, Oxford, 1963.

Etat sommaire par séries des documents conservées aux Archives nationales, Paris, 1891.

EVESHAM, MONK OF, *Historia vitae et regni Ricardi II*, ed. T. Hearne, Oxford, 1729.

Expeditions to Prussia and the Holy Land made by Henry, Earl of Derby, in the years 1390–1 and 1392–3, ed. L. T. Smith, RHS, Camden new series, lii, London, 1894.

FAVENT, T., *Historia mirabilis parliamenti*, ed. M. McKisack, RHS, Camden miscellany xiv, London, 1926.

Foedera, conventiones etc., ed. T. Rymer, Orig. edn, 20 vols, London, 1704–35.

FOWLER, K. A., 'Les finances et la discipline dans les armées anglaises en France au XIVe siècle', *Cahiers vernonnais*, iv (Caen, 1964), 55–84.

FROISSART, J., *Chroniques*, ed. S. Luce, G. Raynaud *et al.* SHF, 14 vols, Paris, 1869–1966, in progress.

——, *Oeuvres*, ed. Kervyn de Lettenhove, 25 vols, Brussels, 1867–77.

GABOTTO, F., *Gli ultimi principi d'Acaia*, Turin, 1898.

Gascon Rolls, 1307–17, ed. Y. Renouard, HMSO, London, 1962.

Guide to the Contents of the Public Record Office, HMSO, 3 vols, 1963–9.

HAMDY, A. H., 'Philippe de Mézières and the New Order of the Passsion', *Bulletin of the Faculty of Arts*, xviii (Alexandria, 1964), 1–105.

Handelingen van de Leden en van de Staten van Vlaanderen, 1384–1405, ed. W. Prevenier, CRH, Brussels, 1959.

Hanserecesse. Die Recesse und andere Akten der Hansetage von 1256–1430, ed. K. Koppmann, 8 vols, Leipzig, 1870–97.

Hansisches Urkundenbuch, 975–1500, ed. K. Höhlbaum, K. Kunze and W. Stein. *Verein für Hansische Geschichte*, 11 vols, Halle, Leipzig, 1876–1916.

HARVEY, J. H., 'The Wilton Diptych – A Reconsideration', *Archaeologia*, xcviii (1961), 1–28.

Histoire civile, ecclésiastique et littéraire de la ville de Nismes, ed. L. Ménard, 2nd edition, 7 vols, Paris, 1750–8.

Histoire générale de Languedoc, ed. C. Devic and J. Vaissete, new edition, 16 vols, Toulouse, 1872–1905.

Index to the Charters and Rolls in the British Museum, ed. H. J. Ellis and F. B. Bickley, 2 vols, London, 1900–12.

Inventaire des archives de la ville de Bruges, I, i: inventaire des chartes, ed. L. Gilliodts van Severen, 7 vols, Bruges, 1871–8.

Inventaire sommaire des archives départementales de la Côte-d'Or, série B, ed. C. Rossignol *et al.*, 6 vols, Paris and Dijon, 1863–94.

Inventaire sommaire des archives départementales du Nord, série B, ed. A. le Glay *et al.*, 10 vols, Lille, 1863–1906.

IORGA, N., *Philippe de Mézières, 1327–1405, et la croisade au XIVe siècle*, Bibliothèque de l'école des hautes études, cx, Paris, 1896.

Istore et croniques de Flandres, ed. Kervyn de Lettenhove, CRH, 2 vols, Brussels, 1879–1880.

Itinéraires de Philippe le Hardi et Jean sans Peur, ducs de Bourgogne, ed. E. Petit, CDIHF, Paris, 1888.

JARRY, E., *La vie politique de Louis de France, duc d'Orléans, 1372–1407*, Paris, 1889.

——, 'La *voie de fait* et l'alliance franco-milanese, 1386–1395', *BEC*, liii (1892), 213–53, 505–70; Reprinted separately, Paris, 1892.

——, *Les origines de la domination française à Gênes, 1392–1402*, Paris, 1896.

JEULIN, P., 'Un grand "honneur" anglais. Aperçus sur le 'comté' de Richmond en Angleterre, possession des ducs de Bretagne', *Annales de Bretagne*, xlii (1935), 380–473.

JONES, M. C. E., 'Brest sous les Anglais, 1342–1397', *Cahiers de l'Iroise*, xvi (Brest, 1969), 2–12.

Joustes de Saint-Inglebert, 1389–1390. Poème contemporain, ed. J. Pichon, *Partie inédite des chroniques de Saint-Denis*, 59–78, Paris, 1864.

KERVYN DE LETTENHOVE, 'Des alliances de la commune de Gand avec Richard II, roi d'Angleterre', *BARB*, 2nd series xx (1865), 304–15.

——, *Histoire de Flandres*, 6 vols, Brussels, 1847–50.

KNIGHTON, H., *Chronicon*, ed. J. R. Lumby, RS, 2 vols, London, 1889–95.

LANGLOIS, C. V. and STEIN, H., *Les archives de l'histoire de France*, Paris, 1891; reprinted 1966.

LARSON, A., 'English Embassies during the Hundred Years' War', *EHR*, lv (1940), 423–31.

LAURENT, H. and QUICKE, F., *Les origines de l'état bourguignon. L'accession de la maison de Bourgogne aux duchés de Brabant et de Limbourg, 1383–1407*, Mémoires de l'Académie royale de Belgique, Lettres, xli(i), Brussels, 1939.

LECOY DE LA MARCHE, R. A., *Les relations politiques de la France avec le royaume de Majorque*, 2 vols, Paris, 1892.

LE FÈVRE, J., *Journal*, ed. H. Moranvillé, Paris, 1887.

LEFRANC, A., *Olivier de Clisson, connétable de France*, Paris, 1898.

LEHOUX, F., *Jean de France, duc de Berri. Sa vie, son action politique, 1340–1416*, 3 vols and index, Paris, 1966–8.

LE PATOUREL, J., 'The Plantagenet Dominions', *History*, l (1965), 289–308.

LEROUX, A., *Nouvelles recherches critiques sur les relations politiques de la France avec l'Allemagne de 1378 à 1461*, Paris, 1892.

Lettres de rois, reines et autres personnages des cours de France et d'Angleterre, ed. J. J. Champollion-Figeac, CDIHF, 2 vols, Paris, 1839–47.

LEWIS, N. B., 'Article VII of the Impeachment of Michael de la Pole in 1386', *EHR*, xlii (1927), 402–7.

——, 'The Last Medieval Summons of the English Feudal Levy, 13 June 1385', *EHR*, lxxiii (1958), 1–26.

LEWIS, P. S., 'Decayed and Non-Feudalism in Later Medieval France', *BIHR*, xxxvii (1964), 157–84.

List and Index Society, IV, Exchequer KR and LTR Memoranda Rolls, London, 1965.

——, *XVII, Exchequer of Receipt: Receipt and Issue Rolls*, London, 1966.

——, *XXXI, Class List of Records of the Exchequer of Receipt*, London, 1968.

——, *XXXII, Class List of Records of the Treasury of Receipt*, London, 1968.

Livre des Bouillons, ed. H. Barckhausen, Archives municipales de Bordeaux, i, Bordeaux, 1867.

LOBINEAU, DOM G. A., *Histoire de Bretagne*, 2 vols, Paris, 1707.

MCKISACK, M., *The Fourteenth Century*, Oxford, 1959.

Mémoires pour servir de preuves à l'histoire ecclésiastique et civile de Bretagne, ed. Dom P. H. Morice, 3 vols, Paris, 1742–6.

Memorieboek der stad Ghent, ed. P. J. van der Meersch, Maatschappy der Vlaemsche bibliophilen, II, xv, 4 vols, Ghent, 1852–64.

MIROT, L., 'Isabelle de France, reine d'Angleterre, comtesse d'Angoulême, duchesse d'Orléans, 1389–1409', *RHD*, xviii (1904), 544–73; xix (1905), 60–95, 161–91, 481–522, reprinted separately, Paris, 1905.

——, 'Une tentative d'invasion en Angleterre pendant la guerre de Cents Ans, 1385–1386', *REH*, lxxxi (1915), 249–87, 417–66.

MIROT, L. and DEPREZ, E., 'Les ambassades anglaises pendant la guerre de Cent Ans', *BEC*, lix (1898), 550–77; lx (1899), 177–214; lxi (1900), 20–58, reprinted separately, Paris, 1900.

MIROT, L. and VIELLIARD, J., 'Inventaire des lettres des rois d'Aragon à Charles VI et à la cour de France conservées aux archives de la couronne d'Aragon à Barcelone', *BEC*, ciii (1942), 99–150.

MOLINIER, A., 'Description de deux manuscrits contenant la règle de la "Militia Passionis Jhesu Christi" de Philippe de Mézières', *Archives de l'Orient Latin*, i, 335–64, 719.

Monumenta Hungariae historia, acta extera, ed. G. Wenzel, 7 vols, Budapest, 1874–8.

Monumenta spectantia historiam Slavorum meridionalium, ed. S. Ljubić *et al.*, Academia scientiarum et artium Slavorum, 43 vols, Zagreb, 1868–1917.

Monuments historiques, cartons des rois, ed. J. Tardif, Paris, 1866.

MORANVILLÉ, H., 'Conférences entre la France et l'Angleterre, 1388–1393', *BEC*, l (1889), 355–80.

——, 'Extraits des journaux du trésor, 1345–1419', *BEC*, xlix (1888), 149–214, 368–452.

MORICE, DOM P. H., *Histoire ecclésiastique et civile de Bretagne*, 2 vols, Paris, 1750–6.

NICOL, D. M., 'A Byzantine Emperor in England: Manuel's visit to London in 1400–1401', *University of Birmingham Historical Journal*, xii (1970), 204–25.

NORDBERG, M., *Les ducs et la royauté. Etudes sur la rivalité des ducs d'Orléans et de Bourgogne, 1392–1407*, Studia historica upsaliensia, xii, Upsala, 1964.

Bibliography

Ordonnances de Philippe le Hardi, de Marguerite de Mâle et de Jean sans Peur, i: 1381–1393, ed. J. Bartier and A. de Nieuwenhuysen, Brussels, 1965.

Ordonnances des rois de France de la troisième race, ed. D. F. Secousse *et al.,* 21 vols, Paris, 1723–1849.

OSTROGORSKY, G., *History of the Byzantine State,* 2nd edition, translated J. Hussey, Oxford, 1968.

PALMER, J. J. N., 'The Anglo-French Peace Negotiations, 1390–1396'. *TRHS,* 5th series xvi (1966), 81–94.

——, 'Articles for a Final Peace between England and France, 16 June 1393', *BIHR,* xxxix (1966), 180–5.

——, 'The Background to Richard II's Marriage to Isabel of France, 1396', *BIHR,* xliv (1971), 1–17.

——, 'England and the Great Western Schism, 1388–1399', *EHR,* lxxxiii (1968), 516–22.

——, 'English Foreign Policy, 1388–1399', *The Reign of Richard II: Essays in Honour of M. McKisack,* ed. F. R. H. du Boulay and C. M. Barron, London, 1971, 75–107.

——, 'The Impeachment of Michael de la Pole in 1386', *BIHR,* xlii (1969), 96–101.

——, 'The Last Summons of the Feudal Army in England, 1385', *EHR,* lxxxiii (1968), 771–5.

——, 'The Parliament of 1385 and the Constitutional Crisis of 1386', *Speculum,* xlvi (1971), 477–90.

——, 'The Peace Negotiations, 1337–1453', *The Hundred Years' War,* ed. K.A. Fowler, London, 1971, 51–74.

——, 'Prêts à la couronne, 1385', *BEC,* cxxvi (1968), 419–25.

PERELHOS, RAMON VICOMTE DE, *Voyage au Purgatoire de St Patrice,* ed. A. Vignaux and A. Jeanroy, Bibliothèque méridionale, 1st series viii, Toulouse, 1903.

PERROY, E., *L'Angleterre et le grand Schisme d'Occident,* Paris, 1933.

——, 'Un evêque urbaniste protégé de l'Angleterre, Guillaume de Coudenberghe, evêque de Tournai et de Bâle', *RHE,* xxvii (Louvain, 1930), 103–9.

——, *The Hundred Years' War,* translated W. B. Wells, London, 1951.

——, 'Louis de Mâle et les négotiations de paix franco-anglaises', *RBPH,* xxvii (1949), 138–50.

PETIT, E., *Ducs de Bourgogne de la maison de Valois, i: Philippe le Hardi, 1363–1380,* Paris, 1909.

Petit Thalamus de Montpellier, Société archéologique de Montpellier, Montpellier, 1836.

PITTI, B., *Cronica,* ed. A. Bacchi della Lega. Collezione di opere inedite o rare dei primi tre secoli della lingua. R. Commissione pe' testi di lingua nelle provincie dell' Emilia, Bologna, 1903.

Polychronicon Ranulphi Higden, ed. J. R. Lumby, RS, 9 vols, London, 1865–86.

POT, J., *Histoire de Rénier Pot, conseiller des ducs de Bourgogne,* Paris, 1929.

Bibliography

Proceedings and Ordinances of the Privy Council of England, ed.
Sir N. H. Nicolas, RC, 7 vols, London, 1834–7.
*Public Record Office Lists and Indexes, XI. List of Foreign Accounts Enrolled on
the Great Rolls of the Exchequer*, HMSO, London, 1900.
——, *XXVII, List of Chancery Rolls, 1199–1903*, HMSO, London, 1908.
——, *XXXV, List of Exchequer Accounts Various*, HMSO, London, 1919.
——, *XLIX List of Diplomatic and Scottish Documents and Papal Bulls*,
HMSO, London, 1923.
*Quelques pièces relatives à la vie de Louis I, duc d'Orléans et de Valentine Visconti,
sa femme*, ed. F. M. Graves, Bibliothèque du XVe siècle, xix, Paris, 1913.
QUICKE, F., *Les Pays-Bas à la veille de la période bourguignonne, 1356–1384*,
Brussels, 1947.
RAMSAY, J. H., *Genesis of Lancaster, 1307–1399*, 2 vols, Oxford, 1913.
*Recueil de pièces servant de preuves aux mémoires sur les troubles excités en France
par Charles II, roi de Navarre, dit le Mauvais*, ed. D. F. Secousse, Paris,
1755.
*Recueil des documents concernant le Poitou contenus dans les registres de la
chancellerie de France*, ed. P. Guerin, Archives historiques de Poitou, xi, xiii,
xvii, xix, xxi, xxiv etc., Poitiers, 1881–1905.
Régestes des délibérations du sénat de Venise concernant la Romanie, i: 1329–1399,
ed. F. Thiriet, Ecole pratique des hautes études, vi: documents et recherches
sur l'économie des pays byzantins, islamiques et slaves, i, Paris, 1958.
Registrum honoris de Richmond, ed. R. Gale, London, 1722.
Rekeningen der stad Ghent. Tijdvak van Philips van Artevelde, 1376–1389, ed.
J. Vuylsteke, Maatschapij nederlandsche letterkunde en Geschiedenis . . .
te Gent, Gent, 1893.
Répertoire numérique des archives départementales du Nord, série B, ed.
M. Bruchet, 2 vols, Lille, 1921.
REY, M., *Le Domaine du roi et les finances extraordinaires sous Charles VI,
1388–1413*, Ecole pratique des hautes études, vi, Paris, 1965.
——, *Les finances royales sous Charles VI. Les causes du déficit, 1388–1413*, Ecole
pratique des hautes études, vi, Paris, 1965.
Rotuli parliamentorum, ed. J. Strachey *et al.*, 6 vols, London, 1767.
RUSSELL, P. E., *English Intervention in Spain and Portugal in the Time of
Edward III and Richard II*, Oxford, 1955.
SALMON, P., *Mémoires*, ed. J. A. C. Buchon, *Collection des chroniques nationales
françaises*, xxv, supplement ii, 1–115, Paris, 1828.
SCHLUMBERGER, G., 'Un empereur de Byzance à Paris et à Londres',
Byzance et les Croisades, 87–148, Paris, 1927.
SCHOOS, J., *Der Machtkampf zwischen Burgund und Orleans*, Publications de la
section historique de l'Institut grand-ducal de Luxembourg, lxxxv,
Luxembourg, 1956.
Séjours de Charles VI, ed. E. Petit, *Bulletin historique et philologique du comité
des travaux historiques et scientifiques*, xi (1893), 45–92.

SHERBORNE, J. W., 'The Battle of La Rochelle and the War at Sea, 1372–1375', *BIHR*. xlii (1969), 17–29.

——, 'The Hundred Years' War. The English Navy: Shipping and Man-power, 1369–1389', *Past and Present*, xxxvii (1967), 163–75.

——, 'Indentured Retinues and the English Expeditions to France, 1369–1380', *EHR*, lxxix (1964), 718–46.

SÖCHTING, W., 'Die Beziehungen zwischen Flandern und England am Ende des Vierzehnten Jahrhunderts', *Historische Vierteljahrschrift*, xxiv (1927–9), 182–98.

Statutes of the Realm, ed. J. Caley *et al.*, RC, 11 vols, London, 1810–28.

STEEL, A., *The Receipt of the Exchequer, 1377–1485*, Cambridge, 1954.

——, *Richard II*, Cambridge, 1941.

STENGERS, J., 'Philippe le Hardi et les Etats de Brabant', *Hommage au Professeur Bonenfant*, 383–408, Brussels, 1965.

TERRIER DE LORAY, LE MARQUIS, *Jean de Vienne, amiral de France, 1341–1396*, Paris, 1877.

THORNE, W., *Chronica de rebus gestis abbatum sancti Augustini Cantuariae, 578–1397*, ed. R. Twysden, *Scriptores Decem, ii*, 2 vols, London, 1652.

TIPTON, C. L., 'The English at Nicopolis', *Speculum*, xxxvii (1962), 528–40.

TOTH-UBBENS, M., 'Een dubbel vorstenhuwelijk in het jaar 1385', *Bijdragen voor de Geschiedenis der Nederlanden*, xix (1964), 101–28.

TOUT, T. F., *Chapters in the Administrative History of Medieval England*, 6 vols, Manchester, 1923–35.

TUCK, J. A., 'The Cambridge Parliament, 1388', *EHR*, lxxxiv (1969), 225–43.

TUCOO-CHALA, P., *La vicomté de Béarn et le problème de sa souveraineté des origines à 1620*, Bordeaux, 1961.

VALE, M. G. A., *English Gascony, 1399–1453: A Study of War, Government and Politics during the Later Stages of the Hundred Years' War*, Oxford, 1970.

VALOIS, N., *La France et le grand Schisme d'Occident*, 4 vols, Paris, 1896–1902.

VAUGHAN, R., *Philip the Bold*, London, 1962.

VIRIVILLE, V. DE, 'Notes sur l'état civil des princes et princesses nés de Charles VI et d'Isabeau de Bavière', *BEC*, xix (1858), 473–82.

WALSINGHAM, T., *Annales Ricardi secundi et Henrici quarti*, ed. H. T. Riley, *Johannis de Trokelowe et Henrici de Blaneforde cronica et annales*, 155–424, RS, London, 1886.

——, *Historia Anglicana*, ed. H. T. Riley, RS, 2 vols, London, 1863–4.

Index

Aardenburg, 60

Abbeville, 148

Ackermann, Francis, of Ghent: English ally, 47, 49, 60, 91, 93, 95–6, 123, 230–1; murdered, 231–2

Adam, Master Peter, 100–1

Adorno, Antonio, 199

Agenais, 13, 145, 147, 153, 238

Albret, Arnaud-Amanieu, lord of (1358–1401), 33, 37, 153, 229

Alençon and Perché, John I, count of (1404–15), 176

Alexandria, 186

Aljubarrota, battle, 68, 69

Amiens, 29–30, 85, 145, 194, 195, 197, 198, 199

Angevin Empire, 29, 170, 171

Angoulême, 145

Angoumois, 15, 147

Anjou, 170, 171, 174, 257; house of, 19, 141, 162, 167, 223

Anjou, Louis I, duke of (1356–84), 5, 13, 192

Anjou, Louis II, duke of (1384–1417), 143, 167, 193

Anjou, Marie, wife of Louis I, sister of John de Blois, 63, 90, 112

Anne of Bohemia, 57, 166

Antwerp, 113, 124

Appellants: victims, 107, 110, 111, 118–19; condemn king's foreign policy as treason, 108–9, 115–19; rebellion, 109, 115, 122, 236; ridicule de la Pole, 110; and Calais, 110–11; reject peace offers, 112; foreign policy, 122–34;

and John of Gaunt, 125–6; and parliament, 130–1, 134–8; and Scotland, 138; initiate peace negotiations, 138–9, 142; failure of policies, 139–40, 142

Aquitaine: and France, 2, 4, 5–6, 7, 9, 12, 67, 74, 152, 225, 234; cost, 11; homage, *ressort* and sovereignty, 15–16, 24, 28–9, 33–42, 144, 145, 146, 148, 153–63; to be alienated to John of Gaunt, 24, 28–42, 118, 144, 148, 150, 152–63, 166–9; annexed to English Crown, 41–2, 155–6, 158, 160, 162, 163; and peace negotiations, 144–9 *passim*, 152–63, 169, 171, 177–8, 204, 207, 256–7; liberties, 154–63; Estates, 154–63; and crusade, 185, 201, 204, 239–40; *see also* Gascon revolt

Aragon, 42, 108, 170, 181, 184, 191, 216, 219; *see also* John I of Aragon; Martin I; Peter III; Yolande

Ardres, 176

Armagh, archbishop of, *see* Colton

Armagnac, counts of, 147, 152–3; house of, 162, 223

Armagnac, John I, count of (1319–73), 153

Armagnac, John II, count of (1373–84), 229

Armagnac, John III, count of (1384–91), 33, 153, 229, 238

Armagnac, Bernard VII, count of (1391–1418), 29, 153–4, 220, 238–9

Armenia, king of, *see* Leo

<h1 style="text-align:center">Index</h1>

Index

Index

Index